Beginning Samsung ARTIK

A Guide for Developers

Cliff Wootton

Apress®

Beginning Samsung ARTIK

Cliff Wootton
Crowborough, East Sussex, United Kingdom

ISBN-13 (pbk): 978-1-4842-1951-5   ISBN-13 (electronic): 978-1-4842-1952-2
DOI 10.1007/978-1-4842-1952-2

Library of Congress Control Number: 2016940104

Managing Director: Welmoed Spahr
Lead Editor: Jeffrey Pepper
Editorial Board: Steve Anglin, Gary Cornell, Louise Corrigan, James T. DeWolf,
    Jonathan Gennick, Robert Hutchinson, James Markham, Matthew Moodie,
    Susan McDermott, Jeffrey Pepper, Douglas Pundick, Dominic Shakeshaft,
    Gwenan Spearing, Matt Wade, Steve Weiss
Coordinating Editor: Melissa Maldonado
Copy Editor: April Rondeau
Compositor: SPi Global
Indexer: SPi Global
Artist: SPi Global

Distributed to the book trade worldwide by Springer Science+Business Media New York, 233 Spring Street, 6th Floor, New York, NY 10013. Phone 1-800-SPRINGER, fax (201) 348-4505, e-mail orders-ny@springer-sbm.com, or visit www.springer.com. Apress Media, LLC is a California LLC and the sole member (owner) is Springer Science + Business Media Finance Inc (SSBM Finance Inc). SSBM Finance Inc is a **Delaware** corporation.

For information on translations, please e-mail rights@apress.com, or visit www.apress.com.

Apress and friends of ED books may be purchased in bulk for academic, corporate, or promotional use. eBook versions and licenses are also available for most titles. For more information, reference our Special Bulk Sales–eBook Licensing web page at www.apress.com/bulk-sales.

Any source code or other supplementary materials referenced by the author in this text is available to readers at www.apress.com. For detailed information about how to locate your book's source code, go to to www.apress.com/source-code/.

Printed on acid-free paper

To my longtime buddy, Pete Willis.

Contents at a Glance

About the Author xxvii

Acknowledgments xxix

Trademarks..xxxi

Foreword xxxiii

Introduction xxxv

■Chapter 1: Getting Started 1

■Chapter 2: Welcome to the Internet of Things 9

■Chapter 3: Hello, ARTIK... 15

■Chapter 4: Understanding Security 41

■Chapter 5: Your Development Kit...................................... 47

■Chapter 6: Getting Your Hardware Together 59

■Chapter 7: Setting Up a Terminal Emulator 81

■Chapter 8: Talking to Your ARTIK..................................... 99

■Chapter 9: Network Configuration 109

■Chapter 10: Configuring and Upgrading 143

■Chapter 11: Programming Your ARTIK............................ 159

■Chapter 12: Using Eclipse IDE 175

■Chapter 13: Using Arduino IDE 195

■Chapter 14: Using the Command Line 219

Chapter 15: Programming in C Language.................................. 239

Chapter 16: Programming with Node.js 257

Chapter 17: Programming with Python 267

Chapter 18: Integrating with SAMI 273

Chapter 19: Integrating with Temboo 301

Chapter 20: Debugging Your Application................................ 325

Chapter 21: Deploying Your Application 333

Chapter 22: Next Steps 341

Index... 347

Contents

About the Author xxvii

Acknowledgments xxix

Trademarks..xxxi

Foreword xxxiii

Introduction xxxv

■Chapter 1: Getting Started...1

Introducing the ARTIK Family 1

Reinventing the Engineering Process..1

About This Book 2

Finding Out About ARTIK..2

Provenance...3

Experience Helps..4

Your Journey Through the Book 4

Do You Use Windows, Linux, or Mac OS X? 4

Get Your Samsung Account 5

Buy an ARTIK Development System Now 5

Would You Like to Know More? 5

What to Read Next..6

Quick Start..6

Chapter 2: Welcome to the Internet of Things 9

What Is the Internet of Things? 9

Concept Map.. 9

An Example You Can Build Today 10

The Internet Is Changing—Rapidly 10

Disruptive Changes... 11

Network Architecture and Design... 11

Sensors... 11

Lifestyle Changes 12

A Revolution in Medicine and the Care Community.......................... 12

Industrial Internet of Things 13

Revenue-generating Opportunities.. 13

Chapter 3: Hello, ARTIK.. 15

What Is an ARTIK Module?... 15

What Is an Ecosystem? 15

The ARTIK Modules.. 16

Software Support 17

The ARTIK Community 17

Security and Privacy Are Core Needs 18

The Connected Cloud Service 19

Sensory Capabilities.. 19

Communications Challenges 19

Integration with Other Platforms.. 20

Benefits to Consumers 21

Introducing the ARTIK 1 21

Functional Organization... 22

Operating System 22

Wireless Communications 22

Spatial Sensors... 23

Computing Capacity... 23

Memory Storage 23

Video Display Output 23

Introducing the ARTIK 5 24

Functional Organization.. 25

Operating System 25

Wireless Communications 25

Networking Protocol Support 26

Computing Capacity... 26

Graphics Processing Unit (GPU).. 26

Memory Storage 27

Hardware Video Codec Support... 27

Introducing the ARTIK 10 28

Functional Organization.. 29

Operating System 30

Wireless Communications 30

Networking Protocol Support 31

Computing Capacity... 31

Graphics Processing Unit (GPU).. 31

Memory Storage 32

Audio Codec Support 32

Hardware Video Codec Support... 33

Comparing the ARTIK Modules 33

Power Management Integrated Circuit (PMIC) 33

Security Management 34

Support for Audio Coding.. 34

Support for Video Coding 34

Physical Connections 35

About the ARTIK Operating Systems 35

Nucleus RTOS 35

Linux: Fedora OS 36

But What Is Yocto? 37

Other Operating Systems 38

Summary 39

■Chapter 4: Understanding Security 41

Risk Factors and Dystopian Futures 41

Security Ecosystem 42

SAMI 42

OAuth2 42

Cloud-based Services 43

Open Technologies for Sharing 43

Keeping Your Data Safe and Secure 43

Secure Operating System 43

Firmware Security 44

Device Authentication 44

Data Encryption 44

Get Your Samsung Account Now 44

Embedded Secure Element 45

Hardware Crypto Engine 45

Segregated Trust Zone 46

Current Status 46

Summary 46

■Chapter 5: Your Development Kit..47

The Developer Reference Board..47

  About the Developer Reference Boards....................................47

What Is in the Box? 48

The Type 1 Developer Reference Board................................50

The Type 5 & 10 Developer Reference Boards (Beta)..........51

Early Production Models..53

Type 5 and 10 Developer Reference Board Connectors 53

Type 5 and 10 Developer Reference Board Switches............55

Type 5 and 10 Developer Reference Board LED Indicators ...55

Type 5 and 10 Developer Reference Board Jumpers 56

Connecting External Devices...56

Summary...57

■Chapter 6: Getting Your Hardware Together 59

Your Workbench 59

Setting Up a Hardware Workbench 59

  Wiring Up Your Circuits 60

  Test Equipment..61

Setting Up a Software Workbench......................................62

  Risk Managing Your Software Development...........................63

Configuring the Developer Reference Board 63

Communicating with Your ARTIK 65

Connecting the ARTIK Development System 66

USB Serial Interfaces 67

  Hooking Up the Serial Interface...68

  Setting Up a USB Serial Interface Driver on Windows 68

  Setting Up a USB Serial Interface Driver on Mac OS X............69

Setting Up a USB Serial Interface Driver on Ubuntu Linux 75

Setting Up a USB Serial Interface on Android Devices 77

USB Vendor IDs 78

Summary 79

■Chapter 7: Setting Up a Terminal Emulator 81

Serial Connections with a Terminal Emulator 81

Installing Your Terminal Emulator 82

Adding a Terminal Emulator to Windows 82

Install PuTTY on Windows 82

Connecting to the ARTIK Development System from PuTTY 84

Closing the Connection 84

Logging the Output to a File 85

PuTTY Log File Naming 85

Using the Default Terminal Application on Mac OS X 86

Closing the Connection 87

Recovering from a Bad Screen Exit 88

Other Useful Screen Commands 89

Logging the Output to a File 89

Log Capture Example 1 (Clipboard Cut and Paste) 90

Log Capture Example 2 (Screen Command Logging) 90

Log Capture Example 3 (Output Redirection) 91

Log Capture Example 4 (Stream Duplexing) 91

Log Capture Example 5 (Script Command Logging) 92

Alternatives to the Mac OS X Terminal App 92

Using the Minicom Terminal Application on Linux 92

Installing Minicom with yum 93

Installing Minicom with apt-get 93

Building Minicom from the Source Code Files 93

Configure Minicom to Talk to the ARTIK Developer Reference Board 94

Connecting to the ARTIK Development System from Minicom 95

Closing the Connection 96

Logging the Output to a File 96

Pausing the Screen Output 97

Using Minicom Inside Your ARTIK 97

Summary 97

■Chapter 8: Talking to Your ARTIK 99

Starting Up the ARTIK 99

The System Administrator Console 99

U-boot Universal Boot Loader Messages 99

Booting the Kernel 100

OS Kernel Startup 101

Setting the Boot Mode Switches 103

Booting Up Your ARTIK Development System 104

Login Credentials 105

Shutdown Commands 106

Shutdown Warnings 107

Shutdown Console Logging Messages 108

Summary 108

■Chapter 9: Network Configuration 109

Networking Your ARTIK 109

Networking Protocol Support 109

Choosing the Best Networking Strategy 110

Wireless Networking 110

Dynamic Name Auto-discovery Support 111

Protocol Support 112

OMA Lightweight M2M Protocol (LW M2M) 112

Constrained Application Protocol (CoAP) 113

Message Queue Telemetry Transport Protocol (MQTT) 113

6LoWPAN Protocol 114

Using ZigBee and Thread Protocols 114

OpenHAB Support in ARTIK 10 Modules 115

OpenStack (Swift) Framework 116

Configuring Your Ethernet Connection 117

How It Works 117

IPv4 Addressing Notation 118

IPv6 Addressing Notation 120

Port Numbers 121

The Switchover 122

IP Address Configuration in Your ARTIK 122

Inspecting the IP Addresses 122

Setting a Temporary IP Address on the Ethernet Interface 123

Setting a Default Persistent Static IP Address 123

Configuring Your ARTIK for IPv6 Operation 125

DNS Configurations 126

Introducing systemd 126

The Impact of systemd on DNS Configuration 126

Statically Configuring Your DNS Servers 127

Getting State of Your IP Links 128

Configure the Wi-Fi Networking 130

Setting Up Wi-Fi Communications 130

Another Way to Configure Your Wi-Fi 133

Troubleshooting FAQ...135

Advanced Wi-Fi Configuration 136

Automatically Reconnect Your Wi-Fi after Each Reboot 136

Connecting with Telnet via SSH...138

Configuring Your Bluetooth Wireless Interface 139

Setting Up Bluetooth for an ARTIK 5 or 10..................................139

Summary...141

■Chapter 10: Configuring and Upgrading 143

Updating Your Operating System..143

Writing Downloaded Images to an SD Card 143

Writing Micro SD Card Images on Windows 143

Writing Micro SD Card Images on Linux...144

Writing Micro SD Card Images on Mac OS X 146

Updating Your ARTIK 5 or 10...152

Known Firmware Versions...155

Installing Software on Your ARTIK 156

Summary...157

■Chapter 11: Programming Your ARTIK...159

Everything Is the Same but Different 159

Programming Your ARTIK..159

Setting Up Your Software Development Environment 160

Code-Editing Tools..160

Folders vs. Directories...161

File-System Path: Folder Separator Characters 161

Spaces in File Names and Paths..162

Upper- and Lowercase Issues 162

Of Camels and Underscores 164

Let the Environment Do the Heavy Lifting 164

Links vs. Aliases 164

Mac OS Resource Forks 165

New-Line Characters... 165

Typographers Quotes... 166

Being in Two Places at Once 166

Developing Your Code.. 169

What Is Cross-Compiling? 169

Building Code for the Correct Target CPU 170

Debug vs. Release... 170

Managing Your Code.. 171

Why Do You Need Java? 172

Checking the Java Version on Windows 172

Checking the Java Version on Mac OS X 172

Checking the Java Version on Linux 173

Installing Java... 173

Do You Need Java on Your ARTIK? 174

Summary... 174

■Chapter 12: Using Eclipse IDE 175

Installing, Configuring, and Using Eclipse IDE 175

Before You Install Eclipse IDE 175

Getting Help.. 175

Installing Eclipse IDE 176

Eclipse on Mac OS X... 176

Workspace Preferences 178

Adding New Tools to Your Eclipse IDE 179

What Is a Toolchain?..180

Installing Support for ARTIK Development...............................180

Why Build Tools Are Needed..181

Installing the GNU ARM Eclipse Plugin on Mac OS X.............181

Installing an ARM Toolchain on Mac OS 182

Configuring Your IDE for Remote Exploring 185

Setting Up a Default Toolchain 188

Semi-hosting Stubs...189

Support for the MIPS Architecture..190

Support for Eclipse Smart Home 190

Making a New ARM Project...190

Deploy the Binary to Your ARTIK..194

Summary...194

■Chapter 13: Using Arduino IDE 195

Installing, Configuring, and Using Arduino IDE 195

Before You Install Arduino IDE 195

How To...195

Recommended Settings for Your Arduino IDE 197

Installing and Configuring libArduino 199

Configuring Your ARTIK for Uploads (Board Setup)................201

Uploading a Sketch to Your ARTIK with Arduino IDE 202

Network Upload Method 202

Serial Upload Method 203

Native Sketch Compilation 203

Recommended Update Cycle 204

Developing with libArduino SDK...204

Arduino Pins: Type 1 Developer Reference Board 204

Arduino Pins: Type 5 and Type 10 Developer Reference Boards.......... 206

System Commands 208

Detecting the Board Version... 208

The Serial Object... 209

The Serial1 Object... 209

The DebugSerial Object... 210

Pin Modes.. 210

Reading Digital Input Pin Values.. 211

Setting Digital Output Pin Values... 211

Setting Analog Output Pin Values 212

Reading the Analog Inputs 213

Serial Peripheral Interface (SPI) 214

Detecting Interrupts 214

Pausing for Breath... 214

Powersaving Mode.. 215

Compiling and Running Sketches Natively... 215

Where to Find Out More 216

Troubleshooting... 217

Managing the Type 5 vs. Type 10 Pin-Number Differences 217

CPU Utilization at 100 Percent... 217

Digital Read Only Ever Reports a 1 Value 217

Porting Projects from Other Architectures... 218

Logic Levels.. 218

Summary... 218

■Chapter 14: Using the Command Line 219

Command-Line ARM Toolchains 219

Ubuntu Linux 219

Debian Linux.. 220

Mac OS X 220

Adding a UNIX Command Line to Windows 221

UNIX I/O Streams and Redirection.. 221

What's Where? 222

File System Mapped Properties Inside the ARTIK...................... 223

What CPU Is Available?.. 223

Detecting Current Processor Speed 224

Connecting to Remote Web Servers 224

Examples with curl.. 225

Useful UNIX Commands Inside Your ARTIK 226

Quitting and Aborting Processes 226

Inhibiting the Debugging Messages 227

Setting the Correct Date 228

Checking Your Memory Usage.. 228

The vi Editor (Why vi?)... 228

How to Use vi.. 229

Open a File for Editing or Create a New One 229

Inside the vi Editor.. 229

Saving and Exiting... 229

Command Mode 230

The GCC Compiler.. 232

Language Support 233

Supporting Libraries 233

GCC ARM Compiler Support... 234

Getting GCC Up and Running 234

Writing a Simple Program (Hello World) 235

Compiler Warnings 236

Next Steps 236

SCP: Secure Copy 236

File Upload to ARTIK Module 237

File Download from ARTIK Module 237

Summary 237

■Chapter 15: Programming in C Language 239

Programming Your ARTIK Natively in C 239

Coding Strategies 239

Creating a Simple Application 240

Looking Deeper Inside Your ARTIK 241

About the /sys Virtual File System 242

GPIO Pins 243

GPIO: Pin Mapping 243

GPIO: Pin Export to the User Domain 245

GPIO: Pin Direction Setting 246

GPIO: Digital Value Setting 247

GPIO: Digital Value Reading 247

GPIO: Edge Detecting 248

Reading Analog Input Values 249

Analog Read Differences Between ARTIK 5 and 10 250

Library Function Toolkit 250

An Example 254

Accessing Remote Systems with libCurl 254

Summary 256

■Chapter 16: Programming with Node.js 257

Developing with Node.js 257

The Architectural Design 258

Compiled Binary Code 259

Checking the Version of Your Node.js Installation 259

Extending Node.js 260

Installing NPM 260

Node Packages and Modules 261

Installing the WebSocket Module 262

Let's Write Some Node.js Code 262

Reading a Pin Voltage with Node.js 262

Sending Data to SAMI with Node.js 264

Summary 266

■Chapter 17: Programming with Python 267

Developing with Python 267

Checking Your Python Interpreter 268

Installing the Python Package Manager 268

Installing Python Packages 269

Run a Simple Python Test 269

Reading a Pin Voltage with Python 270

Summary 271

■Chapter 18: Integrating with SAMI 273

About SAMI 273

What Is SAMI? 274

Interacting with SAMI 275

How SAMI Works 275

SAMI Developer Documentation.. 276

Security 276

Authentication 277

Messages 277

User 278

User ID... 278

Devices.. 279

Device Type 279

Device ID 280

Applications... 280

Application ID 280

OAuth2 Access Tokens 280

Manifest 280

Raw Data... 282

Normalized Data.. 282

The SAMI API 282

Developer SDK Libraries.. 283

SAMI Tools 284

    The Developer Portal 284

    The User Portal.. 285

    API Console... 286

    Device Simulator 286

    Manifest Validator.. 286

User Portal: Managing Devices 286

    Device Details.. 288

User Portal: Managing Rules 289

    Rule-based Actions 290

    Adding New Rules 290

User Portal: Displaying Charts 292

User Portal: Viewing Data Logs 293

User Portal: Exporting Data 294

Developer Portal: Managing Device Types 294

Developer Portal: Managing Applications 295

Connecting to SAMI from Your Applications 295

Acquiring an Access Token for Your Application 296

Getting Data from SAMI for Your Application 296

Sending Data to SAMI from Your Device 297

Try Out More Examples 298

Want to Know More? 298

Summary 299

■Chapter 19: Integrating with Temboo 301

Hello Temboo 301

Developing with Temboo 302

Registering Your Temboo Account 302

Your Temboo Account Dashboard 303

Monitoring Your Activity 304

Your Choreo Library Dashboard 306

Supported Platforms 307

Supported Connectivity 308

Online Data Storage 308

Choreographies 308

Condition Handling 310

Remote Storage in Profiles... 311

Output Filters... 311

Data Streaming 311

Machine-to-Machine (M2M) with Temboo............................... 312

Temboo and ARTIK.. 312

Temboo and ARTIK 5... 313

Getting Ready to Tango with Temboo 313

An Example of Code Generated by Temboo................................ 315

Shared Login Credentials 320

Missing cdefs.h Message... 321

Using CURL via a REST API Instead of C................................... 321

Using Temboo with Node.js 322

Sample Code to Experiment With... 322

Summary... 324

Chapter 20: Debugging Your Application.................................. 325

Debugging Your App 325

Software Debugging with GDB 325

Onboard Native Debugging with GDB... 326

Remote Debugging with GDB 327

IDE Support for Debugging... 328

Emulating Your Hardware with QEMU 329

Using the JTAG Connectors 329

Hardware Debugging with SEGGER J-Link 329

Hardware Debugging with OpenOCD 331

Cleaning Up after Debugging 331

Summary 331

■Chapter 21: Deploying Your Application 333

Getting Ready 333

Deploy Files to ARTIK with scp 333

Deploy Files across the Network 334

Deploy Files to Your ARTIK with a Micro SD Card 334

Deploy Files to Your ARTIK with a USB Flash Drive 337

Prototypes vs. Production 338

Integrating the ARTIK into your Products 338

Summary 339

■Chapter 22: Next Steps 341

What Do You Want to Make? 341

Finding Out about More Project Ideas 343

Becoming a Partner Organization 344

Going Deeper into ARTIK Development 344

My Challenge to You 345

Index 347

About the Author

Cliff Wootton is a Royal Television Society (2002) Innovation award-winning former interactive TV systems architect at the BBC, specializing in content management systems and digital video. He was a guest speaker on pre-processing for video compression at the Apple WWDC 2007 developer conference and presented a technical paper on interactive TV systems at the NAB 2003 conference. He has taught IoT, real-world computing with Arduino, multimedia, video compression, metadata, and how to build multimedia art installations at the master's level at the University of the Arts, London. Cliff now concentrates on research and development projects, building digital media tools for creating audiovisual content, multimedia, electronic book publishing, writing, teaching, and playing the bass guitar.

Acknowledgments

Huge thanks are due to these people who created resources online and contributed ideas and practical help while I was writing this book. Their assistance was truly invaluable and is gratefully acknowledged.

- **Steve Weiss**, **Melissa Maldonado**, **Jeff Pepper**, and **Jonathan Gennick** at Apress–it has been great to work with you guys again

- **Glenn Cameron** at Samsung, who kindly provided prototype hardware and technical resources

- **Curtis Sasaki** for generously contributing the foreword

- **Fred Patton** at Samsung for his excellent photographic contributions and technical support

- **Martin Kronberg** for putting some helpful projects online in the Hackster.io blog

- **Simon Tatham,** who wrote and maintains the PutTTY application

- The minicom project team

- The Temboo team for their generosity in sharing insights into deeply technical interface code through their code-publishing mechanisms

- **Kevin Sharp** for his helpful contributions to the ARTIK blog

- All the artik.io forum posters whose questions inspired me to cover interesting topics

- **Gaynor Bromley** at Panasonic Electric Works UK Ltd for the AXT connector images

- **Joe Geoghegan** and **Bhavin Naik** at Mentor Graphics for technical white papers about Nucleus OS

- **Paul Stoffregen** for developing the Bridge.h library used in the Arduino IDE

- **Tevon Jordaan** for introducing me to Scrivener (an extraordinarily good book-writing tool).

- The Scrivener application developer team (see http://www.literatureandlatte.com)

Trademarks

ARM® is a registered trademark owned by ARM Ltd.

Mali™ is a trademark owned by ARM Ltd.

MIPS® microAptiv™ is a trademark owned by Mentor Graphics.

Linux® is the registered trademark of Linus Torvalds in the United States and other countries.

Java® is a registered trademark of Oracle and/or its affiliates.

All other trademarks are the property of their respective owners.

Foreword

If you follow the tech media at all, you will no doubt have seen plenty of coverage of–and excitement for–the Internet of Things (IoT). The hype surrounding IoT has been palpable. But now we appear to have reached an inflection point, where the hype is becoming reality. IoT is transforming the way people live their lives, with the power to automate, connect, and inform us like never before.

The technology to support IoT is evolving rapidly, with the availability of new, highly-integrated "systems on modules" (SOMs), as well as optimized wireless support and diverse sensor technologies. The most important change however, may be the move back to hardware. Over the past few years, most innovation has been taking place in the cloud and in system software. But with IoT, we are seeing renewed energy and commitment to hardware development. The arrival of low-cost development platforms, such as Arduino and Raspberry Pi, has helped the burgeoning maker community to really take off.

The Samsung ARTIK IoT platform takes this evolution to the next phase with its System on Module (SOM) concept. Designed for both individual developers and those who need it for large-scale production purposes, it features not only the application processor, but also DRAM, flash memory, radios, and advanced security options.

The idea behind ARTIK is simple: reduce the complexity of designing your IoT hardware. Previously, designers often had to do their job twice–once to get a working prototype, and then a redesign for the final production board. With ARTIK, you have the advantage of using the same module in your prototype that you will use in the final production hardware.

Beyond the hardware, the ARTIK platform also delivers a full stack with the latest drivers and tools, as well as a cloud service. And because ARTIK is an open platform, the choice of software is up to you.

As you can imagine, ARTIK is designed to support a broad range of uses, from wearables and products for the smart home to powerful hubs capable of local processing and analytics.

All of us at Samsung are excited to see the creativity that you will bring in leveraging the ARTIK platform, and how your work can change the world around us in positive ways. Of course, having books and documentation to help you get started is always welcome.

We believe that this *Beginning Samsung ARTIK* book and the companion *ARTIK Reference Guide* will provide plenty of inspiration to help you achieve your vision with the ARTIK platform.

—Curtis Sasaki
Samsung ARTIK project leader,
Spring 2016

Introduction

This introductory book will help you start your journey toward becoming an expert ARTIK developer as you develop a new and profitable enterprise.

This book will show you how to set up your own ARTIK development system and get your ARTIK module up and running. Then you can develop your own applications for it. By the end of the book you should have a working system and be able to create and deploy simple applications to your ARTIK module. Then it will be up to you to create something extraordinary. The chapters are arranged in a logical sequence starting with some background information, then how to set up your system, before describing basic programming techniques. External systems such as Temboo and SAMI are covered before rounding things off with debugging and deployment guidelines.

I composed this as I got to know the ARTIK after Glenn Cameron from Samsung kindly sent one to me to work on. As I found out new and interesting things about it, I wrote about what I learned straightaway while the knowledge was still fresh. I tried to maintain the perspective of a new user encountering ARTIK for the first time to avoid making assumptions about what the reader might already know. Some readers will already know about the topics I cover. Even so, the additional background information I provide here will be helpful even to more experienced engineers, designers, makers, and developers.

It is still an early stage in the ARTIK product lifecycle, and many features are still being developed to their full potential. There are topics like video and audio that merit complete books about just that aspect of ARTIK development. Those will come later. For now, it is enough to understand the basics of how ARTIK works so as to have solid foundational knowledge on which to later build the more advanced topics. Some of those topics are mentioned briefly here, but there is not enough space to cover everything in great depth without creating a huge book. For now, let's work on this in more easily digestible stages and get the ARTIK modules up and running first.

The companion *ARTIK Reference Guide* will build on what you learn in this book. It will concentrate on ARTIK internals and provide details for more advanced programming so that you can create more complex applications.

—Cliff Wootton
Crowborough, UK
Spring 2016

CHAPTER 1

■ ■ ■

Getting Started

Introducing the ARTIK Family

Samsung ARTIK is all about versatility. Providing the computing power of a UNIX workstation in a form factor as compact as this will revolutionize the way that smartness is engineered into your products. With computing power delivered as a commodity, ARTIK can make everything smarter.

The Samsung ARTIK platform is designed to jumpstart the development of products that exploit the potential of the Internet of Things (IoT). IoT is a structured way by which all kinds of devices from tiny wearable items to entire homes and factories can communicate with each other. Then they can autonomously adjust their behavior to accommodate real-time changes in their interactions with peers or human operators.

Products like the ARTIK modules are only possible due to the prior success of mobile phone technology. As phones have become smarter and smaller, the integration of memory and computing power into ever-smaller packages can be leveraged to create a general-purpose computer. The further reduction in device size results in technologies such as the ARTIK modules. As these modules become increasingly popular, the economies of scale reduce the unit cost and they can be deployed everywhere.

Reinventing the Engineering Process

Samsung expects ARTIK to be integrated into products, devices, and appliances that the general public will deploy in homes and factories in huge numbers. The SAMI or Temboo ecosystems and others like them will take this integration even further and distribute the smartness across many devices so they work together as a single larger system.

You can retrofit the ARTIK into existing products to make them smarter or include an ARTIK module in the core of a revolutionary new product or service. The ARTIK solution is versatile enough to be deployed in a huge range of scenarios. By developing a base platform, ARTIK helps you leverage all of that technology and concentrate on your value-added innovation. Fundamental capabilities such as communications, media services, sensor integration, security, and compute engines are already up and running. This saves a lot of time when you begin a new design.

Electronic supplementary material The online version of this chapter (doi:10.1007/978-1- 4842-1952-2_1) contains supplementary material, which is available to authorized users.

Using a well-integrated hardware and software solution such as the ARTIK module helps you avoid years of engineering design and development work. Simply add your control interfaces, sensors, and software and let ARTIK take care of the heavy lifting. Because the ARTIK module is built with a lot of well-known open-source technologies, your learning curve can exploit the things you already know. Just fill in the gaps.

About This Book

This is a beginners' guide that will introduce you to developing prototype applications on a Samsung ARTIK module. If you are already an experienced UNIX developer you should feel at home working on ARTIK through the command-line user interface. If you are new to UNIX and the Internet of Things industry, this book will provide useful references to other source material to facilitate your learning experience.

This book will show you how to work with the hardware developer reference board that carries an ARTIK module. The developer board makes access to the pinout connectors on the ARTIK module more convenient for prototyping. The board also provides enhanced hardware debugging connectivity for JTAG probes.

The programming examples in this book are intended to illustrate how to use the application building and deployment commands. They are not very complex, but they do show you in a very brief format how to interact with the hardware from inside your own applications.

The companion Apress *ARTIK Reference Guide* book has more reference material and deeper coverage of the ARTIK internals, along with more extensive coding examples. It will help you move on to more advanced topics and prepare your prototype design for deployment to production.

Finding Out About ARTIK

When a product like ARTIK is so new, the available information about it is scarce. As a developer you need to apply forensic techniques to research-related topics and reverse engineer them to understand what to look for inside the ARTIK module. Once you absorb that knowledge and understand the technology, you are ready to experiment with an idea. It is not always easy, but it is great fun and very satisfying when you get something to work. The Temboo tools are a huge help, because they generate working code that you can learn from. Their code shows you how to access the Arduino compatible pins in your ARTIK module directly from C language or Node.js and other languages.

I was inspired to cover some topics by the posts in the discussion forum, which suggested things that readers would like to know more about. Other content was suggested by reading blogs and tutorials elsewhere on the Internet. Then I concentrated on finding things out by experimentation and documented what I discovered in a logical narrative. The fruits of my own forensic research and experimentation are distilled into this book so you can quickly move on to more advanced things.

I hope this book helps to support developers by answering some of the questions they have asked so far. There will be new questions to answer as we get to know the ARTIK modules better. The Samsung materials are excellent starting points for your learning process. While I have used them as a starting point for my own tutorials, I have added a lot of additional background supporting material around the basic coverage.

Provenance

The book was initially written around the Alpha prototype version of the ARTIK 5 and then upgraded with the information found in the Beta documentation and by testing on a Beta prototype of the ARTIK 5. If you are trying to use the examples in this book on an Alpha prototype ARTIK module, a lot of things had not yet been developed at that point. Some functionality was also not yet available for the Beta prototype, and you will probably observe some functionality differences when you work on the production model.

You might find a practical use for your old Alpha and Beta prototype modules and developer reference boards, but upgrading to a production model ARTIK module when they are available is a good idea. That will ensure a trouble-free development process going forward, and any future software upgrades will be compatible with your prototyping system.

The initial group of ARTIK modules shipped in the spring of 2016 are Commercial Beta version 0.5.0 products. The shipping models will be updated later to production versions as they feed through the manufacturing pipeline. The Commercial Beta is perfectly capable of supporting your prototype product development process. Later on, you may want to risk-manage any potential functional changes by upgrading your ARTIK development systems from time to time as they evolve.

It is natural that things will change inside the ARTIK modules as their design evolves. Where locations within the virtual file system are described, pay special attention to checking these against your own ARTIK module. The fundamental file system organization is dictated by the base operating system (either Nucleus or Fedora). Further changes to the Fedora core are configured by a Yocto profile. There is a possibility that Samsung will move virtual file system locations or change the file names to accommodate new hardware and drivers as they are introduced. It is impossible to predict whether this will happen or when, so you should run some basic checks whenever you upgrade the operating system. Using some intuition and a little forensic research based on what is covered by this book will reveal what you need to know when things move around–as they inevitably will.

Post your observations and discoveries online or submit to the publisher for inclusion in later books. That will help the whole ARTIK community keep up to date.

Although there is some discussion here about the ARTIK 1 modules, this book is primarily concerned with getting your ARTIK 5 and 10 modules working. The ARTIK 1 modules will be delivered in due course, and the knowledge gained from working with the ARTIK 5 and 10 modules can be applied to getting them up and running.

■ **Note** The tutorials and instructions herein are based on what you should observe in a Commercial Beta ARTIK module, with some caveats noted where I found things were not implemented in my earlier Beta test system. My final testing took place on a Commercial Beta unit just as they began to ship.

Experience Helps

To get the most out of a new system, you will rely on a lot of background knowledge and experience that you add to with each new product you work on. That experience takes time to acquire–a lifetime, perhaps. There is always something new being invented to learn about. I realized from the outset that some readers would need to know about important background topics, such as how UNIX works and why IP networks have all those parameters to configure them. Other readers will already be experts in those topics and can safely skip over those sections, although they may need the practical instruction steps. To help readers who are unfamiliar with systems administration, I include basic knowledge to support you during the initial stages. This extra help is not meant to be a complete grounding in UNIX systems administration or how IP networks are implemented. There are many helpful tutorials online and advanced reference books that will go as deeply into those topics as you need if you want to become an expert.

The ARTIK modules run a version of UNIX. Consequently, there are many useful tools that are already installed by default. The vi text editor and gcc compiler are enough to write a simple application without any additional external tool support. If you watch the logging messages during the ARTIK boot process, you will see various other services being started up, such as sendmail. These are all there, ready and waiting to be exploited as part of your design. Get to know these tools well, because the knowledge is career enhancing.

Your Journey Through the Book

Work through the chapters to bring up your development system in an orderly way. If you already have a development environment up and running, just check that your settings are compatible. The earlier chapters are about configuring applications and tools on your workstation. When your development environment is ready, you can interact with your ARTIK module. If you are keen to get started right away, look at the quick-start guide. Not everyone is comfortable with living on the bleeding edge of technology like that and jumping in straight away. Experienced developers enjoy the challenge, however. Gaining a thorough and in-depth knowledge requires a steady step-by-step approach with a gentle learning curve at the beginning. The logos for important software products are included so that when you search for online resources you can identify the correct search results. Some topics have multiple conflicting results that describe products other than the one you need to read about.

Do You Use Windows, Linux, or Mac OS X?

Very often, developer documentation assumes you are working on a Windows workstation. Some professional developers like to use Linux or another UNIX-based system because it is what they grew up with. Recently, and most likely due to the growth in the number of mobile developers writing applications for iOS, a lot of people are using Apple Macintosh computers as a serious platform for their development work.

None of these are necessarily a better solution than the others. They are all different, with Linux and Mac OS sharing some common heritage. A lot of tools have been developed by Apple to replace or supplement command-line utilities that are widely available in Linux. Proprietary Apple tools are not available on Linux, although some open-source projects sponsored by Apple might be. The open-source community plugs the gap with new tools that are usually ported to all three operating systems.

The coverage in this book is balanced across all three development-hosting platforms so as to treat them equally and gives hints about how to resolve any difficulties you encounter. Apress will be delighted to receive advice, comments, and suggestions from readers about improvements to this cross-platform coverage.

■ **Note** Even the core and classic UNIX implementations are fragmented, and there are a few different flavors of Linux. A book like this can cover things from a generic point of view, but the diversity of operating systems, platforms, and versions means that you will often encounter subtle differences. "*Your mileage may vary*".

Get Your Samsung Account

You should sign up for a Samsung account right away. The developer resources for the ARTIK hardware and the SAMI data exchange are only accessible to you when you are logged on with an account. The account is provided free of charge by Samsung for developers and end users. Refer to Chapter 4 ("Security Matters") for an outline of the sign-up process if you are unsure how to do it. The process is straightforward and easy to follow.

Buy an ARTIK Development System Now

The ARTIK 5 development systems went on sale as the Mobile World Conference got underway in Barcelona in February 2016. The supplier is Digi-Key. If you go their website, you can search using the keyword "ARTIK" to find all the Samsung ARTIK products available. Digi-Key has international representation, so you should use the correct version of their site to order in your local currency. The international territories are listed at the bottom of the web page. Here are links to the US and UK ARTIK product searches:

```
http://www.digikey.com/product-search/en?keywords=ARTIK
http://www.digikey.co.uk/product-search/en?keywords=ARTIK
```

Would You Like to Know More?

Some topics of great interest are outside the scope of an introductory book. I will provide a brief mention of them here and provide links to additional material in online resources that I found for you. These resources informed my writing process, but there is much to be gained by your reading them yourself. Most things you need to learn about are based on publicly available knowledge. Explore them to hone your skills and glean more valuable knowledge about the technologies embedded in your ARTIK module.

This curated approach to teaching worked very well in a university environment where the students were expected to use a self-directed study approach to learn what they needed and realize their own project designs.

If you learn something useful and important that is not covered in this book or the companion reference guide, add it to the forum discussions and help your fellow developers at the same time.

There is a small risk that some of the web URLs will move or be deleted in the future. If you cannot find the item listed here, deconstruct the link and look for it using key components of its name. For example, if a blog moves, the articles may still be intact. Take the file-name portion of the URL and search for that using Google, Bing, or any other search engine you prefer.

▦ **Note**   The concept of self-directed learning is best encapsulated by this proverb: "*Give a man a fish and you feed him for a day; teach a man to fish and you feed him for a lifetime.*" I like to teach my students how to catch their own fish!

What to Read Next

There is a lot of ground to cover, and this introductory book is designed to get you up and running without getting too deep into the minutiae of how an ARTIK works. Even at this early stage in the ARTIK world there is more knowledge than I can fit into a beginners' guide. When you need more in-depth knowledge, the more complex and advanced material is published in the companion Apress *ARTIK Reference Guide*. It covers things in much greater detail and has more examples to explain the reference material when necessary.

Quick Start

OK, I know that some of you are impatient to get started with your ARTIK module. If your workstation is not yet able to communicate with your ARTIK module, read Chapter 6 ("Setting Up Your USB Serial Interface") and Chapter 7 ("Terminal Emulators") for help. If you want to live dangerously and try something out now, here are some brief guidelines:

1. Connect your development workstation to the ARTIK developer reference board with the USB cable.

2. Connect to the serial COM port with a terminal emulator. Use PuTTY on a PC, minicom on Linux, or the screen command from a Mac OS terminal window. Run the serial connection at 115200 baud.

3. Power on the developer reference board with the rocker action power switch.

4. Press and hold the power (boot) button down to boot the ARTIK.

5. Watch the verbose output while ARTIK boots.

6. Log in to the ARTIK command line.

   Account: root
   Password: root

7. Go to the temporary files directory:

   ```
   cd /tmp
   ```

8. Use the vi editor to create a C language source file:

   ```
   vi hello.c
   ```

9. Switch to insert mode by pressing the letter [I] key.

10. Type this source code into the editor:

    ```
    #include<stdio.h>

    int main()
    {
    printf("Hello World\n\n");
    return 0;
    }
    ```

11. Press the [**Control**] + [**L**] key combination to refresh the screen if the debugging messages are being displayed at regular intervals.

12. Press the [**Escape**] key to go back to command mode.

13. Press the [:] (colon) key to choose extended command mode.

14. Press the [**w**] key to write the new file contents out to disk.

15. Press the [**q**] key to quit out of the vi editor.

16. Press the [**Return**] key to execute these commands.

17. Now, compile the source code with the gcc command:

    ```
    gcc -Wall hello.c -o hello
    ```

18. Run the compiled program with this command:

    ```
    ./hello
    ```

19. You should see the text "Hello World" echoed on the screen.

Congratulations, you just built an application natively in your ARTIK module and ran it there. Now take a little bit of time to read the rest of this book and get to know your ARTIK module better.

CHAPTER 2

■ ■ ■

Welcome to the Internet of Things

What Is the Internet of Things?

When every electronic and mechanical device is connected to the Internet and has built-in smartness, the Internet becomes a connected web of "things." For years, manufacturers have been making appliances smarter and more automated. There is a limit to how far that can go, because a human being still has to make choices about which kind of washing machine cycle to run or how long the turkey needs to be cooked for Thanksgiving.

Concept Map

The concept map in Figure 2-1 shows how all the new and revolutionary technologies developed in the last few years relate to one another. Some of these concepts are still science fiction, but they are on the horizon. They will soon be in the hands of consumers. Even this concept map is simplified, and many more connections are possible. The Samsung ARTIK is an enabler in all of these concepts.

© Cliff Wootton 2016

C. Wootton, *Beginning Samsung ARTIK*, DOI 10.1007/978-1-4842-1952-2_2

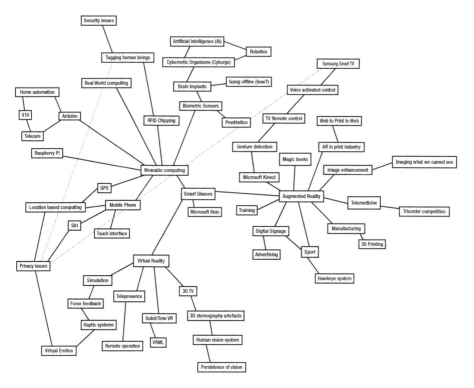

Figure 2-1. *Concept map*

An Example You Can Build Today

Until now, this smartness has been stand-alone. Only the appliance itself knew what it was doing. Today, a cooker could be smart enough to know it is on, and if it also knows it has nothing in it and that you have just left the building, then it could send you a warning. Cookers know nothing about building security, nor should they. Access to the building would be monitored separately. The cooker and access control system could both send a status message to a central decision-making system. The intelligence in that central cortex could use simple, rule-based logic to trigger a warning to a mobile phone and warn you that the cooker is potentially unsafe. Attaching an ARTIK to sensors in a cooker, the front door, and the house security system and then integrating a Samsung SAMI messaging hub provides the means to do this.

The Internet Is Changing—Rapidly

The Internet of Things (IoT) revolution is already rapidly gaining pace. So far, the changes have evolved naturally out of an increasingly connected world. Like most overnight successes, the hard work has taken a long time to come to fruition. The number of devices connected to the Internet already outnumbers the number of people on the planet. This changes the nature of the Internet in subtle ways.

Already, the mobile device explosion has altered the way the Internet is consumed. Website developers have changed their site designs because more people are viewing the World Wide Web on a mobile device. They call this a "Mobile First" strategy, and the desktop versions of their websites take a backseat to the mobile versions.

More evolution will happen as the number of IoT devices increases. The Samsung ARTIK is going to play an important part in that change process.

Disruptive Changes

Publicly available statistics suggest there are about 3.5 billion Internet users. This is equivalent to about half the world population. That total is related to estimates of about 1.7 billion computers and approximately 2 billion mobile devices. Estimating these figures accurately is difficult because many people have more than one Internet-connected device.

The defining point for the Internet of Things revolution is when there are more objects or things connected than people. According to a research paper (The Internet of Things) published by Cisco in April 2011, this statistical cusp would have happened between 2008 and 2009. That is only two years after the introduction of the iPhone in 2007. By 2010, the ratio of connected devices to the population was almost 2 to 1. By 2015, this factor has risen to 3.45, and it is expected that by 2020 there will be more than 6.5 Internet-connected devices for every person on the planet.

These figures do not take into account that a proportion of the world's population has no access to computers at all, so for the developed world, the ratios would be even higher. Early adopters, health monitoring systems, industrial applications, and wired homes may exceed this ratio by an order of magnitude or more.

These estimates are based on what can be engineered with current technology. New inventions will almost certainly increase the rate of change. Cisco predicts that the Internet of Things will result in 40 to 50 billion devices being connected to the Internet by 2020 and that eventually 99% of all physical objects will be connected.

Network Architecture and Design

This shift in technology will have a significant effect on how the Internet works. The way that IP traffic is routed will need to be enhanced to deliver the necessary performance. The implications for security and cyber-attack countermeasures are profound.

Moving from IPv4 to IPv6 protocols removes another important limitation on the number of devices that can be connected and addressed directly.

Sensors

The huge increase in the number of airbags installed in motor vehicles and the sensors that trigger them yielded orders-of-magnitude reductions in the cost of accelerometers. This facilitated motion sensing in phones and tablets at an affordable price.

As the mobile phone market increased in size, the price of sensors has dramatically reduced even further. New kinds of sensors that measure physical characteristics of the real world expand the range of possibilities as they become available. Wireless networking allows new devices to be connected easily, and this communications technology is being integrated directly into the sensors so they can operate independently.

Lifestyle Changes

Evangelists of the Internet of Things (IoT) culture highlight the ways that it can help to solve climate change and energy supply issues, improve living conditions, and potentially eliminate poverty and conflict. Disruptive technology advancements are on the horizon, and the whole application development and deployment environment is likely to change very radically and very quickly.

This might turn out to create as big a change to lifestyles as did the introduction of the Internet. The evolution has been going on quietly in the background for some time. The roots can be traced back to early work at MIT in the late 1990s. The introduction of smartphones in 2007 accelerated the rate of change in the number of devices versus the number of people. Now it has reached a critical mass, and the media has woken up to this fact and started to report on IoT as the next big thing.

A Revolution in Medicine and the Care Community

Some concepts are only possible due to the large number of devices being deployed. The new medical trials initiatives being driven via the open-source HealthKit tools are an example of something that simply was not possible before. IoT will create many more opportunities like that.

Mobile devices such as watches, phones, vehicles, and major transport infrastructure projects are also made smarter by the introduction of IoT technology. IoT has the potential to revolutionize healthcare by pre-empting a risk scenario, such as by early detection of cardiac events, with automated location of the patient and a call for first responder assistance as soon as a situation develops. Related to this are the advanced remote tele-care services. These are assistive technologies for the aged or infirm. There are more advanced prosthetic limbs as well as implant technologies that can restore mobility or replace defective organs. We are living in a time of profound change.

General Electric (GE) has industrialized the sensor processes and gathers large amounts of data from millions of deployed medical devices. This "big data" approach informs new product development and creates huge data sets that facilitate medical breakthroughs. The GE Predix and Apple HealthKit initiatives are two examples of how IoT can revolutionize scientific research.

Industrial Internet of Things

Large corporations are already making significant revenues from IoT. Using IoT on a large scale like this is described as the Industrial Internet of Things (IIoT). GE applies instrumentation to freight trains so they can develop optimized trip plans. These can save millions of dollars' worth of diesel fuel. That translates back to a more ecologically sound approach when applied on a massive scale.

Revenue-generating Opportunities

Revenues are already projected to be several trillion dollars by 2020, rising to several tens of trillions by 2030. These are big stakes indeed.

Several large companies have speculated about future trends. The GE corporation anticipates $500 billion worth of business by 2020 and suggests IoT will add $15 trillion to the global economy by 2030. Cisco believes that the IoT business will be generating $20 trillion in revenue by 2020. The Gartner organization backs these assertions up, although their prediction is slightly more conservative. Even if this is speculative (and the revenue expectations are overhyped), there are certainly big commercial opportunities on the horizon. Some of the revenue-generating opportunities will result from improved efficiency when developing new products or operating existing plants. These are very big numbers indeed and the funding needed to support the emerging IoT business may be taken away from existing industries to resource the new innovations. It is hard to predict which industries will be affected and by how much. There are signs that home automation, medicine, and the automotive industries will be affected. Other industries have the potential to exploit IoT as well.

Your goal is to find a niche where the combination of your knowledge, a Samsung ARTIK module, and these revenue predictions will result in your creating a business that succeeds in generating an income.

## CHAPTER 3

Hello, ARTIK

What Is an ARTIK Module?

Before setting up your development environment and starting work, you need to know what ARTIK is capable of. Spending some time studying the bigger picture will create a better context for a deeper understanding of how it all works.

ARTIK is a family of modules (ARTIK 1, ARTIK 5, ARTIK 10) tailored for the Internet of Things (IoT). With a tiered architecture built for performance, optimized power consumption, and memory utilization and footprint, ARTIK is designed specifically for a variety of applications, from low-end wearable devices to powerful hubs with local processing and analytics. ARTIK's best-in-class security solution includes Embedded Secure Element (ESE) and machine learning for anomaly detection, and Trusted Execution Environment (TEE).

Samsung makes developing for the ARTIK modules as straightforward as possible. In addition to the usual compilers, there are libraries for Java, Python, Temboo, and Arduino, giving you a variety of programming options. You can add others due to the versatile and open nature of the ARTIK design.

What Is an Ecosystem?

The ARTIK ecosystem comprises all the devices you make smarter by integrating an ARTIK module into them, plus the centralized SAMI connecting hub that aggregates all of these sensors and devices into a logical decision-making system. Mobile devices become a dashboard or console with which to control and manage what happens. This is called an ecosystem because it has many dependent parts that operate in a symbiotic fashion. They are all somewhat smart in a self-contained way, but by integrating them, you create a context for very powerful decision making. That is where the true smartness of this approach lies.

An alternative to the SAMI data-aggregation system is the Temboo integrated development and messaging hub. This is a great way to get started with developing your ideas for Internet of Things projects, and the ARTIK module is already pre-configured to integrate with the Temboo ecosystem. Other hub technologies are also feasible to use, or you can create your own if your project design dictates that approach.

© Cliff Wootton 2016

C. Wootton, *Beginning Samsung ARTIK*, DOI 10.1007/978-1-4842-1952-2_3

The ARTIK Modules

The Samsung ARTIK modules are optimized for IoT. Adding an ARTIK module to an appliance or device immediately gives that device an opportunity to integrate with the Internet via cloud services. Add sensors and triggers to your appliance. The ARTIK module can "read" the state of these sensor inputs and communicate them to other devices and services. The ARTIK software you write would take those sensor readings and add artificial intelligence to recognize certain patterns. If a refrigerator starts to have difficulty reaching the correct temperature, perhaps there is something wrong with the cooling system. An engineer can be called automatically and an appointment be made for a maintenance visit. The appliance can be made safe by shutting down the faulty parts, and a warning indicator can be turned on to alert the user.

Some of your project ideas will require much less computing power. Samsung addresses this need by providing small, medium, and large configurations with different feature sets and computing power. The two larger ARTIK modules run embedded UNIX operating systems, while the smallest runs a real-time operating system. All of the ARTIK modules accept a variety of input/output sensors and can use controls to operate other equipment or systems. The ARTIK modules are equipped with wireless communication capabilities to collaborate with one another or via a secure cloud-connected ecosystem. The three ARTIK modules in Figure 3-1 are shown at the same scale to compare the sizes.

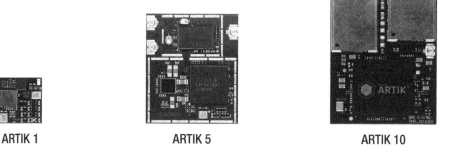

ARTIK 1   ARTIK 5   ARTIK 10

Figure 3-1. *Comparing the ARTIK modules*

The ARTIK modules use a new ePoP (Package on Package) technology that integrates multiple chips onto a single board. This is a robust and very compact form of construction. Samsung calls this technology System on Module (SOM).

The smallest and simplest module is called ARTIK 1. It can be embedded into wearable devices or in places where you only need a very simple computer–perhaps a home media system control surface that is communicating with the central media server to instruct it. This module also has motion sensors included and runs very economically so the battery will last longer between charging cycles. Manufacturer testing indicates that an ARTIK 1 can run for several weeks on a single coin-cell battery.

The medium-size module is called ARTIK 5 and has a more powerful CPU and operating system. In fact, it has multiple CPU cores. It has enhanced audio/visual capabilities too. This is powerful enough to create a home media player attached directly to a video monitor. That creates opportunities to build digital signage systems that can talk to one another and potentially alter their behavior when somebody approaches while they are wearing an ARTIK 1-equipped device. An ARTIK 5 could take over significant responsibilities in running a wired home or a manufacturing process, with the status display being generated onboard and presented on a view screen.

The most capable module is the ARTIK 10. This has significantly more computing capacity with multiple cores and assistive processors for video coding/decoding, graphics rendering, and a very large number of versatile input/output connections. This could operate as either a centralized server or a high-powered media ingest engine.

Software Support

Samsung has created a whole ecosystem of software support for the ARTIK modules. This includes a software stack with all the low-level support you need for accessing the hardware safely and securely.

The ARTIK Community

Sign up for a Samsung ARTIK developer account at the following when you are ready to start developing code for your ARTIK module:

```
https://www.artik.io/developer/users/auth/samsung
```

Once you have signed up, log in with your new ARTIK developer account and explore the resources that Samsung has prepared for you. Having a developer account is not the same as having a Samsung user account registered for use with your smartphone. Register for both kinds of account. Use a unique password for each, and don't use those passwords for anything else in order to protect yourself against identity theft. Make sure that you use a different account as you deploy your software to production, because embedding your own personal login credentials into thousands of shipping devices is a bad idea.

There are many other useful online resources aside from the support materials that Samsung provided. ARTIK is now becoming better known within the IoT community, and support is growing as developers enthusiastically adopt it for experimentation and potential product development. Table 3-1 summarizes where to get more help and advice.

Table 3-1. *ARTIK Community Websites*

Description	URL
Samsung ARTIK blog	`https://www.artik.io/blog/`
Samsung developer pages	`https://www.artik.io/developer`
Instructables	`http://www.instructables.com/member/SamsungIoT/`
Samsung SAMI IO	`https://developer.samsungsami.io/`
Samsung Simband	`https://www.simband.io/`
Samsung Strategy & Innovation Centre	`http://www.samsung.com/us/ssic/`
The ARTIK Forum & Knowledge Base	`http://artie.artik.io/`
ARTIK discussion forum	`http://artie.artik.io/forums/289867-artik`
ARTIK Knowledge Base	`http://artie.artik.io/knowledgebase/articles/all`
Samsung IoT on Instagram	`https://instagram.com/samsungiot/`
Samsung IoT Facebook page	`https://www.facebook.com/SamsungIoT`
Hackster.IO Samsung IoT community	`https://www.hackster.io/samsung`
Samsung IoT on Instructables	`http://www.instructables.com/member/SamsungIoT/`
LinkedIn group	`https://www.linkedin.com/groups/8292561`
Samsung IoT on Twitter	`https://twitter.com/samsungiot`
SmartThings wired home technology	`http://www.smartthings.com/`
Samsung Dev Conference (2016)	`http://www.sdc2016.com/`
Mobile World Congress	`http://www.mobileworldcongress.com/`

Some of these require you to register an account to fully access their resources. Occasionally you will find an online resource that charges a small fee to get access to more value-added and advanced resources, but most are free. Many of these provide newsletter updates via email to alert you to new articles.

Security and Privacy Are Core Needs

Samsung knows that for the ARTIK modules to be reliably deployed, they must remain secure and highly resistant to penetration by hackers. Privacy is also important and is not the same thing as security. IoT devices must communicate securely and privately. At the same time, they need to share information in a controlled way. Data must only be shared with the intended participants and certainly not with strangers or government agencies unless that is beneficial to the end user. Samsung has provided the Embedded Secure Element technology on every ARTIK module. It is implemented onboard as a hardware cryptographic engine.

The first step is to provide sufficient internal capabilities that allow the ARTIK module to sandbox private data within a secure partition that cannot be subverted by external agents. Later on, when the ARTIK needs to share information, those communications must be encrypted. The encryption key is unique to each ARTIK module and is hard-wired or burned-in during the manufacturing process. It cannot be changed or accessed by external processes without destroying the chips. This ensures that every ARTIK can be uniquely recognized and its communications can be encrypted in a very secure fashion.

The Connected Cloud Service

Samsung has worked hard to make sure that the modules are secure and very capable of communicating. Samsung hosts the SAMI cloud-based service that the ARTIK modules can talk to or use to exchange and synchronize information with one another or other devices. Binding these communications to a shared account keeps them separate from other users. This allows a pool of connected ARTIK modules to operate collaboratively but still remain secure. The SAMI cloud service is designed for aggregating, exchanging, and sharing information. SAMI is not intended for mass storage of bulky media assets, but rather it facilitates your access to other separate systems with larger storage capacities that you deploy independently. The SAMI system will be covered in more detail in chapter 18.

Sensory Capabilities

Motion sensors originated in the automotive industry as part of the safety precautions that triggered airbag deployment in the case of a sudden deceleration. As these became more widespread and were fitted to all new cars, the price of the sensors went down. Eventually, they reached a price point where embedding an accelerometer inside a mobile device became cost effective. The first mobile technology application was motion detection in laptops. The motion detector alerts a disk drive that the laptop has been knocked off a table. The hard drive can then park the read/write heads safely in the short time before the laptop hits the ground. Progress in these accelerometers further reduced the price and size. Now they are small and cheap enough to be embedded inside phones and tablets. A gyroscope improves the orientation and position calculations that aggregate all of the sensor values to yield a more reliable output. Nowadays, a magnetometer can augment this to determine the direction the device is pointing. More sophisticated devices are equipped with barometric sensors to work out the height above sea level. This coupled with GPS antennae and knowledge of Wi-Fi and cell tower positions means that location and orientation can be determined very accurately.

Communications Challenges

The sheer number of devices that communications carriers must support simultaneously is a big challenge. As of Q4 2015, the number of mobile phones and tablets has overtaken desktop and laptop devices. The Internet is supporting approximately 4 billion unique devices, and this number is set to increase without IoT making a difference. Predictions vary, but it is possible that by 2020, there could be 50 billion IoT devices competing for the available communications capacity. Increasing the mobile traffic levels by more than an order of magnitude is a challenge to say the least.

Designing your products and services to aggregate multiple devices and connect to the Internet via a hub would help alleviate this problem. Low-power localized personal networks that connect all your wearable or in-car smart devices and use IPv6 protocols will also help.

IoT products must have sufficient intelligence to avoid wasting valuable wireless capacity to reach a simple decision. A farmer might deploy an automated water irrigation system that can measure soil moisture levels, detect daylight, compute time of day, and measure ambient temperature and humidity. Aside from acquiring a weather prediction, it should be smart enough to know when to activate the sprinklers to deliver enough water to the crops at just the right time to be the most effective. This kind of autonomous intelligence is an ecologically sound proposition that minimizes the use of valuable water resources, optimizes crop yields, and should be able to run unattended. Even the weather forecast might be acquired from a digital radio service. Such a system only needs to send a small status message to the farm management system once an hour. Capacity planning is a key component of making successful IoT products work efficiently.

Looking at this problem in the context of an office environment where staff would bring in their own devices forces a completely different approach to provisioning the Wi-Fi services within a building. Capacity planning needs to take into account how many wireless-connected devices each staff member is carrying. Aggregating those devices into a hub application running on a mobile phone is one possible scenario. Only the phone needs to use the Wi-Fi network, which will reduce complexity and traffic. Within the boundary of someone's personal space, all their devices will talk to each other, but privacy is maintained because the central cortex in the phone then only transmits filtered and aggregated data to a remote service.

Integration with Other Platforms

The Samsung ARTIK modules are all certified as being compatible with the Arduino family of modules. This immediately expands the range of sensory possibilities. You could develop Arduino applications and run them directly on an ARTIK. Alternatively, complex pre-processing can be done in an Arduino and then be communicated to the ARTIK. This lightens the load on the ARTIK core processors and allows it to execute the main event loop more efficiently. Arduino modules are well known for their capability to integrate with sensors and for their output connections that can be amplified via driver transistors so as to control very heavy mechanical loads. This driver capability allows an Arduino to operate motors, high-powered lighting systems, servos, hydraulics, and lasers or any similar high-powered machinery. Robotic manufacturing systems and industrial process control become immediately available to your ARTIK-empowered systems. You have the choice to use Arduino boards as delegates or to control and sense things directly from the ARTIK itself.

Benefits to Consumers

Because Samsung now has a core-enabling technology, it can build new consumer products using ARTIK as a foundation. This saves searching for new technologies and keeps all of the research and development in house. Because the ARTIK modules are made with Samsung silicon chips, this also keeps their chip-making foundries busy too. It is a very good solution to a vertically oriented company that can use its own in-house component manufacturing and add more value at each level of the product-design process. Ultimately, this benefits the consumer because the products become more affordable.

Introducing the ARTIK 1

The ARTIK 1 module is extremely compact and is designed for use in scenarios where power consumption, size, and minimal computing power are paramount. The 12mm x 12mm square form factor is good for hiding an ARTIK 1 module inside wearable devices. This is small enough to find space for it in most projects. This ARTIK module is ideal for creating Bluetooth location-based beacons, activity trackers, smart wristband devices, or IoT end nodes that can control digital signage displays or manage appliances. One ARTIK 1 module per room in a wired home could handle environment, lighting, and media control surfaces. Figure 3-2 shows the ARTIK 1 module, enlarged from its 12mm x 12mm size.

Figure 3-2. *The ARTIK 1 module*

The ARTIK 1 module is designed to consume very little power. Nevertheless, you should take power consumption into account when developing your application code. The more CPU cycles you consume, the larger the battery drain. Try to design your application to accomplish as much as possible with as little computing capacity as you can manage.

Functional Organization

A simplified functional breakdown of the ARTIK 1 module is shown in Figure 3-3. This diagram illustrates the major components of the ARTIK 1 internal sub-systems.

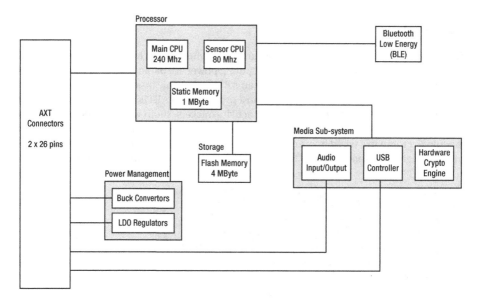

Figure 3-3. *The ARTIK 1 module block diagram*

Operating System

The ARTIK 1 module has an embedded operating system based on the Nucleus Real-Time Operating System (RTOS). The real-time nature of wearable devices needs a more lightweight operating system than the Fedora Linux used in the ARTIK 5 and 10 modules.

Wireless Communications

Communications to the outside world are possible via a Bluetooth transceiver. The communications run in a very low-energy configuration (BLE version 4.0). Use this to exchange messages with a mobile phone, tablet, or watch. Perhaps within close proximity, sensors in an environment can also detect the wearer's presence and location. The signal is transmitted and received by a chip-size antenna that is integrated onto the ARTIK 1 main board.

Spatial Sensors

There is an integrated 9-axis accelerometer and gyroscope for detecting motion and orientation and a magnetometer for detecting the orientation with respect to the Earth's magnetic field. Having a "compass" is useful for augmenting the motion and orientation sensing. The ARTIK 1 will always be able to figure out which way is up and what direction is the shortest way home.

This is the only member of the ARTIK family that has motion-sensing capabilities. Motion sensing can be implemented on products built around the ARTIK 5 and 10 modules by installing external sensors. Perhaps for some solutions, combining an ARTIK 1 and one of the larger ARTIK modules is a good solution. Offload the motion-sensing work to the ARTIK 1 so it can work out gestures. The high-level gesture events are then transmitted to the ARTIK 5 or 10 modules to control an application running there.

Computing Capacity

There are two CPU cores available for running custom application software. One CPU runs at 250MHz and the other at 80MHz. By having two processors, the physical sensing work can be delegated to one of the processors while the other is in control of the main application. This is helpful because a real-time operating system like Nucleus can only run one task at a time, although it can switch tasks very quickly when necessary. The task switch is not managed the way it would be in a general-purpose operating system because an RTOS needs to respond to interrupts and events in a timely manner. Having two CPU cores available makes it easier to delegate one CPU to handling user-generated events while the other manages more compute-intensive tasks.

Memory Storage

For storing and processing data on an ARTIK 1 module, you have 1MB of on-chip memory mapped into the address space of the CPU. Some of this will be devoted to running the operating system. Another 4MB of Flash memory is accessible via a Serial Peripheral Interface (SPI) connection.

The amount of memory in an ARTIK 1 module is significantly more than developers had at their disposal when microprocessors were first used to make personal computers. Sophisticated applications were created in those days with limited resources, and the amount of memory you have available in an ARTIK 1 should be more than enough for the kind of wearable devices or Internet of Things (IoT) endpoints you are creating. Write your code economically and avoid squandering the available resources in your ARTIK to eke out the CPU capacity and battery life.

Video Display Output

The ARTIK 1 module has a WVGA video output driver to put an image on an external display screen. The resolution is 800 pixels wide by 480 high. At an aspect ratio of 15:9, this is almost widescreen. Perhaps it is sufficient for the display on a watch.

Introducing the ARTIK 5

The ARTIK 5 module is more powerful than the ARTIK 1. The ARTIK 5 has faster and more capable CPU cores running at 1GHz. There is also more on-board memory than the ARTIK 1. Because the ARTIK 5 has more connectivity, the board is larger than the ARTIK 1, and it is more carefully screened against radio frequency interference (RFI) because it runs faster. There are more wireless connection options and support for the ZigBee protocol, which is gaining popularity in wired home installations.

The 29mm x 25mm form factor is a significant achievement when you consider the capabilities that Samsung has accommodated in this device.

The ARTIK 5 module also supports the Samsung Secure Element protocols that afford robust protection against hacking at the module level. Integrate your distributed systems so they can collaborate by connecting them together via the SAMI cloud-based protocols.

This ARTIK module can also decode a variety of video playback formats and present the output directly on an attached video monitor. The ARTIK 5 is well suited for building smart home hubs, high-end smart watches, drone flight controllers, and embedded IP-based camera management systems. Figure 3-4 shows the ARTIK 5 module with its radio frequency (RF) shielding removed.

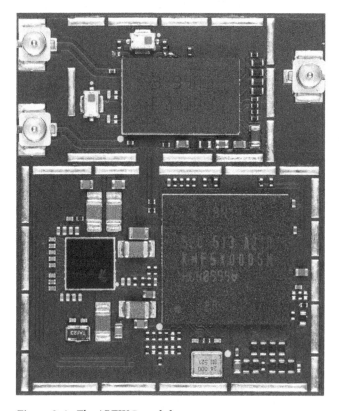

Figure 3-4. *The ARTIK 5 module*

Functional Organization

A simplified functional breakdown of the ARTIK 5 module is shown in Figure 3-5. This diagram shows the important sub-systems inside an ARTIK 5.

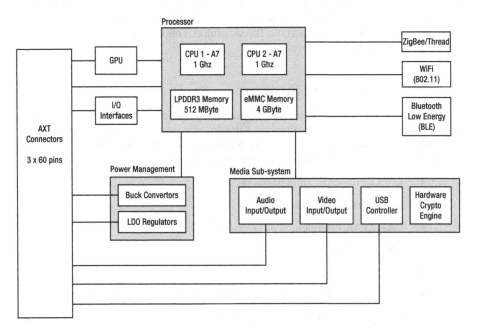

Figure 3-5. *The ARTIK 5 module block diagram*

Operating System

The same version of Fedora Linux is used in the ARTIK 5 and 10 modules. Fedora is a multi-process UNIX OS usually found in mainstream computers. The performance is optimized for throughput to get the maximum compute performance, as opposed to the Nucleus OS in an ARTIK 1 that is optimized for responsiveness. This additional computing power lets you build more sophisticated products. The embedded version of Fedora in the ARTIK modules has been generated with Yocto templates that pare down and configure the Fedora distribution to make it small enough to embed.

Wireless Communications

The ARTIK 5 module supports the Bluetooth low-energy communications (BLE version 4.0) for attaching close-proximity peripherals.

Because this module is not designed to be the core of a wearable device, it also has Wi-Fi support for the IEEE 802.11 b/g/n protocols. The newer IEEE 802.11 ac and ah versions are not currently supported.

For wired home automation enthusiasts, the ARTIK 5 module supports the ZigBee (IEEE 802.15.4) communications standard. The competing Thread Group protocol is also supported. They both operate in a similar way, but there are differences in their capabilities. Thread has a longer reach than ZigBee, but ZigBee can support many more devices within a local mesh. ZigBee has been available for at least a decade. The Thread protocols are based on IPv6 and are a result of the Nest learning thermostats from Google. Samsung and ARM actively support the Thread project. Following the progress as it evolves will inform your future strategy.

Networking Protocol Support

The ARTIK 5 natively supports the following networking protocols. Add others if you have the necessary source code for the libraries. Samsung may add other communications protocols at a later date. Refer to chapter 9 ("Networking Your ARTIK"), where these are described in more detail, to avoid repeating the same discussion for each module:

- OMA Lightweight M2M protocol (LW M2M)

- Constrained Application Protocol (CoAP)

- Message Queue Telemetry Transport (MQTT)

- IPv4 via Ethernet

- IPv6 via Ethernet

- IPv6 via Low-power Wireless Personal Networks (6LoWPAN)

- Multicast Domain Name System for Wi-Fi (mDNS)

Computing Capacity

The CPU in the ARTIK 5 is a dual-core ARM A7 processor similar to that found in many mobile devices. Both cores run at 1GHz, providing plenty of computing leverage for your applications. This is capable of loading the attached graphics processor with new instructions very quickly.

Graphics Processing Unit (GPU)

In addition to the compute engines, there is an embedded graphics co-processor. The ARM® Mali™ - 400 Graphics Processing Unit (GPU) supports OpenVG version 1.1 for vector graphics and OpenGL ES1.1/2.0 for 3D rendering.

Open GL for embedded systems is a sub-set of the full Open GL specification. This implementation maps functionality from OpenGL 1.1 and 2.0. The OpenVG implementation provides hardware-assisted vector-graphics drawing tools.

This is a very powerful graphics engine and provides a serious level of graphics capability. In a process-control application, the production workflow can be rendered as a mimic display showing an entire manufacturing process or perhaps a railway network in a transport management and control system. Find out more about these graphics capabilities here:

```
https://en.wikipedia.org/wiki/Mali_(GPU)
http://www.arm.com/products/multimedia/mali-cost-efficient-graphics/
mali-400-mp.php
https://en.wikipedia.org/wiki/OpenGL
https://en.wikipedia.org/wiki/OpenGL_ES
https://en.wikipedia.org/wiki/OpenVG
```

Memory Storage

The ARTIK 5 modules have 512MB of fast-access, low-power DDR3 (LPDDR3) memory directly connected to the CPU. This is similar to the kind of memory you have in a laptop computer but requires much less power to operate. Everything about the ARTIK modules is designed to conserve power, and the memory architecture is carefully designed to drain the minimum power from a battery.

Additional storage capacity is implemented with a larger 4GB bulk memory attached as eMMC storage. This is effectively a memory card that is permanently bonded to the ARTIK module. It is enough to be able to store and process video or draw large animated graphic scenes. A vertically integrated manufacturer such as Samsung has a lot of the technology needed to create an ARTIK already established in-house.

Hardware Video Codec Support

The ARTIK 5 module includes hardware for a variety of video formats summarized in Table 3-2. Encoding and decoding support varies depending on the codec. Not all codecs are supported in both modes, and the encoding is powerful enough to support HD video as 30 frames per second (FPS) with 720 lines. This is not the full HD 1080p image size delivered by a Blu-ray disk player.

Table 3-2. *ARTIK 5 Video Support*

Codec	Encode	Decode
H.263	√	√
H.264 (AVC, MPEG 4 part 10)	√	√
VP8	√	√
MPEG-2		√
VC1		√
Xvid		√

Introducing the ARTIK 10

The ARTIK 10 is the most capable and powerful of all the modules in this family. It has more of everything compared with the ARTIK 5. In terms of computing capacity it has 8 CPU cores in all. There are many more connector outputs, and it can handle a higher quality HD video output or encoding throughput. This would make a very capable starting point for building TV set-top boxes with interactive TV capabilities. It is probably powerful enough to create a home Intranet server or media hub for a digital entertainment system. If you delegate more of the hard work to a centralized ARTIK 10, you can use ARTIK 5 modules in your client players instead of needing to deploy more ARTIK 10 modules. If you construct a home Intranet around an ARTIK 10, that could also provide a personal cloud integration for all the devices around the home and then provide gateway access to the Internet via a single interface. If an ARTIK 5 is not powerful enough for your needs, an ARTIK 10 is certainly up to the task of managing the throughput for all kinds of smart machines.

The 29mm x 39mm form factor is astonishing when you consider this is a fully featured UNIX computer with high definition video encode/decode capabilities integrated into the module.

This module is powerful enough to live encode incoming video for onward delivery to a media storage system. This opens up possibilities for use in security monitoring and personal video recorder products. It could also find applications in the broadcast industry for building master control and file-based edit/storage systems.

The ARTIK 10 module also supports the Samsung Secure Element protocols that afford robust protection against hacking at the module level. Integrate your distributed systems via the SAMI cloud-based protocols.

This ARTIK can also decode a variety of video playback formats and present the output directly on an attached video monitor. Figure 3-6 shows the ARTIK 10 module.

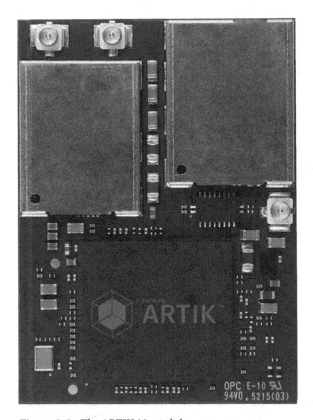

Figure 3-6. *The ARTIK 10 module*

Functional Organization

The functional breakdown of the ARTIK 10 module is shown in Figure 3-7. This diagram shows the main internal sub-systems in an ARTIK 10.

29

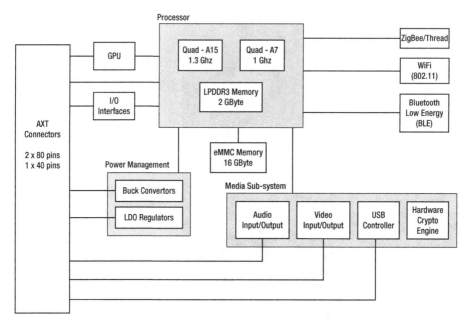

Figure 3-7. *The ARTIK 10 module block diagram*

Operating System

The operating system is the same version of Fedora Linux as the ARTIK 5 uses, although there are some differences in the installed libraries and supporting code. The additional computing power of the ARTIK 10 lets you build more sophisticated products with faster performance or higher throughput. The embedded version in the ARTIK modules has also been generated with the Yocto templates that pare down the Fedora distribution to make it small enough to embed.

Wireless Communications

The ARTIK 10 module supports Bluetooth low-energy communications (BLE version 4.0) and Wi-Fi support for the IEEE 802/11 b/g/n protocols. The newer IEEE 802/11 ac version is not currently supported.

Like the ARTIK 5, the ARTIK 10 module supports the ZigBee (IEEE 802.15.4) communications standard. The competing Thread Group protocol is also supported, and your software designs that work on the ARTIK 5 should be easily ported to the ARTIK 10 if you need the additional computing resources.

Networking Protocol Support

The ARTIK 10 module natively supports the following networking protocols. Add others as part of your project implementation if you need them. Samsung may add other protocols to the ARTIK 10 module at a later date. Refer to chapter 9 ("Networking Your ARTIK"), where these protocols are described, to avoid repeating the same discussion for each module:

- OMA Lightweight M2M protocol (LW M2M)
- Constrained Application Protocol (CoAP)
- Message Queue Telemetry Transport (MQTT)
- IPv4 via Ethernet
- IPv6 via Ethernet
- IPv6 via Low-power Wireless Personal Networks (6LoWPAN)
- Multicast Domain Name System for Wi-Fi (mDNS)
- OpenHAB-based framework
- OpenStack (Swift) Framework

The ARTIK 10 is the only module that natively supports OpenHAB and OpenStack networking. If you have access to the source code, they could be ported to an ARTIK 5 if you are prepared to do the work.

Computing Capacity

The CPU support in the ARTIK 10 comprises a quad-core ARM A15 processor plus a quad-core ARM A7 processor. The A15 runs at 1.3GHz and the A7 at 1GHz, providing a lot of computing power. This is equivalent to a small laptop computer or a high-end tablet device.

Graphics Processing Unit (GPU)

The ARTIK 10 has a more powerful graphics co-processor than the ARTIK 5 has. The ARM® Mali™ - 628 Graphics Processing Unit (GPU) supports a variety of graphics frameworks to generate images very quickly. See Table 3-3 for a summary.

Table 3-3. ARTIK 10 GPU Support

Framework	Version
OpenGL ES	1.1/2.0/3.0
OpenCL	1.1
OpenVG	1.0.1
DirectX	11
Google Renderscript	

31

OpenGL for embedded systems is a sub-set of the full OpenGL specification. This implementation maps functionality from OpenGL 1.1, 2.0, and 3.0. The OpenGL implementation in an ARTIK 10 module has additional higher-version support than the ARTIK 5 does.

The OpenVG implementation provides hardware-assisted vector graphics drawing tools.

The Microsoft DirectX support will assist in porting applications and frameworks from projects that are built for Windows operating systems.

The Google Renderscript support is compatible with the framework developed for use in the Android operating system.

This GPU also supports OpenCL, which provides additional computing capacity to the ARM CPU's. The CPU can delegate work to the GPU, such as video compression or big data computations on large arrays.

This is a very powerful graphics engine that provides a serious level of graphics capability. Find out more about these graphics capabilities here:

```
https://en.wikipedia.org/wiki/Mali_(GPU)
http://www.arm.com/products/multimedia/mali-cost-efficient-graphics/
mali-t628.php
https://en.wikipedia.org/wiki/OpenGL
https://en.wikipedia.org/wiki/OpenGL_ES
https://en.wikipedia.org/wiki/OpenVG
https://en.wikipedia.org/wiki/OpenCL
https://en.wikipedia.org/wiki/DirectX
https://en.wikipedia.org/wiki/Renderscript
```

Memory Storage

The ARTIK 10 module has 2GB of low-power DDR3 memory (LPDDR3) on board. This is similar to the kind of memory you have in a laptop computer but requires much less power to operate. This memory is directly connected to the CPU. An additional 16GB of eMMC memory capacity is attached through a slower interface. This is the equivalent of approximately 20 CD-ROMs or a couple of DVD disks. If you compress the audio, perhaps a thousand or more songs could be stored inside the ARTIK 10 module.

Everything about the ARTIK modules is designed to conserve power, and memory architecture is carefully designed to drain the minimum power from a battery.

Audio Codec Support

The ARTIK 10 provides audio codec support for surround sound and multi-channel mixing. This is all done in hardware that avoids using up valuable computing capacity on the CPU. The surround sound delivery is done via the I2S bus. The multi-channel support is implemented as an 8-channel Time Division Multiplexor (TDM) routed to a hardware mixer for mix-down and routing to the output.

Hardware Video Codec Support

The ARTIK 10 module includes hardware for higher quality video formats (summarized in Table 3-4) than the ARTIK 5 has. Encoding and decoding support varies depending on the codec. Not all codecs are supported in both modes, and the encoding is powerful enough to support HD video at 120 frames per second (FPS) with 1080 lines. This is better than the quality you would have delivered from a Blu-ray disk player. The higher frame rate will make sports footage and other rapidly moving objects easier to see on the screen due to the reduced motion blur artifacts.

Table 3-4. *ARTIK 10 Video Support*

Codec	Encode	Decode
H.263	√	√
H.264 (AVC, MPEG 4 part 10)	√	√
VP8	√	√
MPEG-2		√
VC1		√

Comparing the ARTIK Modules

The ARTIK module family spans a huge range of capabilities. At the smallest scale, you have a very compact and lightweight module (ARTIK 1) that is ideally suited to developing wearable devices or being embedded inside consumer products. At the other end of the scale, the ARTIK 10 is a hugely powerful media processing–capable 8-core computer with a lot of onboard capabilities and many interfacing possibilities due to the range of I/O processors integrated with the CPU. In the middle ground, the ARTIK 5 has media-processing playback capabilities and also has a generous complement of inputs and outputs.

Many features are engineered and implemented across all ARTIK modules. The only difference is the scale or number of component items supported. ARTIK 1 has the fewest, and the ARTIK 10 has more because it is designed for larger and more complex tasks.

Power Management Integrated Circuit (PMIC)

Power consumption is reduced to a very low level across all ARTIK modules. The same kind of embedded power management controller is used across all ARTIK modules. This maintains a steady power source for all the chips on the board and the voltages being supplied to externally connected devices.

The PMIC is a critically important part of the power management that extends the life of the battery providing power to your ARTIK module. The buck convertors step down the incoming power supply to the correct regulated voltage to deliver power to the onboard processor and other components. The low-dropout (LDO) circuits maintain the supply when the battery runs down.

The PMIC support in the ARTIK 10 has more buck convertors and LDOs for regulating the power supply when compared with an ARTIK 5 or ARTIK 1. Learn more about PMIC concepts here:

```
https://en.wikipedia.org/wiki/Low-dropout_regulator
```

Security Management

The ARTIK modules implement the hardware-encrypted Secure Element system that Samsung provides across the whole ARTIK range. Refer to chapter 4 ("Security Matters") for more details about how this works.

Support for Audio Coding

At this very early stage of the ARTIK product lifecycle, the audio capabilities are present but unsophisticated. There is an API to access the inbuilt audio mixer, and the ARTIK can run various open-source applications, such as mPlayer, to process the audio.

This functionality will become more capable and sophisticated as Samsung continues to develop the ARTIK products, and third-party developers also have an opportunity here to extend the capabilities by their own ingenuity.

The foundation of the audio support is built on the Advanced Linux Sound Architecture (ALSA) project. This is a standard set of tools for audio processing in Linux. ALSA provides support for MIDI in addition to the sampled audio support. Access the ALSA project and explore the open source and guidance on using the tools here:

```
http://www.alsa-project.org/main/index.php/Main_Page
http://alsa.opensrc.org/
```

Find out more about the audio toolkits and capabilities in the companion Apress *ARTIK Reference Guide* book.

Support for Video Coding

Digital video is a complex topic. The ARTIK 10 has sufficient computing power to encode video from a camera or digital video interface. The ARTIK 5 is capable of playing back high-quality video.

The documentation relating to UVC camera drivers for Linux lists various compatible cameras and how to interact with them. Find out more about UVC here:

```
http://www.ideasonboard.org/uvc/
```

The ARTIK OS has the popular ffmpeg video-coding tool installed by default. The aplay and mPlayer tools should get you started with playing video clips.

This is an advanced topic and requires a good deal of careful integration. It is dependent on the make and model of your video input/output devices and on what you plan to do with them. Consult the *ARTIK Reference Guide* for more details.

Physical Connections

The connections are all brought out of the ARTIK modules via Panasonic AXT multi-pin connectors on the underside. Build receptacles for these connectors on your interface inside the product you want to empower with the ARTIK. Allow sufficient vertical space in your mechanical design to accommodate these connectors–and the ARTIK when it is plugged into them. Look at the developer reference boards to see these connectors under your ARTIK module. Check out the companion Apress *ARTIK Reference Guide* for detailed information about the pinouts and connectors. The configuration of these connectors is different for each of the ARTIK module variants. An example connector is shown in Figure 3-8.

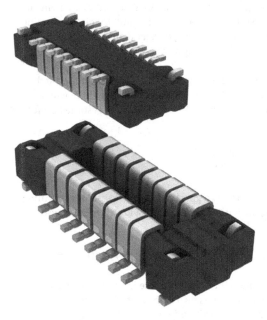

Figure 3-8. *Panasonic AXT connectors*

About the ARTIK Operating Systems

The ARTIK 5 and 10 modules run a version of Linux. You should become familiar with UNIX commands, scripts, and how the file system works. It helps to know about regular expressions and how to pipe the output of one command into another. There are many books available that will teach you about the UNIX command-line shells.

Nucleus RTOS

The Nucleus real-time operating system in the ARTIK 1 module is unique to that device. The larger ARTIK modules use a Linux general-purpose operating system (Fedora), which works quite differently.

NUCLEUS

Figure 3-9. The Nucleus OS logo

Because the ARTIK 1 is used in a different context, it needs a real-time operating system (RTOS) rather than a traditional time-sharing process multiplexed operating system. A traditional operating system focuses on getting as much work done within the shortest time span. This sometimes affects its response to external stimulations. A real-time operating system has a predictable response time. There are a lot of similarities, but an RTOS will generally break down a computing task into smaller slices that are ready to receive new input when called for. RTOS systems are also more event driven. The coding of RTOS internals is more efficient and constrained so as to execute more quickly than a traditional time-sharing OS. This allows an RTOS-equipped system to respond to real-world trigger events right away.

The Nucleus RTOS was developed by Mentor Graphics and is already embedded in several billion consumer devices. Because it has been widely adopted, there will be a large number of other useful resources available on the Internet. Here is some helpful documentation to start with:

```
https://www.mentor.com/embedded-software/nucleus/
https://en.wikipedia.org/wiki/Nucleus_RTOS
```

The Nucleus community discussion forum is a good place to go for solutions. Any questions you will come up with during the early part of your research have probably come up before and been answered already:

```
https://communities.mentor.com/community/embedded_software/nucleus_rtos
```

Nucleus is less capable of being modified than Fedora since it is managed as a closed-source project. If you plan to embed Nucleus into a product of your own design, the commercial license permits you to see the source code. The Samsung engineers would have access to add features and bind the OS to their hardware but as third party customers, we cannot obtain the source code and add our own enhancements. This suggests that ARTIK 1 software development should focus on writing applications, because the OS is harder to access for modification.

The Nucleus kernel only consumes about 2KB of your available memory. Beyond this, memory consumption depends on what additional operating system services you have configured. When you write your application, be aware of the limited amount of memory and only use what you need. Concentrate hard on removing potential memory leaks, and recycle the memory allocations to avoid filling it up. Be as economic as you can with CPU processing capacity to avoid draining the battery.

Linux: Fedora OS

The operating system in the ARTIK 5 and 10 modules is based on Fedora Linux and has more capabilities than the Nucleus OS found in the ARTIK 1.

Figure 3-10. *Fedora Linux logo*

These larger modules have more hardware interfaces to control and require libraries of supporting code that the ARTIK 1 does not need. Fedora is not a real-time OS because an ARTIK 5 or 10 works like a conventional computer and does not expect to respond to outside stimuli as immediately as an ARTIK 1 does. Find out more about Fedora here:

```
http://www.linux.com/directory/Distributions/popular-distributions/fedora
https://en.wikipedia.org/wiki/Fedora_(operating_system)
https://fedoraproject.org/wiki/Overview
https://getfedora.org/
https://docs.fedoraproject.org/en-US/
```

The Alpha prototype versions of the ARTIK modules shipped with Fedora 20. The Beta prototype modules upgrade that version to Fedora 22, which has many more capabilities. Fedora will be upgraded as new releases are developed, so your production revision ARTIK modules may be running a later version. It is quite easy to detect what version you have from inside your applications. A simple example in chapter 15 illustrates how to do this with only a few lines of code.

Fedora focuses on rapid and regular release cycles, with new features being added often. It is used as the basis of the Redhat Linux distribution that powers many corporate systems. CentOS is a community-supported derivative used in many virtual private servers that power the World Wide Web. Because of this relationship, the Fedora-based operating system is well supported by a large community, and there are lots of resources to support your development activity.

But What Is Yocto?

The Yocto project is not an operating system itself but rather is a template for taking an existing Linux distribution and paring it down to be embedded onto a single-board computer. The ARTIK modules use the Fedora Linux distribution as a basis for the Yocto embedding process.

Figure 3-11. *Yocto project logo*

Samsung has joined with a lot of other companies that produce consumer products to form the Yocto Long-Term Support Initiative (LTSI). This is designed to provide stable and ongoing support for products based on this template-driven embedded operating system infrastructure.

Enthusiasts debate online whether Yocto is the optimum choice for the ARTIK modules. Samsung does not want to exclude any OS version that ARTIK developers might use. Theoretically for now, you could build your own embedded Linux operating system and install it. The resources you need to create a device tree and include a board support package have not yet been published. As ARTIK becomes more widely known, the user community will develop solutions like that for everyone to share. ARTIK modules running Tizen and Snappy Ubuntu have already been demonstrated. You have to make a solid business case to justify the amount of effort needed to port a new operating system to the ARTIK. For most users, the default OS will be just fine.

Here is the home page for the Yocto project. This is a good place to start searching for resources:

```
https://www.yoctoproject.org/about
```

Other Operating Systems

ARTIK discussion forum postings asked whether other operating systems could be ported to the ARTIK. The simple answer is yes, because it is based on a UNIX-driven hardware architecture, and therefore any UNIX variant is feasible in principle. The more complex answer is that while anything is possible, some things are easy and others are a bit harder. Provided you build a bootable eMMC image small enough for the embedded OS to work within the available memory in the ARTIK, this should be doable.

As an example of running other operating systems, the ARTIK 5 and 10 modules were demonstrated at the 2015 Samsung Tizen developer conference with a special build of the Tizen operating system. Tizen is an operating system developed by Samsung for use in TV set top boxes. This was also integrated with the SAMI system for exchanging IoT data between devices. Dr. Luc Julia demonstrated how to create a Tizen TV Manifest in SAMI, get real-time data, and have the Tizen TV interact with other devices already connected to SAMI after the Manifest was created.

A Snappy Ubuntu core running on an ARTIK module was demonstrated at the Mobile World Conference–Barcelona in February 2016, further proving that if you have the resources and knowledge, porting a different OS to the ARTIK is not an impossible task.

Summary

Now that you are getting to know the ARTIK modules and how the three different models compare with one another, it is time to look more closely at the ARTIK features and capabilities. Although the modules are different and there are two kinds of operating system in use, the modules all work in fundamentally the same way. The next chapter will examine the security features of the ARTIK modules. Security is fundamental to building a reliable and robust Internet of Things ecosystem. Samsung has built security support into the hardware that makes it much more difficult to subvert.

■ ■ ■

## CHAPTER 4

Understanding Security

Risk Factors and Dystopian Futures

Taking security seriously is more important than ever before when it comes to IoT systems. IoT systems must be 100 percent robust, secure, and private too. There are three perspectives on this–the Good, the Bad, and the Arguable.

1. Smart vehicles within a transport infrastructure can leverage their location information to add new capabilities. Knowing that your car is moving and that its location is not adjacent to any of your nominated drivers is a good indication that it has been stolen. Self-driving cars will always be location tracked and can be controlled or immobilized remotely. Car theft will be much more difficult, because vehicles can be immobilized remotely. Even vehicle ownership is being questioned as a consequence of using self-driving vehicles.

2. On the other side of this scenario are the risk factors. Developers should seriously consider the dark side of this equation. Hacking a self-driving car could be a way to cause an accident or gain unauthorized access to the car to steal its contents.

3. There are grey areas where trading a little privacy in exchange for improved services and infrastructure is beneficial. Everything will be trackable, including every individual person and their property. Governments can use this tracking technology as a way to price the transport infrastructure. This makes it very easy to introduce congestion charging as a way to alter the driving habits of the population at large without massive infrastructure needing to be built. That may lead to less stressful commuting. It remains to be seen whether the revenues would be invested in improving the transport system as a whole. Insurance companies are already considering how to personalize policies by aggregating big data sources to know more about your lifestyle.

© Cliff Wootton 2016
C. Wootton, *Beginning Samsung ARTIK*, DOI 10.1007/978-1-4842-1952-2_4

Take into account all of these perspectives and ensure the security of your design is well conceived, operates as you intend, and cannot be subverted by third parties. Protect the privacy of your customers to avoid unwanted intrusions into their lifestyles.

Security Ecosystem

Securing your ARTIK-based products against intrusion, interference, and data theft is a critical part of your design process. Samsung has built tools into the ecosystem that help you with that. You are free to develop a security system of your own, but the combination of the built-in security tools and the SAMI cloud-based data exchange can take a lot of the hard work out of building a secure and robust architecture for your product.

Read this blog article by Kevin Sharp that explains the whole security issue in an interesting way:

```
https://www.artik.io/blog/2015/iot-101-security
```

SAMI

SAMI can provide an application standard for a market like IoT where interoperability and security are essential. The design emphasizes data-driven development. Writing a manifest decouples the framework from having to hardwire support for devices and also helps you manage the extensibility that is vital to being able to support new and as yet unknown devices. Think beyond single devices and consider instead how data belonging to different users and devices can be connected to generate new insights. By adding rules that trigger actions, the data exchange becomes much more than a simple data conversion nexus. Samsung describes this as *data fusion*.

OAuth2

Security in the ARTIK and SAMI ecosystems is handled with OAuth2 protocols. These are well known in the industry, and there is a lot of documentation and support for them. Because Samsung has already done all the hard work of embedding them, you need not delve into their inner workings. It is beneficial to know how OAuth2 works so that you can diagnose problems if they crop up. There is OAuth2 support and toolkits for all the languages you are likely to use for ARTIK and SAMI software development. Find out more about them and OAuth2 here on the home page:

```
http://oauth.net/2/
```

Cloud-based Services

The purpose of the SAMI data-exchange approach is to build a unified ecosystem for IoT. Samsung also provides the SmartThings OpenCloud. SmartThings is a software and data aggregation service built on top of SAMI that can send and receive all data formats between all devices, and store them for analytics. It is especially well suited to building smart home systems.

Open Technologies for Sharing

The IoT industry needs open standards that reflect the best system architecture designs. Developers must be able to easily connect different kinds of applications so they can communicate with one another. A single developer may not be in control of all the applications that they depend on. An open but secure data exchange needs to allow multiple developers to share data with one another. Creating order amongst a chaotic tangle of competing devices and protocols, and fostering a collaborative approach to development, goes hand in hand with setting a secure foundation for IoT. The world cannot afford to sacrifice functionality and security on the altar of market share and dominance by a single provider.

Keeping Your Data Safe and Secure

Samsung has engineered a lot of security support into the ARTIK designs to protect your privacy. The ARTIK hardware and software control who is permitted to access the device, what they can do with it, and what information they are allowed to view. The ARTIK modules also have smart-machine learning for identifying unusual behaviors that compromise device security. If you insist on building a fundamentally insecure application or device, ARTIK cannot protect you from your own stupidity, but it can give you enormous help in building secure and intrusion-proof systems without your needing to become a security expert in the first place.

Secure Operating System

The ARTIK 5 and 10 modules run a variant of the Linux operating system. The security support in Linux is inherited from UNIX, which has been around for a long time and has matured into a secure and robust environment. That is not to imply that other operating systems are not secure, but they are proprietary. A Linux solution is a good choice because it has an open-source heritage that makes it very easy to introduce corrective patches when a potential security flaw is detected.

Firmware Security

The ARTIK ecosystem supports secure firmware-updating principles. Samsung will from time to time release updates that are installed under control of the trusted execution environment.

Device Authentication

Authenticate your ARTIK module by registering it with your SAMI account, and use the SAMI data exchange to aggregate feeds from several devices. This uses a three-element key that is cryptographically secured by the embedded secure element support:

- Device type ID
- Unique device instance ID
- OAuth2 token for the data-exchange transactions

Data Encryption

The hardware crypto engine inside your ARTIK's embedded secure element encrypts data that is transmitted to a remote service, such as the SAMI data exchange. Because this is hardware-based security, it is much more robust than a software solution and is very resilient to intrusion.

The transmitted data is based on Datagram Transport Layer Security (DTLS), which operates deep down in the networking protocol at the most fundamental layer. This makes the transmission secure at a foundational level. Read more about how this works on Wikipedia:

```
https://en.wikipedia.org/wiki/Datagram_Transport_Layer_Security
```

Get Your Samsung Account Now

You need a Samsung account of your own to access the SAMI services. This will associate all the data streams your devices create with the same account, where it is aggregated and maintained in private. A Samsung account also grants access to the online ARTIK developer resources. Follow these steps to register and verify an account to use for your prototyping research:

1. Go to the Samsung account front page:

   ```
   https://account.samsung.com/
   ```

2. Click on the "Sign Up" link at the top right.

3. Enter your e-mail address that will be used as your Samsung account ID.

4. Enter a robust password.

5. Confirm your password in the second textbox.

6. Add your name and personal details.

7. Type the captcha text to indicate that it is a human being applying for the account and not a web crawler.

8. Choose whether to receive marketing communications from Samsung.

9. Read and agree to the Terms & Conditions.

10. Read and agree to the Samsung Privacy Policy.

11. Read and agree with the Data Combination Policy.

12. Click on the Continue button.

13. Samsung sends an e-mail verification message to you at the mailbox you specified as your Samsung account ID.

14. Check your e-mail and click on the verification link to confirm that your e-mail account is working and to tell Samsung your account was created by the e-mail account owner.

15. Use these credentials to sign in to your Samsung account to access the SAMI system as a user or developer. The same account will access the ARTIK developer resources.

Embedded Secure Element

ARTIK was built with security in mind. All three ARTIK modules have an embedded secure element (SE) that can be used to protect sensitive information stored on a device using traditional cryptography, and to store any cryptographic materials used to encrypt a user's data. These security features are very important because they facilitate a secure integration of IoT devices with the SAMI data exchange.

Hardware Crypto Engine

The ARTIK module maintains a closed storage container where cryptographic keys can be locked away safely. These keys are used to encrypt and decrypt messages between your ARTIK module and the SAMI data exchange, for example. They could secure any kind of encrypted messaging. The keys are unique to each ARTIK and are "burned in" as the modules are manufactured. No two ARTIK modules share the same credentials, and because this storage is inaccessible to the user space, neither users nor developers can extract the keys and subvert them. This is fundamental to making ARTIK communications secure.

The secure element support is integrated at the chip level with each ARTIK as it is manufactured. This is a hardware-implemented crypto engine, and penetration attempts will destroy the chip, causing any attempt to physically hack the devices to fail. Software-based attacks are prevented because there is no route to access the secured storage from the user space.

Segregated Trust Zone

A segregated trust zone, also known as a trusted execution environment (TEE), is accessible only by authenticated services. This prevents access by malicious attackers attempting to negotiate a route around the secure element support. Only those processes running within the TEE can access secure content within the protected parts of the module.

Current Status

As of the Alpha and Beta prototypes of the ARTIK modules, the embedded secure element support is not yet complete. This blog article describes how to accomplish a useful level of security for the time being with a SAMI-based data exchange:

```
https://blog.samsungsami.io/topics/security/
```

Summary

The security features must work in the background without the developer needing to worry or intervene. The hardware crypto support in an ARTIK module ensures that HTTPS protocol connections to SAMI (for example) are secured without any help from your application code. This partition of responsibilities makes things more secure, as there is no software component exposed in source code and, therefore, nothing to be subverted. The hardware crypto support is impenetrable from the software, and physically accessing the internals of the crypto engine would destroy the contents of the chip beyond repair; the ARTIK module would cease to work.

The next step is to get to know the ARTIK developer reference board that facilitates the prototyping of new project ideas. This brings all the connections out to more easily accessible switches, sockets, and connector pins.

CHAPTER 5

Your Development Kit

The Developer Reference Board

The ARTIK modules are small and easily damaged. You should avoid handling them unnecessarily. They have specialized multi-pin Panasonic AXT connectors on the underside to avoid having to solder connections directly onto them. The best way to start learning how the ARTIK modules work is to use the developer reference board. This extends the connectivity of the ARTIK out to connectors that you will be more familiar with. The developer reference board also provides debugging facilities through its JTAG connector.

The developer reference board is designed to safely mount your ARTIK so you can work on your product design without constantly handling the module. This will protect it from undue wear and tear and the risk of static discharge damage. Even so, you should always make sure you have grounded yourself and the equipment you are handling before touching it in order to dissipate any gradual build-up of static charges.

About the Developer Reference Boards

There are several different developer reference boards available for mounting your ARTIK modules in a test harness for connection to your hosting development workstation. Each kind of ARTIK module has a board specifically designed for it.

The ARTIK 1 is small enough to be used in wearable products. It has fewer connecting pins than the other ARTIK modules, which need to support connections that the ARTIK 1 does not need. Consequently, the Type 1 is a quite different developer reference board design.

There are multiple versions of the developer reference board that have evolved from the original Alpha prototype. The Beta prototype integrated the serial interface onto the main board and eliminated the need for the extra debug board and USB-Serial adapter. Table 5-1 is a summary of the different versions and release dates to help you identify the different boards and ARTIK modules.

C. Wootton, *Beginning Samsung ARTIK*, DOI 10.1007/978-1-4842-1952-2_5

Table 5-1. *Developer Reference Board and Module Versions*

Prototype	Type	Version	Date	Description
Alpha	1	0.2.0	2015-04-21	Compatible with ARTIK 1 only
Alpha	2	0.2.0	2015-04-20	Universal developer board, compatible with ARTIK 10 and with the addition of a small mezzanine adapter the ARTIK 5 can be mounted on the same board.
Beta	5	0.3.0		Development prototype
Beta	10	0.3.0		Development prototype
Beta	5	0.3.1	2015-09-02	Compatible with Beta ARTIK 5
Beta	10	0.3.1	2015-09-02	Compatible with Beta ARTIK 10
Beta	5	0.3.2	2015-10-22	Compatible with Beta ARTIK 5
Beta	5	0.5.0	2015-12-23	At launch, ARTIK 5 modules will be this Commercial Beta version
Beta	10	0.5.0	2015-12-23	At launch, ARTIK 10 modules will be this Commercial Beta version
Production	5	1.0.0	Later	ARTIK 5 production modules
Production	10	1.0.0	Later	ARTIK 10 production modules

This introductory book will review the best information we have on the currently shipping versions of the reference board as of spring 2016. As the product evolves, the changes do become smaller and subtler. The Commercial Beta revisions are close enough to the production version to be suitable for early adopters to use.

■ **Note** Because Samsung is still developing the ARTIK platform, the developer reference board and the ARTIK modules will change from what is documented here.

What Is in the Box?

When you open the developer kit, you will find all the accessories needed to get started with your research project right away. A typical developer kit is shown in Figure 5-1.

Figure 5-1. *Typical developer kit*

- One of the ARTIK 5 or 10 modules already safely mounted on the developer reference board. The board will be a Type 5 or Type 10 variant. Some pinouts and jumpers are different between the two kinds of developer reference board. Alter your application code depending on the one you are using.

- A USB-A to USB-Micro-B cable that replaces the USB-Serial adapter that was required for the Alpha prototypes. The serial adapter is now an integral part of the developer reference board. Just connect this USB cable to your development workstation.

- A 5-volt DC power supply pod that operates worldwide at 100 to 240 volts AC.

- A set of wireless communications antennas for use with the Wi-Fi and ZigBee SMA connectors.

The Type 1 Developer Reference Board

The Type 1 developer reference board shown in Figure 5-2 is self-contained and has Panasonic AXT connectors configured to mount a single ARTIK 1 module. There are breakout connectors for all of the services and signals that the ARTIK 1 supports. These provide easier access than trying to make your own direct connections to the two small AXT connectors on the bottom of the ARTIK 1 module.

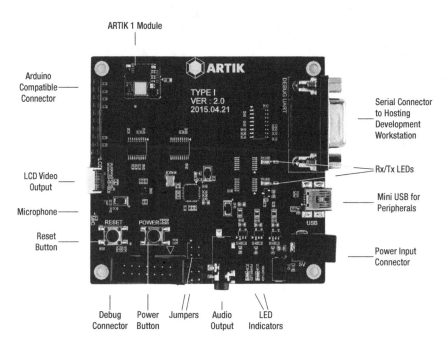

Figure 5-2. *ARTIK 1 developer reference board*

Table 5-2 lists the switches, jumpers, and connectors found on the Type 1 developer reference board. Configure their operation once you have the system up and running.

Table 5-2. *Type 1 Developer Reference Board Connections*

Connector	Description
Power Port	5-volt power input
JTAG	14-pin JTAG hardware debugging connector. Attach a Segger JTAG debugging hardware tool here. You may need a 14- to 20-pin adapter cable to match the JTAG pinouts.
Serial Connector	This is a generic DB9 serial connector. Plug this into the serial interface you have configured on your computer.
LCD Video	Video output to a small wearable LCD display
Microphone	Audio input via a microphone on the developer reference board
Mini USB	Connect downstream USB peripherals here.
Audio	3.5 mm headphone-compatible jack output socket
Arduino Connector	A sub-set of the pins found on an Arduino
AXT CPU Socket	This is where your ARTIK module will be connected to the outside world. The developer reference board may already have the ARTIK fitted.
Power Button	Power up U-Boot call to action. The boot button.
Reset Button	Reset action
Jumper pins	Configuration jumpers 1 to 4. Their functionality is currently undocumented.
RXD LED	Located near the serial connector. This should flash when the board receives serial data from your computer.
TXD LED	Also located nearby, this should flash when the developer reference board is sending data back to your computer.
Power LED	Illuminates when the power is turned on
Reset LED	Illuminates when the reset button is pressed

The Type 5 & 10 Developer Reference Boards (Beta)

With the introduction of the Beta versions of the ARTIK modules, the developer reference boards have been updated. The Alpha prototypes shared the same Type 2 universal developer reference board for both ARTIK 5 and 10 modules. Now there is a different developer reference board for each of them. There are pinout differences between these boards to account for in your code. The Type 5 board shown in Figure 5-3 is for developing your applications with an ARTIK 5 module. The newer design eliminates the external ribbon cable–connected debug board and integrates an onboard USB-Serial interface. This illustration shows the board fitted with a Beta version of the ARTIK 5. The layout of the production model is slightly different, with the three coaxial connections on the ARTIK module arranged in different positions.

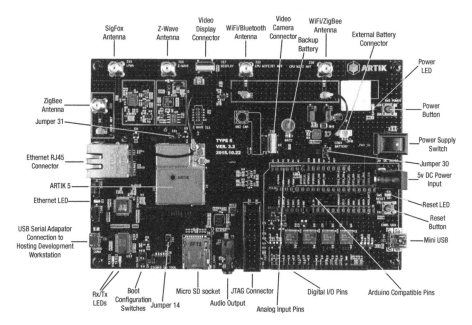

Figure 5-3. *Type 5 Beta developer reference board (Ver 0.3.2)*

The Type 10 developer reference board shown in Figure 5-4 is for developing applications with an ARTIK 10 module. Like the Type 5 board, this one has a USB-Serial interface integrated directly onto the board. This example is a Commercial Beta revision that will be shipped to early adopters.

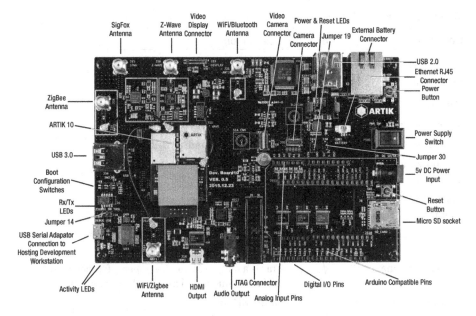

Figure 5-4. *Type 10 Commercial Beta developer reference board (Ver 0.5.0)*

Early Production Models

The ARTIK 5 and 10 modules will be shipped to the early-adopting consumers on a version 0.5.0 developer reference board. These early production boards are functionally similar to the Beta version, but some of the connectors are moved to different locations. Samsung describes this revision as a Commercial Beta model.

Type 5 and 10 Developer Reference Board Connectors

Table 5-3 lists the connectors on the developer reference board and what they are for. Any configuration of these connectors and their operation needs to be done once you have the system up and running. Edit configuration files in the operating system or send messages to the kernel to set things up exactly how you want them. The kernel is an important part of the operating system that interfaces to the ARTIK hardware and provides an API for your application code to call.

Your developer kit includes wireless antennas. Attach these depending on what kind of wireless communications you want to use. Purchase additional antennas if you want to activate all of the Wi-Fi capabilities at once. Be careful to order extra attachable antennas with the correct kind of SMA connector, as there are several different configurations.

You will notice that the board layout changes with each revision, so although the same connectors are present, they might not be in the same place. You should inspect your board carefully to find the correct ones, and some experimentation may be necessary.

Table 5-3. *Type 5 and 10 developer reference board connections*

Connector	5	10	Description
Power port	√	√	5v power input
MicroHDMI		√	HDMI video output
Camera	√	√	Video camera input
Secondary camera		√	Additional camera input
ZigBee antenna	√	√	ZigBee smart home antenna
Combo Wi-Fi & BT antenna	√	√	Combined Wi-Fi & Bluetooth antenna
Combo Wi-Fi & ZigBee antenna	√		Additional antenna on the Type 5 only
Z-Wave antenna	√		This is a feature of the developer reference board and is not integrated into the ARTIK module.
SIGFOX antenna	√	√	This is a feature of the developer reference board and is not integrated into the ARTIK module.
Backup battery	√		Onboard battery
External battery	√	√	Connection to an external backup power supply
Ethernet RJ45	√	√	Wired Ethernet connections
Micro USB 3.0	√		Micro-sized connector on Type 5 only
USB 3.0		√	Full-sized USB 3 connector on Type 10 only
USB 2.0 Type A		√	Secondary USB interface on Type 10 only
Micro SD Card Receptacle	√	√	For loading software
Audio output socket	√	√	3.5 mm stereo jack socket
Arduino compatible Pinouts	√	√	Arduino-compatible pins. Some differences between the addressing and pin availability between the Type 5 and 10 boards.
Analog input pins	√	√	GPIO analog inputs. Some differences between the Type 5 and 10 boards.
Digital I/O pins	√	√	GPIO input/outputs. Some differences between the Type 5 and 10 boards.
CPU socket	√	√	This is where the ARTIK module will be connected. The developer reference board should already have this fitted.
JTAG	√	√	20-pin ARM JTAG hardware debug connector. Attach a Segger JTAG hardware-debugging probe here.
USB Serial adapter	√	√	USB connection to the hosting development workstation. Install the appropriate drivers to support the built-in USB-to-serial interface.

Type 5 and 10 Developer Reference Board Switches

The switches listed in Table 5-4 control the developer reference board and the embedded ARTIK that you have mounted on it.

Table 5-4. *Type 5 and 10 Developer Reference Board Switches*

Switch	What It Controls
Power Switch	The power switch powers up the board and turns on the LEDs.
Power Button	This should be called a Boot button because pressing it will trigger the boot strap loader.
Reset Button	The reset button illuminates the Reset LED but appears to do nothing while the ARTIK is running. The hardware address for this switch is currently undocumented but it might be accessible to your software as a GPIO input.
Boot Mode Selector	Choose either the embedded OS or the OS installed on the SD card.
eMMC11 Selector	Choose the kind of memory to map in.

Type 5 and 10 Developer Reference Board LED Indicators

The LED indicators on the developer reference board and what they tell you are summarized in Table 5-5.

Table 5-5. *Type 5 and 10 Developer Reference Board LED Indicators*

Indicator	Details
Reset state active	This illuminates when the Reset button is pressed. This is near the Reset button on the Type 5 developer reference board and near the secondary camera connector on the Type 10.
Power on	Indicates that the developer reference board is powered up. This is near the Power button on the Type 5 developer reference board and near the secondary camera connector on the Type 10.
Ethernet activity	Adjacent to the Ethernet connector
USB activity	Adjacent to the USB connectors
RXD	Located near the serial connector. This should flash when the board receives serial data from your computer.
TXD	Also located nearby, this should flash when the developer reference board is sending data back to your computer.

(continued)

Table 5-5. (*continued*)

Indicator	Details
SIGFOX	This LED indicator is only present on the Type 10 boards and indicates SigFox activity.
USB	This LED indicator is only present on the Type 10 boards and indicates USB 2.0 activity.
PGANG	This LED indicator is only present on the Type 10 boards. The functionality is currently undocumented.

Type 5 and 10 Developer Reference Board Jumpers

The developer reference boards contain several jumpers (as listed in Table 5-6). These will reconfigure the board and (possibly) the ARTIK behaviors when the pins are shorted together. Unless you know what the purpose of a jumper is, you should not just connect them and experiment. Your ARTIK module may not boot as a consequence. Take care to only alter jumpers if you know what they do. Check that the jumper pins are straight and unbent. Sometimes they can become damaged in transit and accidentally short together.

Table 5-6. *Type 5 and 10 Developer Reference Board Jumpers*

Jumper	Description
J20	ARTIK revision 3 configuration
J33	ARTIK revision 3 configuration (Type 5 board only)
J36	ARTIK revision 3 configuration (Type 10 board only)
J30	Functionality undocumented (Type 5 & 10)
J14	Functionality undocumented (Type 5 & 10)
J31	Functionality undocumented (Type 5)
J19	Functionality undocumented (Type 10)

Connecting External Devices

The developer reference boards provide connectivity for a variety of external hardware. There are camera connections directly on the ARTIK modules for feeding video in. At present the video support for these is still being developed and is quite primitive. That will change as more developers try things out and publish their results. Plug additional hardware into the USB connector and install suitable drivers for it. Optionally, write new drivers or recompile the existing ones to be compatible with the ARM CPUs. The USB port provides a way to add large amounts of external storage for surveillance- and video-related products such as media servers or video recorder applications. Your ARTIK may not be able to provide sufficient power for those external devices, so they should have their own independent power supply.

Summary

This introductory book focuses on using the developer reference boards to exercise your ARTIK modules. The internals of the ARTIK modules–and how to use them in your own product designs–are covered in the companion Apress *ARTIK Reference Guide* book. Now that the different versions of these developer reference boards have been examined, the next step is to set up a development workstation to interact with them.

■ ■ ■

## CHAPTER 6

Getting Your Hardware Together

Your Workbench

Having a dedicated place to work on your projects is helpful. Set up a software environment and a place to do hardware engineering at the same time. Be careful to keep your machine shop separate from your ARTIK or development workstation. Dropping metal filings onto electronic circuit boards is a recipe for disaster. Keep the two workspaces apart as far as possible.

Setting Up a Hardware Workbench

Equip yourself with some electronics tools and components. Gathering a stock of components and organizing them into storage containers will ensure you have everything ready to roll when you have a great idea. Check out the Arduino suppliers (Oomlout, Sparkfun, Adafruit, etc.) for starter kits with LEDs, resistors, and capacitors. They also supply kits with a few motors, solenoids, and sensors. Use plastic storage containers to keep things neat and tidy. Have a supply of connecting cables or reels of insulated wire. Stock a few mechanical components. A collection of miscellaneous brackets, nuts, bolts, and washers for assembling hardware would be useful.

You should have a range of tools that include good quality pliers, wire cutters, and a soldering iron. You should invest in a static electricity dissipating strap. Wearing this and tethering it to the grounded earth terminal of your workspace should prevent your generating a static discharge and blowing up your ARTIK. If you do not have one, touch something that is grounded first and then only handle your ARTIK module by gripping it by the edges.

A small vice, metalworking tools, and needle files are useful for cutting out control panels and brackets. Buy a few things at a time as you need them, and before long you will have a fully equipped workshop.

Apress publishes several useful handbooks about setting up your electronics workspace. They also have helpful guides on soldering and how electronic circuits work.

© Cliff Wootton 2016
C. Wootton, *Beginning Samsung ARTIK*, DOI 10.1007/978-1-4842-1952-2_6

Wiring Up Your Circuits

Check out the connectors on the development system. Having some compatible connectors with wire tails is useful for connecting your breadboard or printed circuit board (PCB) designs to the development system.

Stick to the accepted conventions on wire coloring to diagnose problems with your designs more easily. Ribbon cables with multi-colored wires are useful for connecting multiple signals over some distance. Work out the connections based on color and position within the ribbon. The common conventions are listed in Table 6-1, but these are not mandatory.

Table 6-1. *Wire Color Conventions*

Color	Meaning
Black	Negative DC and also common ground plane
Red	Positive DC power supply
Green	Earth
Yellow	Signal - Perhaps for Rx when setting up communications
Blue	Signal - Perhaps for Tx when setting up communications
Orange	Connecting to a driver for amplifying a current to supply high power
Grey	Connecting to an external switcher

Prototyping your circuit design on a breadboard (see Figure 6-1) is useful for trying things out quickly. Once your design is stable, you should then solder things together on a circuit board for a more permanent)solution that stays in one piece while you work on it.

Figure 6-1. *Breadboard (courtesy of Oomlout)*

Test Equipment

A digital multimeter (see Figure 6-2) is useful for measuring voltages and resistors, and for testing circuit continuity. Test circuits for continuity with a battery and LED indicator if you do not have a multimeter, but make sure you include a limiting resistor to control the LED current.

Figure 6-2. *Digital multimeter (courtesy of Binarysequence)*

An oscilloscope (see Figure 6-3) is very useful for observing time-varying values. This would be very useful for establishing the timing differences when comparing an ARTIK module and an Arduino board. Timings are interesting to look at if you are programming the Pulse Width Modulated (PWM) digital output pins. More sophisticated oscilloscopes support logic probes. These logic analyzers are high-end devices, and you only need this kind of expensive equipment if you plan to take this very seriously.

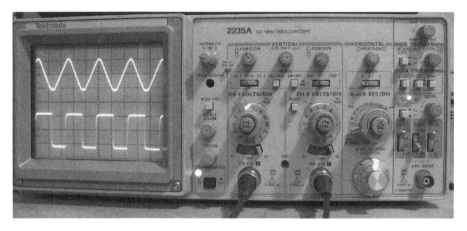

Figure 6-3. *Oscilloscope (Courtesy of Xato)*

Setting Up a Software Workbench

Use Windows, Macintosh, or Linux as your development platform and add a couple of applications to build projects with. Similar tools are available for all platforms. The Linux and Macintosh operating systems are UNIX based, which might be helpful when you are developing your ARTIK software. Even though Windows is not a UNIX-based operating system, it is very easy to add a UNIX command-line shell by installing Cygwin and the PuTTY terminal emulator.

The Samsung ARTIK developer resources describe in detail how to set up a cross-compiler to develop ARM software with a Windows-based development system. Some coverage in the Samsung notes applies to Linux workstations too. ARTIK early adopters requested additional coverage for the Macintosh platform, which is addressed in this book. The cross-compiler tools in particular are somewhat different for the Macintosh platform because the Linaro toolchain cannot be used there. The cross-compiling toolchain on Mac OS is explored in this book without duplicating what Samsung already makes available online for Windows and Linux users.

If you are not used to installing software, reading all of the notes that come with the software before you begin is a good idea. Keep the installation package archived safely so you can review the documentation and use it again. Make a note of the website where the installation packages are maintained and check for updates periodically or when you need them.

Risk Managing Your Software Development

If possible, you should commit a single computer to your ARTIK work. If something goes badly wrong and it trashes the system, you avoid wiping out your favorite games machine or the place where you administer your accounts and paperwork. The shared family computer is also not the best place to do this. If you only have one computer then you have no choice. In that case, at least create a special login account to do the development work in. The chances of trashing your workstation when developing ARTIK software are small but not zero–much less than if you were developing kernel driver code to attach new hardware directly to your workstation. Some scenarios with an embedded ARTIK need complex workstation setups. Assess and manage the risks accordingly. Keep lots of backups, preferably offline on another device or system. That way, your recovery process should be quick and easy.

Configuring the Developer Reference Board

On the Type 5 and 10 developer reference boards, there are two configuration jumpers that must be set correctly in order for the board to operate with the revision of the ARTIK module you have plugged in. Your developer kit should be shipped to you with these configured correctly for the ARTIK provided with it. You only need to be concerned with this if you are swapping out an old ARTIK module for a newer one that requires a different jumper configuration.

Figures 6-4 and 6-5 show the location of the jumpers on the developer reference boards. The location is similar on the Type 5 and 10 boards of the same revision, but they might be in a different place on a later version of the board. However, the jumper pins are numbered differently on each type of developer reference board.

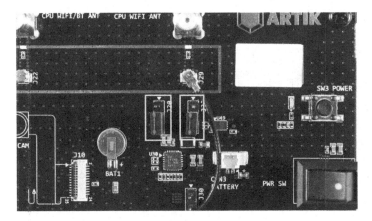

Figure 6-4. *Type 5 jumper locations (version 3.2)*

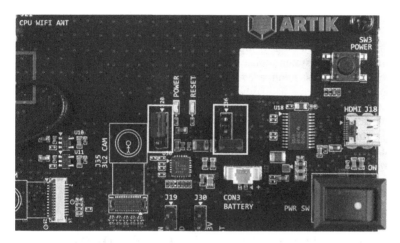

Figure 6-5. *Type 10 jumper locations (version 3.2)*

If your ARTIK module is earlier than version 3, the jumpers should be configured as shown in Figure 6-6.

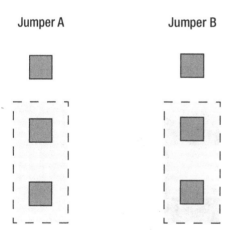

Figure 6-6. *Jumper configuration for pre–version 3 ARTIK modules*

If your ARTIK is a version 3.0, 3.1, or later model, use the configuration seen in Figure 6-7 instead.

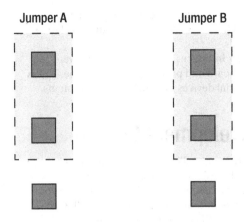

Figure 6-7. Jumper configuration for version 3.0 and later ARTIK modules

The jumper numbers on the developer reference boards are shown in Table 6-2.

Table 6-2. Developer Reference Board Configuration Jumpers

Jumper	Type 5	Type 10
A	J20	J20
B	J33	J36

If you did this correctly, your ARTIK module and developer reference board are now compatible, and everything should work as intended.

Communicating with Your ARTIK

The ARTIK modules have a command-line console accessed through a serial interface. This is a classic and "old-school" way to interact with a computer. Prior to the Xerox SmallTalk systems and the Apple Lisa computer (these were the first computers to offer a graphical user interface to the general public), this was the only way to interact with a computer.

This is daunting if you have never worked like this, but it is not very complicated. A simple terminal emulator application can talk to the ARTIK console. You type a command and the ARTIK executes it and gives you the result and waits for your next instruction. This is challenging at first because there are a lot of new commands to learn and it is a very powerful environment. If you take small, careful steps and learn one thing at a time, you will make steady progress. Familiarize yourself with the command-line instructions by exploring them carefully one at a time. When you become adept at using them, you can string them together into more powerful combinations by redirecting their I/O or writing a shell script to automate them.

Initial communications with the ARTIK module take place through a serial interface. After configuring the network support the ARTIK can be reached across the Local Area Network (LAN) using telnet and other protocols.

Serial interfaces are sometimes called TTY interfaces. Serial connections were originally used with an electric typewriter keyboard and printer called a Teletype. This is abbreviated to TTY and is used to name the serial devices in UNIX operating systems.

Connecting the ARTIK Development System

There are two SMA antenna connectors that deliver Wi-Fi on the newer developer reference boards. One is a combination of Wi-Fi and Bluetooth and the other is a combination of Wi-Fi and ZigBee. Choose one of these to attach the antenna to so you can configure the Wi-Fi. After checking your configuration jumper settings, follow the following steps to connect and power on your ARTIK development system:

1. Connect a wireless antenna to the connector labeled "CPU WIFI ANT." (labelled J23 on the Commercial Beta developer boards)

2. Connect the board to your development workstation using the USB cable. There is only one micro-USB connector on the developer reference board.

3. You should see the Rx and Tx LED indicators light up.

4. Make sure the power switch on the developer reference board is set to the off position.

5. Plug your 5V power supply into your power outlet.

6. Insert the small DC power plug into the power port on the developer reference board.

7. Flip the power switch on the developer reference board to the on position.

8. The LED indicator next to the SW3 POWER button should illuminate.

9. Your developer reference board is now powered up, but your ARTIK is not yet booted.

Your ARTIK 5 setup should look something like the example shown in Figure 6-8. The picture in Figure 6-9 illustrates an early Beta Type 10 developer board with an ARTIK 10 module installed for evaluation. The production models may look slightly different.

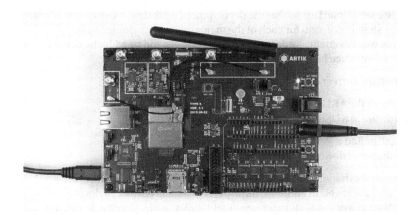

Figure 6-8. *Type 5 developer reference board all hooked up*

Figure 6-9. *Type 10 developer reference board all hooked up*

Now that your developer reference board and ARTIK are up and running, move on to the next step to check that your USB serial connections are working before booting the operating system in the ARTIK.

USB Serial Interfaces

Early ARTIK developer systems shipped with a separate external USB interface. This often used the Prolific Technologies driver. The Beta version of the developer boards integrated the serial interface directly onto the board. This interface requires a different driver from FDTI, which you may need to install separately depending on your operating system version.

Setting up the serial interface so that the development workstation can communicate with the ARTIK is slightly different for each of the major operating systems. Some operating systems will automatically detect the USB hardware and provide the correct driver for the serial interface hardware. These are the main steps:

1. Install the correct driver for the serial interface hardware.

2. Connect the ARTIK developer reference board serial interface hardware to a USB port on the computer.

3. Install or find a terminal application that can talk to the ARTIK via the serial device driver that the operating system has set up.

There are several variations of Linux. They have minor differences in how you install new software packages. In addition, third-party installers have been developed independently. Your driver installation process might look slightly different. In general though, it should be similar enough to follow what is happening.

Hooking Up the Serial Interface

Plug the USB connector into your development workstation before powering on the developer reference board. If the serial interface is not immediately recognized, one of the following may be the reason:

- The correct driver software may not be installed.

- Alternatively, if the driver is installed, it might not be configured properly.

- The driver might require the dev board to be powered on to see it.

When you power on the ARTIK it should wake up the serial driver in your development workstation. Some USB interfaces must be unplugged and plugged in again to wake the driver up. The default settings should work without your needing to delve into the complexities of serial communications.

Setting Up a USB Serial Interface Driver on Windows

When you plug the serial interface into your USB port, your Windows operating system should tell you that new hardware has been detected. This might trigger a software update if it needs to install a driver. It depends on the make and model of your serial interface and the version of Windows you are using. Some drivers are pre-installed in the Windows operating system. If a software update is required, follow the instructions on your screen. A reboot of your Windows computer may be called for. After the driver is installed, check it out with the Device Manager in the Windows Control Panel.

One of the ARTIK Discussion Forum members shared this link to download a USB driver for Windows when you are using a Trip·Lite USB-Serial adapter (thanks Thierry):

```
http://www.tripplite.com/shared/software/Driver/U209-000-R- Driver-For-
Windows-2000-Or-Later.zip
```

You may need a different driver if your OS does not have built-in support for the Beta (and later) developer reference boards with an integrated FTDI serial interface.

Setting Up a USB Serial Interface Driver on Mac OS X

The operating system uses the product and vendor ID values to select the right driver. You might have to manually install another driver if you change to a different serial interface.

OS X and Security Issues

Apple has a determined policy of keeping operating systems and products secure against any risk of intrusion. This is always in the best interests of the consumers, but there are a few consequences for developers. Apple will continue to close access to more of the operating system internals and special files as OS X advances. As a rule, Apple replaces the casual developer's access to system files with frameworks that allow application developers to still achieve their goals. In the margins are developers who want to create systems administration tools. This affects ARTIK developers, because a special driver might need to be installed for the serial interface. A few more steps are necessary on recent operating system versions to accommodate the Apple security countermeasures. The details might be slightly different for each version of the OS X operating system as Apple introduces new constraints. Guidance is presented here based on what has been happening with the latest OS X releases.

Is a New Driver Necessary?

Your Mac OS X operating system should automatically configure the correct driver for the USB serial interface if it has one available. As I moved from using an Alpha prototype board to the Beta version of the ARTIK, the OS X kernel attempted to load a built-in FTDI driver for the new serial interface. On a test system running an older version of OS X, that driver turned out to be incompatible with the ARTIK hardware. Work through a few diagnostic steps to make sure you have the right driver installed and selected. Install a new one if necessary.

Is the Hardware Detected?

Inspect the system configuration on Mac OS X via the "About this Mac" item on the Apple menu. Click on the More Information button to call up the System Profiler application or run it directly from the "Utilities" folder. If the serial adapter is plugged in, you should see it listed as "USB-Serial Controller D:" in the USB device tree. Select that item in the list to see the properties in the System Profiler app.

Depending on the USB serial device name in the system profile display, follow the most appropriate instructions as follows.

Installing a Driver (USB-Serial Controller D)

Figure 6-10 illustrates what you might see on a Mac OS X system when you try to use an Alpha prototype developer reference board and an external USB serial adapter based on the Prolific Technology chipset. Note that many different manufacturers use this chipset and they will all look very similar, and might all work with the same driver.

USB-Serial Controller D:

```
Product ID:               0x2303
Vendor ID:                0x067b  (Prolific Technology, Inc.)
Version:                   4.00
Speed:                    Up to 12 Mb/sec
Manufacturer:             Prolific Technology Inc.
Location ID:              0xfa130000 / 6
Current Available (mA):  500
Current Required (mA):   100
```

Figure 6-10. *Prolific USB serial device properties on Mac OS X*

▪ **Note**   Because this USB serial interface is based on the Prolific Technology chipset, you should use their driver. As time goes on, conventions are developed between competing manufacturers and they may emulate one another's products. Drivers that did not previously work gradually become compatible with new hardware. There is no way to predict this, and the provenance of your driver should be consistent with the hardware manufacturer for best results.

Now that the hardware is installed, the next job is to install a driver for it. Table 6-3 summarizes some possible drivers for the PL2303 chipset. Installing a driver from any of these sources will probably work because they all communicate with the same chipset. The driver name is mirrored in the USB vendor ID that is defined by Prolific Technologies–the company that makes the interface chips.

Table 6-3. *Prolific 2303 Driver URLs*

Interface	Driver
Tripp·lite U209-000-R	http://www.tripplite.com/support/downloads
Pluggable PL2303-DB9	http://plugable.com/drivers/prolific/
Generic PL 2303 compatible	http://www.prolific.com.tw/US/support.aspx

The version 1.5.1 driver is compatible with Mac OS X 10.6 and higher. The product ID (2303) and the vendor ID (067B) match the values shown in the System Profile. This driver should be good for most current Mac OS X scenarios using the Prolific chip set. Download the installer package (PL2303 Prolific Mac OS X 10.6 and newer v1.5.1) and un-archive the zip file. Open the folder and read the installation instructions in the enclosed PDF. The Read-Me document lists the vendor and product ID values if you want to check them. The instructions show you how to install a driver that you did not obtain via the Apple App Store. This is important now that Mac OS X is being made more secure. If necessary, bypass the Apple App Store Gatekeeper to install an unsigned kernel extension. These basic steps show you how:

1. Download one of the drivers. This one is easy to find:

   http://plugable.com/drivers/prolific/

2. Open the System Preferences window.

3. Find the Security and Privacy settings pane.

4. Unlock the preference panel with an administrator password to make changes.

5. Turn off the gatekeeper by choosing the "Anywhere" option in the Allow Applications section.

6. Unpack and run the installer package file to install the new driver package.

7. Restart the computer.

8. Go back to the Security and Privacy control panel and turn the gatekeeper back on if you turned it off earlier.

9. Open a terminal window.

10. List the logical devices under the /dev/ path to see if the interface is visible with this command:

    ls /dev/ | grep usb

11. You should see a list with /dev/.cu.usbserial included, if the driver has been activated.

12. Alternatively, your devices might be named like this:

    tty.usbserial-{dev_board_ID}

13. Note the name of the driver that you see, because you will need that when you connect to the ARTIK module from your terminal session.

14. If you go back to the System Profile, the serial device should still be visible in the USB tree. It might not be displayed if it has not been woken up. Power cycling your ARTIK developer reference board may help. Unplugging and plugging in the USB cable again may also make it show up.

15. Refresh the device list each time by pressing the [Command] + [R] key combination.

Installing a Driver (FT232R USB UART)

The device report in the system profiler looks different when you connect a Beta version ARTIK Type 5 or 10 developer reference board. Figure 6-11 illustrates what you might see if you connect an ARTIK with an FTDI serial interface. This serial adapter is integrated onto the developer board and you do not need a separate interface.

FT232R USB UART:

```
Product ID:              0x6001
Vendor ID:               0x0403  (Future Technology Devices International Limited)
Version:                  6.00
Serial Number:           AI02ZIIU
Speed:                   Up to 12 Mb/sec
Manufacturer:            FTDI
Location ID:             0xfa130000 / 7
Current Available (mA):  500
Current Required (mA):   90
```

Figure 6-11. *FTDI USB serial device properties on Mac OS X*

This board uses the Future Technology Devices International (FTDI) drivers that are commonly used on Arduino boards. FTDI drivers are available from a variety of sources.

Apple has included a default FTDI driver from OS X 10.9 upwards. This driver (and its useful companion file) is documented in a technical note here:

```
https://developer.apple.com/library/mac/technotes/tn2315/_index.html
```

Testing the Beta version ARTIK developer reference board on Mac OS X 10.11 worked without problems, connecting via the default Apple FTDI driver. No additional software installation was necessary. Connecting the serial interface cable into the USB port on the Macintosh immediately created a device at this location:

```
/dev/cu.usbserial-AI02ZIIU
```

The part of the device name following the dash might be different on your development workstation. Note this down carefully for reference later on. Operating systems earlier than Mac OS X 10.9 will require an FTDI driver to be installed so they can work with the Beta developer reference boards. From OS X 10.9 upwards, try the built-in driver first and only replace it with a new one if it does not work.

Follow these instructions to check for an incompatible FTDI driver and move it to one side. Install a new driver compatible with the FTDI-equipped Beta ARTIK developer reference board. Always be careful that you keep safe copies of any files you move in case you need to restore things later.

1. Open a terminal window to access the file system from a command line.

2. Change your working directory to where the FTDI kernel extension is located within the IOUSBFamily bundle:

    ```
    cd /System/Library/Extensions/IOUSBFamily.kext/Contents/PlugIns
    ```

3. List this directory to see if there is an FTDI kext file:

    ```
    la -ll
    ```

4. You should see something like this:

    ```
    AppleUSBCDC.kext
    AppleUSBCDCACMControl.kext
    AppleUSBCDCACMData.kext
    AppleUSBCDCDMM.kext
    AppleUSBCDCECMControl.kext
    AppleUSBCDCECMData.kext
    AppleUSBCDCEEM.kext
    AppleUSBCDCWCM.kext
    AppleUSBEHCI.kext
    AppleUSBFTDI.kext ◄ This is the existing driver
    AppleUSBHub.kext
    AppleUSBMergeNub.kext
    AppleUSBOHCI.kext
    AppleUSBOpticalMouse.kext
    AppleUSBUHCI.kext
    AppleUSBVideoSupport.kext
    AppleUSBXHCI.kext
    IOUSBCompositeDriver.kext
    IOUSBHIDDriver.kext
    IOUSBHIDDriverSafeBoot.kext
    IOUSBLib.bundle
    IOUSBUserClient.kext
    ```

5. The FTDI kext (kernel extension) may not be present. This could explain why your Beta developer reference board is not recognized. If the FTDI driver is there, set it aside and install a replacement. Use this command to disable it:

    ```
    sudo mv AppleUSBFTDI.kext AppleUSBFTDI.disabled
    ```

6. Enter an administrator password.

7. Download the replacement driver. Make sure you use the correct one for the version of OS X you are using:

    ```
    http://www.ftdichip.com/Drivers/VCP.htm
    ```

8. Mount the disk image.

9. Because the version 2.2.18 driver is unsigned, you must tell the gatekeeper to allow applications to be installed from anywhere.

10. Go and change your gatekeeper settings in the Security and Privacy control panel if necessary.

11. Run the installer.

12. Reset your gatekeeper protection to block unsigned installations again if necessary.

13. Now, when you plug in the developer reference board, the USB serial interface identifier should show up in the device listing. Type this command to confirm it is there:

    ```
    ls /dev | grep usb
    ```

14. On my Mac OS X 10.8.5 system, I see these devices listed. These are the USB serial interface identifiers:

    ```
    cu.usbserial-AI02ZIIU
    tty.usbserial-AI02ZIIU
    ```

15. Open a terminal window if you have one available and use the screen command to connect to your ARTIK developer reference board using the serial interface. The USB serial interface identifier you just discovered should be substituted in place of the example shown here:

    ```
    screen /dev/tty.usbserial-AI02ZWTO 115200
    ```

FTDI Driver Versions

There are many driver versions available from FTDI. You should use the correct one for your OS X version. Make sure you choose the correct 32- or 64-bit variant. Table 6-4 lists the available driver versions and their corresponding target OS releases.

Table 6-4. *FTDI Driver Versions vs. OS X Versions*

OS X Version	FTDI Driver Version	Notes
10.3	2.2.18	Install the special 10.3 (Panther) package.
10.4, 10.5, 10.6, 10.7, 10.8	2.2.18	Install the 10.4–10.7 package.
10.9, 10.10, 10.11	2.3	Only install this if the Apple built-in driver does not work. Apple signs this driver.

Drivers vs. Device Names

If you configure an outboard USB-Serial adapter with the Prolific USB driver, your serial port will have a different device name compared with the connection to an integrated serial interface on the Beta versions of the developer reference boards. The examples in this introductory book are updated with the latest available information, but if you have a different setup, see the device names in Table 6-5 for guidance on what to look for in your system.

Table 6-5. *USB Serial Adapter Driver Names*

Device name	Provenance
cu.usbserial tty.usbserial	Prolific USB-Serial adapter driver connecting to an Alpha developer reference board.
cu.usbserial-{dev_board_ID} tty.usbserial-{dev_board_ID}	Apple FTDI driver connecting to an integrated serial interface on a Beta developer reference board.

Setting Up a USB Serial Interface Driver on Ubuntu Linux

Setting up a USB serial driver on Linux is straightforward provided you work through these steps carefully one at a time. There is more information available on this web page:

```
http://pensacola-tech.com/pensacola/2010/06/01/↵
        how-to-enable-usb-serial-port-adapter-on-ubuntu-2/
```

Here are the instructions for a typical Ubuntu Linux system:

1. Log in to the root account on your Linux system.

2. Plug the USB-Serial adapter into one of your USB ports on the computer.

3. Wait for a few seconds to give the operating system time to notice the new hardware and load a driver for it if it has a suitable one available.

4. Type this command:

   ```
   dmesg
   ```

5. The dmesg command will echo back the most recent few lines of the system message console, and you should see something like this:

   ```
   usb 2.0: new full speed USB device using uhci_and address 2
   usb 2.0: configuration #1 chosen from 1 choice
   ```

6. Unplug the USB-Serial adapter to see a list of USB devices without it being plugged in.

7. Type this command to list the USB devices:

   ```
   lsusb
   ```

8. You should see a list of USB devices that looks like this:

   ```
   Bus 003 Device 001: ID 0000:0000
   Bus 002 Device 007: ID 03f0:4f11 Hewlett-Packard
   Bus 002 Device 006: ID 05e3:1205
   Bus 002 Device 004: ID 15d9:0a33
   ```

9. Now plug the USB-Serial adapter back in discover the bus device assignment.

10. List the USB devices again:

    ```
    lsusb
    ```

11. Compare the list with the previous one. The additional line is highlighted:

    ```
    Bus 003 Device 001: ID 0000:0000
    Bus 002 Device 007: ID 03f0:4f11 Hewlett-Packard
    Bus 001 Device 002: ID 4348:5523 ◄ This is a new device
    Bus 002 Device 006: ID 05e3:1205
    Bus 002 Device 004: ID 15d9:0a33
    ```

12. Determine the vendor ID and the product ID by inspecting this additional line. In this example they are 4348 and 5523. For a Trip·Lite USB-Serial adapter, they are 2303 and 067B.

13. Load the kernel module called usbserial and pass the vendor and product ID values to it. The driver can then associate itself with the correct hardware device on the USB bus. Type this command, making sure you substitute the correct vendor and product ID values for your interface hardware:

```
sudo modprobe usbserial vendor=0x4348 product=0x5523
```

14. Now view the system console log again with this command:

```
dmesg
```

15. You should see messages like this:

```
usbserial_generic 2.0:1.0: generic converter detected
usb 2.0: generic converter now attached to ttyUSB0
usbcore: registered new interface driver usbserial_generic
```

16. This tells you that the device is mapped to the /dev/ttyUSB0 serial port.

17. List the devices under the /dev/ path to see if the interface is visible with this command:

```
ls /dev/
```

18. Instruct Ubuntu to load this module automatically by including the following line in the /etc/modules file. Substitute your own vendor and product ID if they are different.

```
usbserial vendor=0x4348 product=0x5523
```

Other Linux distributions may use different commands to discover the hardware ID values and the name of the kernel extension containing the driver.

Setting Up a USB Serial Interface on Android Devices

If you are connecting an Android device with a USB-to-Serial adapter cable, the USB connector on the phone or tablet will need an adapter to convert from micro USB to full-sized USB connectors. Solve this by using a USB Host Mode (OTG) cable to connect to your serial interface. These adapters come with straight or right-angled connectors that help you position the phone and ARTIK module more conveniently. These adapters are inexpensive and easy to obtain online. Figure 6-12 shows two examples with alternative micro USB connectors at one end.

Figure 6-12. *Micro USB OTG adapter cable*

Alternatively, buy a single cable with the correct micro USB connectors on both ends. It is impossible to predict exactly what sort of cable you will need because it depends on your hosting device, but fortunately they are easy to find in online stores and all of the potential combinations are available.

USB Vendor IDs

Table 6-6 provides a short list of useful USB vendor and device identifiers. This may help you diagnose driver activation issues when connecting an ARTIK serial interface to your development workstation or when attaching an Arduino to your ARTIK or workstation.

Table 6-6. *USB Vendor Identifiers*

Product ID	Vendor ID	Details
0x6001	0x0403	Future Technology Devices International Limited UART fitted to a Beta ARTIK Type 5/10 developer reference board
0x2303	0x067b	Trip·Lite USB-Serial adapter with Prolific Technology chips used with Alpha ARTIK Type 2 developer reference boards
Device specific	0x2341	Genuine Arduino (cc) boards
Device specific	0x2A03	Arduino-org boards made by Arduino SRL

Get an up-to-date list of USB vendor and device ID values from the following URL. This is a community-generated table and not a copy of the official USB registry database. It relies on the efforts of volunteers for accuracy and may not include the very latest devices:

```
http://www.linux-usb.org/usb.ids
```

Summary

Now that you have a place to work, set up a terminal emulator to communicate with your ARTIK module and start it up. The next chapter will show you how to install, configure, and use a terminal emulator application to connect via the serial interface you just installed.

■ ■ ■

## CHAPTER 7

Setting Up a Terminal Emulator

Serial Connections with a Terminal Emulator

Connecting your development workstation to an ARTIK module with a serial interface and a USB adapter solves the hardware connectivity issue. Now, use a terminal emulator application to send instructions to the ARTIK and receive its responses. Anything you type on your keyboard will be transmitted to the remote system, and anything the ARTIK outputs will then be echoed on the screen of your terminal.

Terminal emulator applications are available for all types of workstations and operating systems. They are based on the old-fashioned tele-typewriter devices that you see in 1950s movies. A lot of that "old-school" technology influences what things are called inside modern computers and smart mobile devices. When you see devices named TTY, it is an echo from an earlier and much less sophisticated age when computers were rare, expensive, and very large.

Open a session with your terminal application. This gives you a command line on your development workstation where you can execute a screen command (or an equivalent) to connect to your ARTIK developer reference board via a serial interface. That interface then passes your keystrokes to the ARTIK. Any characters echoed back from the ARTIK follow the same route back to your terminal emulator screen. Figure 7-1 shows how the various processes connect together.

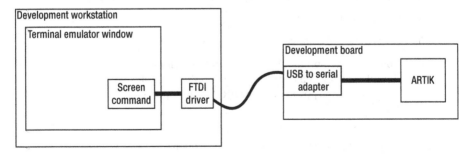

Figure 7-1. *Connecting to ARTIK*

© Cliff Wootton 2016

C. Wootton, *Beginning Samsung ARTIK*, DOI 10.1007/978-1-4842-1952-2_7

Installing Your Terminal Emulator

Some operating systems already have a terminal application installed. These next steps are optional depending on your configuration. There are alternatives to all of these, and you may prefer to use a different terminal emulator application if you are already familiar with one. Table 7-1 recommends the applications suitable for each operating system.

***Table 7-1.** Terminal Emulators for Different Operating Systems*

OS	Terminal Emulator App
Windows	Install and configure PuTTY
Macintosh	Use the built-in Terminal application but establish the serial connection from the command line. Or install iTerm and use that to establish the connection, as it has better log-capture tools.
Linux	Install and configure the minicom package.

Adding a Terminal Emulator to Windows

The PuTTY application is developed and maintained by Simon Tatham. Installers are available for all the variants of the Windows operating system.

Install PuTTY on Windows

Here are the basic instructions for installing PuTTY and configuring it to connect to your ARTIK developer reference board.

1. Go to this website:

    http://www.putty.org/

2. Download the installer.

3. Run putty.exe to install the PuTTY terminal app.

4. Connect a USB serial interface to the PC.

5. Open the Device Manager in the Windows Control Panel.

6. Note the COM port number for the USB serial interface. This should appear when you connect the USB serial cable to the PC. If necessary, power cycle the ARTIK developer reference board.

7. If the COM port connection is not detected, temporarily power on the ARTIK developer reference board.

8. Go to the PuTTY terminal app.

9. Open the PuTTY configuration screen.

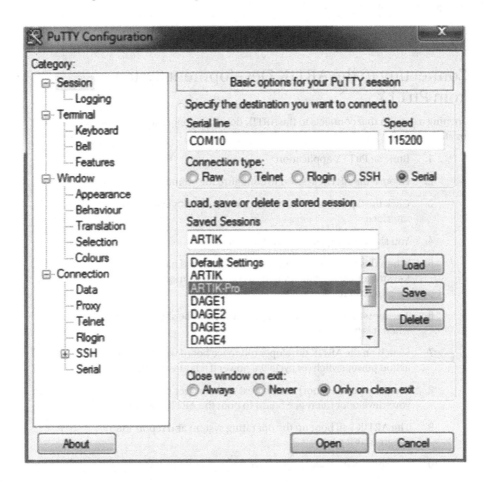

10. Set the selected serial line to the COM port you noted just now.

11. Set the connection speed to 115200.

12. Set connection type to Serial.

13. Name this session to find and restore it later.

14. Save the session.

15. The PuTTY console screen will be blank until you reset the developer reference board and boot the ARTIK.

16. Exit the PuTTY application, unless you want to connect to the ARTIK.

The PuTTY documentation is here in case you want to explore more detailed configuration options:

```
http://www.chiark.greenend.org.uk/~sgtatham/putty/docs.html
```

Connecting to the ARTIK Development System from PuTTY

Opening a session that connects to the ARTIK developer reference board is very similar for all operating systems.

1. Run the PuTTY application.

2. Choose the ARTIK session to configure the connection.

3. Click the Open button to connect to the ARTIK via the serial interface.

4. You should see a terminal window open.

5. When this is the active window, your keyboard has focus. Keystrokes will be transmitted to your ARTIK module and be executed there.

6. The messages from your ARTIK module will be shown here when it is turned on.

7. Switch on the ARTIK developer reference board with the rocker action power switch (or cycle the power if it is already on).

8. Press the power (boot) button next to the power switch on your developer reference board to boot the ARTIK module.

9. The ARTIK will boot up the operating system and report the progress as it goes.

10. The serial output will be displayed on the screen of your workstation.

11. Eventually the ARTIK login prompt will be displayed.

12. Log in to the ARTIK system administrator root account with the root password.

Closing the Connection

You should always exit from a command-line session in an orderly way. Follow these steps to shut down the PuTTY session with your ARTIK.

1. Close the logged-in session on the ARTIK with the exit command.

2. Quit the PuTTY application.

If you are quitting for the day and will not be logging in again, shut down the ARTIK instead of exiting from the session. This is better, because it allows the operating system to tidy things up.

Logging the Output to a File

By default, PuTTY will discard the session data after you exit. Tell it to preserve the output in a file to archive it, read it later, or use it to build automated scripts. It is extremely useful to capture session dialogs in order to create documentation from them. They are almost ready to use as a step-by-step example. Annotate the listing with your own comments and remove sensitive information that needs to be kept private. Here is how to turn on the logging:

1. Open the PuTTY settings panel.

2. On the left, there is a tree-structured list.

3. Find the item called Session.

4. Unfold it with the disclosure widget.

5. Click on the Logging item.

6. Set up the kind of session logging you need.

7. The recommended item is "All session output."

8. Either type in the full path name of the log storage file or browse to locate the folder where it will be written and add the name.

PuTTY Log File Naming

Use special meta-characters to automatically generate your log file name. This will create a new log file every time you run PuTTY. Your logs will be better organized, and you will be able to find specific sessions more easily. You could always rename the session logs to describe what you did and archive them if you want to keep a permanent record. The PuTTY log file-naming meta-characters are enumerated in Table 7-2.

Table 7-2. *PuTTY Log File-Naming Meta-characters*

Meta-character	Meaning
&H	Host name for the session
&Y	Four-digit year number
&M	Month number
&D	Day date number
&T	Time string

These meta-characters are usually only used as part of the log file name. Keep session data separate based on the target host name by using a meta-character as a directory-naming component. This would store all logs in one directory:

```
D:\putty-log\&H-&Y&M&D-&T.log
```

This would store logs in separate directories on a host-by-host basis:

```
D:\putty-log\&H\&Y&M&D-&T.log
```

Note the subtle difference by adding an extra directory level backslash (\) after the host name in place of the dash separator (-).

Using the Default Terminal Application on Mac OS X

The Macintosh operating system has a built-in Terminal application for executing command-line instructions. Starting it up opens a window on your Macintosh in which to type UNIX commands and interact directly with OS X. Follow these instructions to run a dialup connection tool from the Mac OS X command line and tell it where and how to connect to the ARTIK development system.

1. The Terminal application lives in the Utilities folder (inside the Applications folder). Use the keyboard shortcut that takes you straight to the Utilities folder from the Finder:

    ```
    {your_boot_disk} ➤ Applications ➤ Utilities ➤
    Terminal app
    ```

2. Press the [Command] + [Shift] + [U] key combination.

3. Scroll down and double-click on the Terminal application icon to run it.

4. List the logical devices and filter them with a grep command to find the correct identifier for the ARTIK USB serial interface. Use this command (note the vertical bar that pipes the output of the ls command to the input of the grep command):

    ```
    ls /dev | grep usb
    ```

5. You should see one item listed that has a name prefixed by cu.usbserial or tty.usbserial followed by your USB serial interface ID.

6. An example with a real USB serial interface device identifier looks like this:

```
cu.usbserial-AIO2ZIIU
tty.usbserial-AIO2ZIIU
```

7. At the prompt, type this command with your own USB serial interface device identifier substituted in place of the example one:

```
screen /dev/tty.usbserial-AIO2ZIIU 115200
```

8. When this is the active window, your keystrokes will be transmitted to your ARTIK for execution there.

9. The messages from your ARTIK module are displayed here when it is turned on.

10. Switch on the ARTIK developer reference board with its rocker action power switch (or cycle the power if it is already on).

11. Press the power (boot) button next to the power switch on your developer reference board to boot the ARTIK module.

12. The ARTIK will boot up the operating system and report the progress as it goes.

13. The serial output will be displayed on the screen of your Macintosh.

14. Eventually the ARTIK login prompt will be displayed.

15. Log in to the ARTIK system administrator root account with the root password.

Closing the Connection

When you are finished, follow these steps to cleanly exit out of the screen command:

1. Close the logged-in session on the ARTIK with the exit command.

2. Press the [Control] + [A] key combination.

3. Press the [Control] + [\] key combination.

4. You will be prompted to close all the windows.

5. Press the [Y] key to exit the screen command.

6. Now you are back at the command-line prompt for your Macintosh.

7. Exit by closing the window or quitting the terminal application.

Recovering from a Bad Screen Exit

If you do not exit the screen command in an orderly manner, the screen process will continue to run in the background. While it is running, it will stay connected to the ARTIK and block any further access to the serial interface. Resolve that by searching for the screen process with the ps command and signaling it to stop with the kill command when you know the process ID (PID). Follow these steps to find the PID and close a screen command that is blocking your serial port:

1. Find the process ID (PID):

    ```
    ps -ef | grep usb
    ```

2. This should display a matching process like this:

    ```
    501 1185 1 0 2:47pm cu.usbserial 0:01.16 SCREEN
    /dev/cu.usbserial 115200
    ```

3. Note the second number (1185 in this example). That is the PID for your application process. The first number is the parent PID that is probably the process running your command-line shell. You should see that value repeated a few times. The application PID you are interested in will only be listed once.

4. Now kill the screen process by sending a signal to the process. Substitute the correct PID value in this command:

    ```
    kill -9 1185
    ```

5. Check that it has stopped by listing the processes again with the ps command.

■ **Note** **DO NOT ACCIDENTALLY KILL THE PARENT PROCESS.** If you do, your workstation session might be forcibly aborted. This is a bad thing as it can corrupt files, and in extreme cases it can blow away the partition map and destroy the main hard disk. Rebooting your workstation is now the only solution unless your application was running in a sub-shell. You should run a disk repair with the fsck tool or the Disk Utility immediately in case something was broken. Your Macintosh or Linux workstation may take a little longer to start up the first time while it checks the integrity of your hard disk.

Other Useful Screen Commands

Read the UNIX manual page for the screen command to find out what other command-line options to use with it. Add the -L option to log the output to a file.

Pressing the [Control] + [A] key combination enters command mode. Follow that with the [?] key to see the keystroke commands available. The manual page has more details. Type this command to see it in your terminal window:

```
man screen
```

If you prefer to read the command-line manual pages in a web browser, the manual pages are available on the Apple developer website. The top level is located here. Navigate into section 1 and scroll down the list to find the page for the screen command:

```
https://developer.apple.com/library/mac/documentation/Darwin/Reference/
ManPages/
```

The examples here are based on using the screen command because it is included by default in Mac OS X. Alternative serial terminal applications will work too.

Logging the Output to a File

This used to be configurable in the Mac OS X Terminal application preferences in a similar way to in PuTTY, but that feature was removed a few OS versions back. The current version of the Terminal application in the Mac OS utilities logs output in a scroll-back buffer. This is less intuitive and it's harder to capture all the output.

Although these examples are described for the benefit of Mac OS X users, you can use variations of the techniques in Cygwin for Windows and in Linux terminal sessions.

Log Capture Example 1 (Clipboard Cut and Paste)

In earlier versions of the Terminal application, there was a preference setting to tune the length of the scroll-back buffer. Setting it to unlimited was useful, but performance degraded when it got very long. Now that this option has been removed, it is hard to predict what gets put into the scroll-back buffer. If you bring up a manual page, the scroll-back buffer contains the text you view, but when you exit the manual page it gets cleared from the buffer. There are a few useful work-around approaches to capture the screen output. Copy the scroll-back buffer to the clipboard with these steps:

1. Open a destination file with a text editor so you have somewhere to past the log.

2. Click in the terminal window to give it focus.

3. Use a Select All instruction:

   [Command] + [A]

4. Copy the screen content into your clipboard:

   [Command] + [C]

5. Paste the result into your text editor:

   [Command] + [V]

6. Save the log file.

Log Capture Example 2 (Screen Command Logging)

To record a log within a screen command session, append the -L option to the screen command when you open the session. Follow these steps to run the session and log the output:

1. Start the serial session like this:

   ```
   screen -L /dev/tty.usbserial-AIO2ZIIU 115200
   ```

2. The session will be recorded to a file called screenlog.{n} where n is a number from 0 to 9. The output is flushed periodically to the file and also when you exit the session.

3. Toggle the logging on and off by going into command mode with a [Control] + [A] key combination and executing a [Shift] + [H] key combination.

4. Press the [Control] + [A] key combination.

5. Then press the [Shift] + [H] key combination.

6. The screen session will echo a message to your console about the logging process.

Log Capture Example 3 (Output Redirection)

This capture method will record the output of a specific command by redirecting it to a temporary file for analysis later. In the examples, the tilde character (~) is shorthand for accessing sub-directories within your own home directory. Log a session to a file like this:

1. List the contents of a directory to a new file:

   ```
   ls -la > ~/Desktop/myoutput.log
   ```

2. Append to an existing log file:

   ```
   ls -la >> ~/Desktop/myoutput.log
   ```

3. This will not capture the error messages to the log file. Capture those separately to another file:

   ```
   ls -la 2> ~/Desktop/myerrors.log
   ```

4. Capture the standard output and merge the error messages with it:

   ```
   ls -la 2>&1 ~/Desktop/myoutput.log
   ```

Log Capture Example 4 (Stream Duplexing)

Another possible approach to capturing logs is to pipe the output of your command to the tee command, which splits the input into two streams that can be redirected independently. One would still go to your screen, the other to a file:

1. Capture the standard output to a new file:

   ```
   ls -la | tee ~/Desktop/myoutput.log
   ```

2. Append the standard output to an existing log file:

   ```
   ls -la | tee -a ~/Desktop/myoutput.log
   ```

Log Capture Example 5 (Script Command Logging)

This technique uses the `script` command to capture the terminal output. The example tells the `script` command to flush the output to the log file every 15 seconds:

```
script -t 15 ~/Desktop/myoutput.log ls -lt
```

Set this up as a default command to be executed every time a terminal window is opened. Additional line feeds may be recorded and must be cleaned out before using the output file. There is a race hazard risk with this approach if you have more than one window open with both of them logging their output to the same file. It is better to only log the output when you need it.

The command that you previously typed at the start of the line is now presented as a parameter to the `script` command. Use the `script` command as follows to spawn a new command line and log all of the output to the file:

```
script -t 15 ~/Desktop/myoutput.log
```

Remember to always exit out of the `script` command session with a [Control] + [D] key combination.

Alternatives to the Mac OS X Terminal App

The CoolTerm application is a good alternative to the Mac OS Terminal app. CoolTerm is useful for managing the serial connection to your ARTIK separately from running a command line through the Terminal app. Get a CoolTerm installer here:

```
http://freeware.the-meiers.org/
```

Another possibility is using the shareware iTerm application as a complete replacement for the standard Terminal app. The iTerm application has a very elegant solution for capturing the logs via a menu item to start and stop the logging. This is a more sophisticated emulator than the Apple Terminal Emulator app. This is useful if you spend a lot of time in a command-line environment. The iTerm home page is here:

```
https://www.iterm2.com/
```

Using the Minicom Terminal Application on Linux

If your development workstation is running the Linux operating system, use the minicom application to interact with a command-line shell. Depending on your Linux distribution (flavor), the `yum`, `rpm`, or `apt-get` installers will add new packages if minicom is not installed by default. Download the source code files and compile the software tools yourself if you prefer to ensure they are 100 percent compatible with your operating system configuration. There is more information available on the minicom web pages:

```
https://alioth.debian.org/projects/minicom/
https://help.ubuntu.com/community/Minicom
https://apps.fedoraproject.org/packages/minicom
```

Installing Minicom with yum

The Redhat, CentOS and Fedora distributions use the yum command to install new packages. The yum tool is smart enough to search for and download packages from a central package repository. Use this command to install minicom with yum on compatible Linux distributions:

```
yum install minicom
```

Installing Minicom with apt-get

Some versions of Linux manage their installations with the apt-get command rather than the yum command. Debian Linux uses this, for example. Installing the minicom terminal emulator is straightforward if apt-get is supported by your system:

```
sudo apt-get install minicom
```

Building Minicom from the Source Code Files

If the apt-get installer is not available, follow these instructions for building and installing using the source code files:

1. Go to the Debian packages web page for minicom.

   ```
   https://packages.debian.org/search?keywords=minicom
   ```

2. Download the installation package and note where it was dropped on your system.

3. Open a command-line terminal window on your Linux workstation.

4. Change to the minicom-$VERSION directory (where $VERSION indicates which revision you have).

5. Optionally, check out the configuration help with this command:

   ```
   ./configure --help
   ```

6. Run the configuration script to build a source code image ready to compile:

    ```
    ./configure
    ```

7. Build the application:

    ```
    make
    ```

8. Install the application:

    ```
    make install
    ```

9. Log in as root or use the sudu command to modify the /etc/minicom configuration file.

10. Run minicom in configuration mode:

    ```
    minicom -s
    ```

11. Change the configuration options to suit what you want to do.

12. Choose "Save setup as dfl" from the configuration menu to save the changed settings as system defaults.

13. Add every user who should be allowed to use minicom to the user group of the corresponding character devices (e.g., /dev/ttyS0). On Debian this group already exists and is called dialout. Your Linux OS might call it something else.

Configure Minicom to Talk to the ARTIK Developer Reference Board

Now that you have minicom installed and ready to use, configure it to connect to your ARTIK developer reference board via the USB serial interface. The minicom serial configurations are described here:

```
https://help.ubuntu.com/community/Minicom
```

Here are the configuration steps:

1. Log on as the root user or use the sudu command prefix to run a command as if you were the root user.

2. Get a list of your serial ports with this command:

    ```
    dmesg | grep tty
    ```

3. For USB-to-Serial adapters, you might see something like this:

```
[0.000000] console [tty0] enabled
[5.065029] usb 4-3: pl2303 converter now attached to ttyUSB0
```

4. Note the name of the serial port listed for the USB interface. In this example it is ttyUSB0.

5. Now run minicom in a configuration mode to adjust the serial connection settings:

```
sudo minicom -s
```

6. From here, choose "Serial port setup."

7. Alter the various settings to configure in the correct device (we are using ttyUSB0 here).

8. Set the communications speed to 115200.

9. The default settings for data size, parity, and stop bits are usually OK.

10. Choose "Save setup as dfl" from the configuration menu to save the changed settings as system defaults.

11. Exit the minicom application.

The minicom application keeps the default startup configuration in the /etc/minicom/minirc.dfl file. Make a backup copy of this file for safekeeping. Experienced system administrators may edit this file directly, but since minicom provides a configuration mode that is rarely necessary.

Connecting to the ARTIK Development System from Minicom

Running the minicom application on Linux is similar to using the screen command on Mac OS X.

1. Open a command-line window on your Linux desktop.

2. Start minicom, with no options to run with the default configuration:

```
minicom
```

3. When this is the active window, your keystrokes will be transmitted to your ARTIK module and processed there.

4. Messages from your ARTIK module will be displayed in the minicom window when it is booted.

5. Switch on the ARTIK developer reference board with its rocker action power switch (or cycle the power if it is already on).

6. Press the power (boot) button next to the power switch on your developer reference board.

7. The ARTIK will boot up the operating system and report the progress as it goes.

8. The serial output will be displayed on the screen of your Linux workstation.

9. Eventually the ARTIK login prompt will be displayed.

10. Log in to the ARTIK system administrator root account with the root password.

Closing the Connection

When you are finished, follow these steps to cleanly exit out of the minicom session:

1. Close the logged-in session on the ARTIK with the exit command.

2. Press the [Control] + [A] key combination to get a message bar at the bottom of the minicom terminal window.

3. Press the [Shift] + [X] key combination to exit the minicom application.

4. Now you are back at the command-line prompt for your Linux workstation.

5. Exit by closing the window.

Logging the Output to a File

Add the capture option to minicom when you start it up. This will store all screen output in the indicated log file:

```
minicom -C /var/log/mylogfile.log
```

■ **Note**   Make sure that you type an uppercase letter [C] key or your log file will not be created. The lowercase letter [c] key is reserved for setting up the screen colors.

Toggle the logging stream on and off by pressing the [Control] + [A] key combination followed by a [Shift] + [L] key combination.

Pausing the Screen Output

The terminal emulator application supports software flow control that is useful for pausing the output to the console screen. Pressing the [Control] + [S] key combination (equivalent to the ASCII control code XOFF) will stop the flow. Restart it by pressing the [Control] + [X] key combination (equivalent to XON). This might also work in other terminal emulator applications on other platforms.

Using Minicom Inside Your ARTIK

If you intend to connect external devices to your ARTIK module, you may choose to do so with a downstream serial interface, perhaps with a serial adapter connected to the USB connector. Because the ARTIK runs Linux, you may be able to get minicom up and running inside your ARTIK. This would make debugging your downstream serial connection much easier. Porting and recompiling minicom for the ARM CPU architecture may be challenging if a compatible version is unavailable. If you modify the source code to make it work, submit your changes back to the minicom project team or post an article online to help the rest of the ARTIK community.

Summary

Things are about to get very interesting. You have just set up the terminal emulator you will use to talk to your ARTIK. The next step is to switch it on and start it up. This is an important milestone in your journey, because you will then be ready to begin to explore the internals of the ARTIK operating system.

CHAPTER 8

Talking to Your ARTIK

Starting Up the ARTIK

Now that you can communicate with the ARTIK module you are ready to start it up. At first this can seem very confusing because the ARTIK will display a long list of messages as individual processes are started. This verbose messaging can be turned off when you ship your production devices. In a development context it is useful to see what is running at boot-up time. Customize the startup process to turn off unwanted services or add new ones to the boot sequence. The onscreen feedback shows you whether that configuration worked correctly. You will soon become familiar with the contents of this message stream, and if anything goes wrong you will spot it right away.

Capturing this message stream to a log file from your terminal emulator application and reading through it carefully will teach you a lot about how your UNIX systems start up. There are useful and important values revealed for use in your ARTIK applications.

The System Administrator Console

When your ARTIK starts up, it displays status messages on the system administrator console about each process or utility as it is initiated. That console output is presented on your terminal emulator screen. If you start the emulator first and connect to the serial port before starting up your ARTIK, you can capture the log and inspect it. Some messages are a little opaque, but with practice you will be able to recognize whether there are any problems with your configuration due to your alterations. Gradually, you will learn what all of this means, and reviewing these messages is a good way to get to know your UNIX systems. Sometimes, the messages will tell you a useful identifier for use later when you use the command line to interact with a process.

U-boot Universal Boot Loader Messages

These messages are generated by the initialization code when the U-Boot Universal Boot Loader runs. This U-Boot software presents a description of the hardware and CPU model. On a PC, the equivalent would be the BIOS, and on a Macintosh it would be the EFI Firmware. This brings up the hardware to a point where it can look for an operating system kernel and get that running. Press any key to halt the automatic loading of the operating system and interact with U-Boot to explore your ARTIK hardware. See Listing 8-1 for an example of what happens when you boot a Beta revision ARTIK 5 module.

Listing 8-1. U-Boot Startup Messages (Beta)

```
U-Boot 2012.07 (Nov 09 2015 - 13:32:25) for ARTIK5

CPU: Exynos3250 [Samsung SOC on SMP Platform Base on ARM CortexA7]
APLL = 700MHz, MPLL = 800MHz

Board: ARTIK5
DRAM:   504 MiB
WARNING: Caches not enabled

TrustZone Enabled BSP
BL1 version: 20140203

Checking Boot Mode ... EMMC4.41
MMC:    S5P_MSHC0: 0, S5P_MSHC2: 1
MMC Device 0: 3.6 GiB
MMC Device 1: [ERROR] response error : 00000006 cmd 8
[ERROR] response error : 00000006 cmd 55
[ERROR] response error : 00000006 cmd 2
In:    serial
Out:   serial
Err:   serial
rst_stat : 0x10000
Net:   No ethernet found.
Hit any key to stop autoboot:g
```

If you press any key at this point, the booting process will stop. Only interact with the U-Boot command line if you are confident and know what you are doing. This is not a place where you can casually tinker with settings, because you might not be able to get it to work again. The U-Boot environment is an advanced topic, and there is nothing to do there from a beginner's perspective; it is best to just let it continue and start the kernel automatically.

Booting the Kernel

If you did not purposely halt the U-Boot autoloader, the OS kernel will be started up automatically once the operating system has been retrieved from its secure storage. See Listing 8-2.

Listing 8-2. Reading the OS Image from Secure Storage (Beta)

```
reading zImage
4367680 bytes read in 17600 ms (242.2 KiB/s)
reading exynos3250-artik5.dtb
38241 bytes read in 11667 ms (2.9 KiB/s)
```

```
reading uInitrd
1353683 bytes read in 25638 ms (50.8 KiB/s)
## Loading init Ramdisk from Legacy Image at 43000000 ...
   Image Name:   uInitrd
   Image Type:   ARM Linux RAMDisk Image (uncompressed)
   Data Size:    1353619 Bytes = 1.3 MiB
   Load Address: 00000000
   Entry Point:  00000000
## Flattened Device Tree blob at 40800000
   Booting using the fdt blob at 0x40800000
   Loading Ramdisk to 43eb5000, end 43fff793 ... OK
   Loading Device Tree to 43ea8000, end 43eb4560 ... OK

Starting kernel ...
```

If you interrupted the auto boot and want to start the kernel manually, type the following command into the U-Boot command line:

```
boot
```

The ARTIK will only take a few seconds to boot up to the login prompt.

OS Kernel Startup

First the hardware is prepared. Then the operating system (Fedora in this case) is located and the startup scripts are executed to bring up the system in an orderly fashion. Study the boot listing on your own ARTIK and inspect the messages about these services as they start. The Fedora boot process carries out these steps as it starts up:

- Prepares the hardware

- Locates the operating system image to be booted

- Runs the OS startup scripts

- Locates encrypted volumes

- Sets up memory swap space

- Configures memory into privileged space and user space

- Starts journal logging

- Sets up file system and mounts volumes

- Sets up serial TTY

- Created NFS file system for remote file system mounts

- Creates device virtual file system

- Initializes random number seed

- Locates MMC memory device

- Mounts boot file system

- Locates sound card

- Loads kernel extension modules

- Initializes Remote Procedure Call support

- Starts time synchronizer

- Configures hardware timers

- Sets up DNS bind

- Sets up D-Bus

- Starts Avahi mDNS

- Establishes login service

- Starts GSS Proxy daemon

- Starts PWM audio services

- Initializes Bluetooth firmware

- Starts network manager

- Starts OpenSSH server

- Notifies NFS peers that a restart has happened

- Presents the login prompt to the user

See Listing 8-3 for the last few lines of a kernel startup log recorded from a Beta model ARTIK 5 as it boots up.

Listing 8-3. Kernel Startup Log and Fedora Startup Messages

```
[0.059426] /cpus/cpu@0 missing clock-frequency property
[0.059454] /cpus/cpu@1 missing clock-frequency property
[0.284917] cw201x 1-0062: get cw_capacity error; cw_capacity = 255
[0.619665] (unregistered net_device): timeout waiting for reset completion
[0.666998] jpeg-hx2 11830000.jpeg: failed to get parent1 clk
[0.782503] exynos-adc 126c0000.adc: operating without regulator vdd[-19]
[3.834717] s5p-decon-display 11c00000.fimd_fb: wait for vsync timeout
Loading, please wait...

Welcome to Fedora 22 (Twenty Two)!

... Many lines of boot messaging omitted here to save space ...
```

```
Fedora release 22 (Twenty Two)
Kernel 3.10.9 on an armv7l (ttySAC2)

localhost login:
```

Log in to the root account now and explore your ARTIK from the command line.

Setting the Boot Mode Switches

Alter the way your ARTIK boots when it is running on the developer reference board by setting the boot mode switches. Orient the developer reference board with the boot configuration switches facing you, as shown in Figure 8-1. Find the Micro SD socket as well.

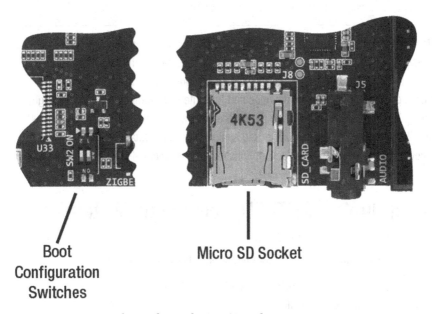

Boot Configuration Switches

Micro SD Socket

Figure 8-1. *Boot mode switches and Micro SD socket*

The boot mode switches labeled 1 and 2 should both be set to Off. This means the board is in eMMC boot mode and will look for an eMMC memory image that contains a viable and bootable operating system kernel.

To set the board to SD card mode, set switch 2 to On and leave switch 1 set to Off. This mode is used to install a new kernel or firmware updates. In SD boot mode, the ARTIK will look for an attached SD card and try to locate a viable and bootable OS kernel there.

If you try to boot an ARTIK with an empty SD card, even the most basic parts of the boot process will not work. Make sure you install an SD card with a genuinely bootable image if you set the switches to boot from it. Table 8-1 summarizes the boot switch possibilities:

Table 8-1. *Boot Mode Switch Settings*

Switch 1	Switch 2	Setting Description
Off (0)	**Off** (0)	eMMC boot mode to run the OS installed in the internal secure memory
Off (0)	**On** (1)	SD boot mode to install a new OS from the Micro SD card
On (1)	**Off** (0)	Undocumented state
On (1)	**On** (1)	Undocumented state

▥ **Note** These switches and the Micro SD socket are not always in the same place, and when viewed from the edge of the board the switches may be oriented upside down, which makes the On and Off settings look as if they are the opposite way around. Later revisions of the developer reference board have relocated these items several times, and this might happen again. There is some conflict in the source documentation describing the settings shown in Table 8-1, which has been checked against Alpha and Beta versions of the ARTIK developer reference boards. Earlier descriptions incorrectly reversed some switch positions.

Booting Up Your ARTIK Development System

Follow these steps to boot up your ARTIK:

1. Connect the power cable to the reference board and plug it in.

2. Start up your terminal emulator application.

3. Open the serial console.

4. Turn the log capturing on if you want to store the boot messages for inspection later.

5. The rocker action power switch powers up the board and turns on the LEDs.

6. The LED indicators labeled RXD and TXD will illuminate to indicate traffic flowing through the serial interface to your development workstation.

7. Now press the power (boot) button next to the power switch on your developer reference board to boot your ARTIK module.

8. Some of the LED indicators will blink.

9. Booting messages will appear on the serial console.

10. Wait until you receive a login message.

11. Log in to the ARTIK system administrator root account with the root password.

Login Credentials

The system administrator of a UNIX system is described as the root user. This user has sufficient permission and privileges to completely destroy the operating system and render the ARTIK un-bootable. You must always be very careful when you are logged in as the root user. Always think about what you are about to type at the command line. The initial login credentials are listed in Table 8-2.

Table 8-2. *Login Credentials*

Account	Password	Description
root	root	Summer 2015 pioneer edition ARTIK modules onwards (including Beta & Spring 2016 launch models)
root	f@s)P!A$RTNER	Early firmware Alpha prototype ARTIK modules

Earlier prototype versions of the ARTIK firmware have a different initial root password. This indicates that you have older firmware that should be updated:

f@s)P!A$RTNER

You should change the administrator password immediately. Changing default passwords is very important when you go into production with a new product design that has an ARTIK embedded within it. Make sure the new password is something you can remember. Be sure to carefully note the new password, because if you lock out the root account, gaining access to the system again is difficult. Reinstalling the operating system from scratch may be necessary.

Use the passwd command on the ARTIK command line to alter the root account password. Enter your password carefully twice to confirm that you typed it correctly. They must both match or the password change will be aborted. This is a safety feature to avoid setting the password to something unintentional. Type it slowly so that each keystroke is correct. The ARTIK operating system suggests that any passwords shorter than eight characters are weak. Follow these steps to change the password for the root account:

1. Decide what your new password is going to be. It should fit the following criteria:

   • Easy to remember

   • At least eight characters long

   • Mix of upper- and lowercase letters

   • Mix of letters and numbers

   • The strongest passwords include punctuation characters

2. Log in to the root account.

3. Type the password-changing command:

   passwd

4. Carefully enter your new password for the first time.

5. Carefully enter your new password again to confirm it.

6. Note your new password in a safe and secure place.

Shutdown Commands

If you are reconfiguring your ARTIK or building applications and services to be reconnected at boot time, you will want to shut down the ARTIK and reboot it to test your changes. Be careful not to accidentally shut down your development workstation instead of your ARTIK module. Power cycling an ARTIK without gracefully shutting it down would also work, but it is never a good idea to just remove the power from a running UNIX system. It is much better to shut it down in an orderly way. This gives the OS an opportunity to record important information about the system and restore it when the system restarts. Use the shutdown command with options to modify its behavior:

shutdown {control_options} {time_value} {warning_message_text}

The most useful command-line options are listed in Table 8-3. Use the man shutdown command to see all the descriptive help pages.

Table 8-3. *Shutdown Command Options*

Option	Description
--help	Displays a brief help message
-H	Halts the ARTIK
-P	Powers off the ARTIK. Restart it again by pressing the power (boot) button
-r	Shuts down and reboots the ARTIK from the U-Boot as if the power (boot) button has been pressed
-c	Cancels a pending deferred shutdown command

The time values can be specified as a specific hh:mm time in 24-hour format. Use the keyword now to indicate the shutdown must happen right away. Alternatively, use the +{minutes} format to indicate a delay measured in minutes before the shutdown happens. Without a time value, the shutdown command assumes +1 by default and waits 60 seconds before shutting down. When you indicate a delay, the operating system will inhibit new logins for the 5 minutes prior to the shutdown.

Sending a message to your users makes sense in the context of a delayed shutdown. The warning message will be sent to all logged-in users. When you add a message, you must specify a time value to avoid the message being misinterpreted as command-line options.

If you are shutting down now, your users will not have any chance to see the message or take any action before the shutdown happens but their terminal screen will at least display it until they reset. The message may still be helpful to warn them about why the system is shutting down right away and when it will be up again.

Table 8-4 illustrates a few example shutdown command variations.

Table 8-4. *Example Shutdown Commands*

Command	Description
shutdown -r now	Shut down gracefully right away and run the Universal Boot Loader again to restart the ARTIK.
shutdown -P now	Shut down gracefully right away and return the ARTIK to the initial powered on but not yet booted state.
shutdown -r +5	Reboot the ARTIK in five minutes.
shutdown -r 11:55	Reboot the ARTIK just before midday. That would be tomorrow if the command is typed in the afternoon.
shutdown -c	Cancel a pending shutdown.
shutdown --help	Display the list of commands.

■ **Note**   You can use the systemctl utilities to power off and reboot the ARTIK if you prefer, but the time-honored shutdown command works just fine and is easy to use.

Shutdown Warnings

When you tell the ARTIK to shut down without specifying a time delay the default timeout is assumed and the message shown in Listing 8-4 appears on the console display.

Listing 8-4. Shutdown Messages

```
Broadcast message from root@localhost.localdomain (Wed 2014-01-01 12:20:32 UTC):

The system is going down for power-off at Wed 2014-01-01 12:21:31 UTC!
```

Override this message with your own text, provided you indicate a time value so your users will see the message in time to respond to it.

Shutdown Console Logging Messages

The operating system displays a log of what is happening as it closes down any running processes and returns to a quiescent state. Execute this command to shut down and see the messages on your console screen as the operating system tears down all the processes that it started when the system was booted:

```
shutdown -P now
```

Shutting down in an orderly manner is always the recommended approach so as to avoid corrupting your ARTIK operating system files.

Summary

If everything went correctly up to this point, you should be able to boot and log in to your ARTIK and start to explore the internal layout. At the moment, you can only communicate via a serial interface. The next priority is to get the other network connections and protocols up and running. Once you have done some internal configuration, your ARTIK will be ready for application coding.

■ ■ ■

## CHAPTER 9

Network Configuration

Networking Your ARTIK

Now that your development workstation is able to talk to the ARTIK via a serial interface connection, you can start up, shut down, and reboot the ARTIK operating system. The next task is to configure the network connectivity in the ARTIK. Less sophisticated product designs might not need network capabilities, but it will help to integrate the software tools in the development workstation if they are able to communicate across the network. Your ARTIK needs to have some network connectivity set up first. There are three basic kinds of networking available:

- Ethernet wired connections accessible via a sub-net or local area network (LAN)

- Wi-Fi connections using one of the IEEE 802.11 protocols

- Bluetooth connections to peripheral devices that the ARTIK module will manage

The first two are the most helpful for integrating the developer tools. The serial connection is still available for debugging but has no inherent smartness. Connect a JTAG hardware-debugging probe to communicate with the internals of running applications as you develop them. There are several useful ways to talk to your ARTIK and the processes inside it. Add other communications devices by plugging adapters into the ARTIK's peripheral USB interface and then install drivers to support them.

Networking Protocol Support

The ARTIK 5 and 10 modules support a variety of networking protocols that are available courtesy of the Linux operating system. You can provide the necessary service endpoints, supporting libraries, and drivers yourself to add protocols that are not already supported by default.

Kevin Sharp has produced a series of useful blog articles to get you started. Read about connectivity and IoT networking technologies here:

```
https://www.artik.io/blog/2015/iot-101-networks
https://www.artik.io/blog/2015/iot-101-connectivity
```

© Cliff Wootton 2016
C. Wootton, *Beginning Samsung ARTIK*, DOI 10.1007/978-1-4842-1952-2_9

Choosing the Best Networking Strategy

Choose the best network connection strategy by balancing bandwidth, range, and power consumption as the key factors. The complexity of the chosen transmission protocol is also relevant because more energy is consumed when the CPU needs to work harder to encode and decode messages.

If your product is stationary and never likely to move, a hard-wired Ethernet-connected solution is best. Maximum network throughput is achieved with a physical cable connection, although modern wireless connections are getting faster. The configuration instructions for your Ethernet connector describe how to set up an IP address for IPv4 and IPv6.

An Ethernet-based configuration will expend less energy than using a Wi-Fi connection. In a hard-wired scenario, you can also permanently power the unit so that a limited battery life is of no consequence. Then you are free to choose whatever protocol you need.

Wireless Networking

When you are selecting a communications technology, it helps to compare like for like. Figure 9-1 illustrates comparative range and power consumption for the wireless communications supported by the ARTIK modules. The data transfer capacity is indicated by the size of the circles. A few of the protocols are emulated on the developer reference board and are not available directly from the ARTIK module when it is embedded in a stand-alone configuration. If you need those protocols, your product design must implement its own support for them. Those protocols may eventually migrate into the ARTIK in which case they will be natively supported.

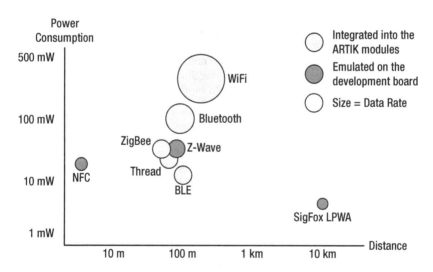

Figure 9-1. *Power consumption vs. range*

If range is important, choose IEEE 802.11 Wi-Fi. This has good bandwidth but consumes more energy than the alternatives. Manage the state of the Wi-Fi link up and down to conserve battery power in a mobile scenario. There are three variants of the protocol supported. The 802.11b, g, and n variants are all available. Variants b and g are similar in performance to Bluetooth Low Energy and only provide a little more bandwidth. IEEE 802.11n is the best solution if you choose this kind of networking. The newer ac and ah variants are not yet available on ARTIK modules.

If your product is part of a Personal Area Network combining several wearable devices, Bluetooth is the best option. Choose Bluetooth Low Energy (BLE), as this has the best power consumption profile and the communications range is good (within the context of a wearable device). Classic Bluetooth performs less well in terms of power and range.

The ZigBee and Thread protocols are extremely low power options. These will sip their power; a small coin cell battery will last for a very long time. Managing your connections and turning things off when they are not needed is always a good design strategy and will enable the battery to last longer.

Table 9-1 summarizes the different protocols supported by each ARTIK module.

Table 9-1. *Wireless Protocols Supported by Each Module Type*

Protocol	ARTIK 1	ARTIK 5	ARTIK 10	Dev board
Bluetooth		√	√	
Bluetooth Low Energy (BLE) 4.0	√	√	√	
Wi-Fi (IEEE 802.11		√	√	
ZigBee		√	√	
Thread		√	√	
Z-Wave				√
NFC				√
SigFox LPWA				√

Dynamic Name Auto-discovery Support

The Multicast Domain Name System for Wi-Fi (mDNS) is a zero-configuration Dynamic Name System resolver for use in small networks such as those found on a Wi-Fi installation. It is able to coexist with a traditional unicast DNS resolver. In Apple networks, this is compatible with the Rendezvous/Bonjour protocols.

When an mDNS client process needs to resolve a host name, it sends an IP multicast query message over the local area network (LAN). All hosts on that LAN see the message. It asks the host having that name to identify itself. That target machine then multicasts a message in reply that includes an IP address. All machines in that sub-net can then use that information to update their own private mDNS caches.

Each node on the network must be configured with a unique IP address. If an IP address collision happens, the integrity of the mDNS is compromised and parts of your network (or possibly all of it) will cease to function.

The service is managed with the `avahi` daemon, which needs to be running in order for mDNS to work. The ArchLinux wiki has set up instructions for configuring `avahi` services, which include file sharing and AirPrint access to printers. Find out more about mDNS here:

```
https://en.wikipedia.org/wiki/Multicast_DNS
https://tools.ietf.org/html/rfc6762
https://wiki.archlinux.org/index.php/avahi
```

Protocol Support

A protocol is an agreed upon format for sending messages between systems. Typically you would send a request from a client process to a service, which would reply with a message that the client could understand.

Messages are sent in a variety of different ways, perhaps by tunneling via an `HTTP:` protocol. This might look very similar to a form submission from a web browser. The service might respond to a request like that with a response encapsulated in XML or JSON. A JSON-formatted response is more compact than XML and easier to parse. Rather than use `HTTP:`, you could transmit an XML-formatted request to a SOAP service using WebSockets.

A more compact message format uses less CPU power to encapsulate and unwrap the transactions, and that directly affects the power consumption of your design. The size of the message affects transfer speed and also the data transfer budget that your customers pay for. Network traffic for IoT products should be kept to a minimum and made as efficient and compact as possible.

OMA Lightweight M2M Protocol (LW M2M)

The Lightweight M2M protocol from the Open Mobile Alliance is designed to support communications from mobile to mobile (M2M) devices. It facilitates Internet of Things device management. The LWM2M support defines the communications protocol between an LWM2M server and an LWM2M client in another device. Because it is targeting mobile devices, the protocol is very economical in terms of the message size of the underlying data model. It is frequently used with CoAP (explained next). The LWM2M protocol is especially optimized to manage functionality over mobile phone networks or meshes of sensors. Find out more about this protocol here:

```
https://en.wikipedia.org/wiki/OMA_LWM2M
```

Temboo has introduced support for this in their web-based code design workbench. Incorporate it into your Temboo project with their point-and-click GUI-based code builder to generate the code to embed into your application.

Constrained Application Protocol (CoAP)

The Constrained Application Protocol allows very simple electronics devices to communicate over the Internet. It is particularly useful for miniature low-power sensors, switches, valves, and similar components that are operated or monitored remotely. The CoAP protocol can tunnel via HTTP: for integration with the web. Connecting directly without tunneling is more efficient, and this protocol consumes much less bandwidth than sending HTTP: requests. The CoAP protocol also supports multicast messaging.

The core of the protocol is specified in RFC 7252; important extensions are in various stages of the standardization process. CoAP messages are transported via fast UDP connections. Because there is no flow control, they are not as robust as TCP-connected messaging. Message Queue Telemetry Transport Protocol (MQTT) is better if you need guaranteed delivery as opposed to speedy delivery.

CoAP is built around a REST API programming model and is easy to manage via a proxy when you want to interact with a web-based application. Find out more about CoAP here:

```
https://en.wikipedia.org/wiki/Constrained_Application_Protocol
https://tools.ietf.org/html/rfc7252
```

Message Queue Telemetry Transport Protocol (MQTT)

Message Queue Telemetry Transport (MQTT) services run directly on top of the TCP/IP protocol. TCP guarantees that all message packets will arrive in sequence and takes care of retransmission and assembly into the correct order. The downside is that this requires some buffering, because packets arrive by different routes and hence out of sequence. A small delay is introduced while the data is reconstructed. This delay is the built-in latency of a protocol such as MQTT. UDP can be used for transmission if speed is of the essence, but you lose the guaranteed chronological order and completeness of the transacted packets.

This protocol is built around a publish/subscribe programming model and is more efficient than CoAP. Choose this protocol when message size is most important.

The publish/subscribe messaging pattern requires a message broker. Messages are sent to the broker and redistributed to interested client processes that have registered with it. The broker may decide to route messages only to a subset of the clients based on their content.

The MQTT protocol has been around since 1999 when it was invented by IBM and delivered as part of their message queuing solution. The naming of this protocol does not imply that all implementations will support queuing but rather is a historical hangover from its origins. The current version of the standard is 3.1 and is published by OASIS for download here:

```
http://docs.oasis-open.org/mqtt/mqtt/v3.1.1/mqtt-v3.1.1.html
```

Prominent users of MQTT are Amazon IoT and Facebook Messenger, although they only use sub-sets of the protocol. If you have the necessary permissions, you can synthesize messages and transmit them into these systems. Your application should authenticate first. A license and permission from the service providers are sometimes necessary for commercial applications. A variation of the protocol is called MQTT-SN and can be used on non-TCP networks such as ZigBee. Find out more about MQTT on Wikipedia here:

```
https://en.wikipedia.org/wiki/MQTT
```

6LoWPAN Protocol

The protocol name 6LoWPAN is condensed from "IPv6 over Low power Wireless Personal Area Networks." The original concept asserts "the Internet Protocol could and should be applied even to the smallest devices." It is fundamental that low-power devices with limited computing power should be able to participate in the Internet of Things.

The 6LoWPAN standards working group has defined protocols that allow IPv6 packets to be sent and received over ZigBee-based networks (IEEE 802.15.4). This protocol wrapping is necessary because although IPv6 is derived from IPv4, they work differently than the IEEE 802.15.4 networking protocols and must tunnel through the wireless infrastructure, using it as a transport mechanism. Find out more about this protocol here:

```
https://en.wikipedia.org/wiki/6LoWPAN
https://tools.ietf.org/html/rfc4944
https://tools.ietf.org/html/rfc6282
https://tools.ietf.org/html/rfc6775
https://tools.ietf.org/html/rfc4919
```

Using ZigBee and Thread Protocols

Your ZigBee protocol connection can be configured to create a mesh of interconnected devices that increases the range of a single node. The nodes in the mesh can then reach further by forwarding messages for each other. This is a more lightweight communications protocol than Bluetooth or Wi-Fi and has an embedded security model. Stay up to date with all matters relating to security in case there are weaknesses discovered that allow unwanted intrusions into your ZigBee infrastructure. Make sure your ZigBee mesh does not interact with your neighbor's system if they have ZigBee deployed too.

Although the ZigBee and Thread Group systems are competitors, they have agreed to work on joint standardization of the protocols. The systems will then collaborate rather than compete when a user implements both within the same environment. See the following:

```
https://en.wikipedia.org/wiki/ZigBee
```

There is a detailed article in the Samsung developer blogs that describes how to install the Ember debugging system for ZigBee. Read this blog article for details if you want to exercise the ZigBee capabilities of your ARTIK 10 module:

```
http://artie.artik.io/knowledgebase/articles/755967-artik-zigbee-manual
```

OpenHAB Support in ARTIK 10 Modules

The Open Home Automation Bus (OpenHAB) creates a common framework for managing home automation devices and applications. This should aid interoperability between devices and software from different manufacturers. OpenHAB will run anywhere a Java VM runtime environment is available. It requires at least Java version 1.7 in order to work properly. This allows it to run in your ARTIK 10 module and in your development workstation, regardless of the platform it is based on. There are also user interfaces and API support for Android, iOS, and web-based applications. Integrating OpenHAB with any mobile device should therefore be straightforward.

New devices are integrated with OpenHAB through the addition of bindings and bundles. A bundle contains the optional plugin code support that talks to a particular product. Samsung provides a bundle for connecting to their consumer TV products. Bindings are used to integrate with software products and online API frameworks. A binding is delivered as a Java JAR file. Visit the OpenHAB website and find the "Supported Technologies" web page for more help.

OpenHAB is currently undergoing an evolution from version 1 to version 2. The focus of this work is to make it easier to administer OpenHAB installation. In OpenHAB 1, the configuration requires you to hand edit various configuration files. OpenHAB 2 adds administrative tools to help you do this. The developers have made the decision to base version 2 on the Eclipse Smart Home project.

There are also links to helpful blog articles in the Git repository for OpenHAB 2. Find out more about the OpenHAB project there. The website has a useful "Getting Started" article that will help you with your development process:

```
http://www.openHAB.org/
https://github.com/openhab/openhab
https://github.com/openhab/openhab2
https://en.wikipedia.org/wiki/Draft:OpenHAB
http://www.openhab.org/getting-started/
http://www.openhab.org/features/supported-technologies.html
http://kaikreuzer.blogspot.de/2014/06/openhab-20-and-eclipse-smarthome.html
http://www.eclipse.org/smarthome/
```

A pre-installed framework on the ARTIK 10 module natively supports OpenHAB. This is not currently installed on ARTIK 5 modules. The location of this framework can be determined with the find command via a case-insensitive search:

```
find / -iname \*openhab\* -print
```

This grep command will locate files whose names do not contain the string 'OpenHAB' but whose content mentions it. The first example command may take some time to execute because it searches though the entire file system in the ARTIK. You can just search in specific directories such as /etc as shown in the second example:

```
grep -r -i -H 'OpenHab' /
grep -r -i -H 'OpenHab' /etc
```

OpenStack (Swift) Framework

OpenStack is an object-based data storage system for sharing assets between systems. Use it to create private or public cloud-based systems of your own. The objects are distributed across a cluster of OpenStack nodes.

The API to OpenStack is implemented as a REST API interface called Swift that is built on top of OpenStack and provides additional features. This is also wrapped in language support for most popular development languages.

A Swift OpenStack cluster server implements four basic process types to communicate with:

- Proxy
- Account
- Container
- Object

Run a proxy process by itself to create a proxy node that gives a more secure kind of access to the cluster. Installing the other three process types on a server creates a storage node. Nodes can be organized into zones and regions that are interconnected transparently. Other internal processes are also running so as to manage consistency across all nodes in the cluster regardless of how widely they are dispersed in a distributed cluster configuration.

Interact with a Swift OpenStack cluster via the curl command-line tool or with libCurl from your C language applications. These are the basic Swift HTTP verbs:

- GET—downloads objects, lists the contents of containers or accounts
- PUT—uploads objects, creates containers, overwrites metadata headers
- POST—creates containers if they do not exist, updates metadata (accounts or containers), overwrites metadata (objects)
- DELETE—deletes objects and containers that are empty
- HEAD—retrieves header information for the account, container, or object

Read more about the Swift OpenStack framework and its associated projects that provide bindings to your favorite programming languages at the URLs that follow. The bindings encapsulate calls to the `curl` tool so as to access them more conveniently from your own applications:

```
http://www.openstack.org/
https://swiftstack.com/openstack-swift/
http://docs.openstack.org/developer/swift/associated_projects.html
https://wiki.openstack.org/wiki/SDKs
```

■ **Note**   The Swift OpenStack framework has no relationship to the Swift programming language that Apple provides for creating applications for the App Store ecosystem. Now that Apple's Swift programming language is published as an open-source project, you may accidentally discover that project when you are searching for OpenStack.

Configuring Your Ethernet Connection

The ARTIK developer reference board has an RJ45 Ethernet connector for IP networking support. Although the serial interface is useful, bringing up an IP network connection to use the Secure Telnet protocol to make the ARTIK available from anywhere on your network.

The Internet Protocol version 4 has been the basis for the Internet revolution since it was developed in the late 1970s. All the expectations for the number of nodes that can be mapped with this protocol have been exceeded, and it is being replaced with version 6 to increase capacity.

Log in to your ARTIK module via the serial connection to configure your Ethernet IP connectivity.

■ **Note**   As of the very early Beta release of the embedded operating system firmware, Ethernet connectivity is not yet supported on the ARTIK 5 module. If you have a Beta or earlier version of the ARTIK 5, you can still connect using Wi-Fi. Later Beta firmware added this functionality. It is supported on the shipping Commercial Beta units.

How It Works

The IP protocols that the Internet depends on are maintained and standardized by the Internet Engineering Task Force (IETF). They publish numbered documents calls RFCs. The RFC documents are the definitive reference for matters concerning Internet standardization. Higher-level capabilities such as web standards are managed by organizations such as the World Wide Web Consortium (W3C). These documents show you how your application needs to be built to interact appropriately with the rest of the world. Here are some useful places to look for Internet-related standards documents:

```
https://www.ietf.org/
https://www.ietf.org/rfc.html
https://en.wikipedia.org/wiki/Request_for_Comments
http://www.w3.org/
```

IPv4 Addressing Notation

The IPv4 protocol describes each unique address on the Internet with a 32-bit value. By convention this is broken down into a dotted quad format where each group of 8 bits is described as a decimal value separated by dots. Typical IPv4 addresses look like this:

```
172.16.254.1
192.168.1.32
```

Figure 9-2 shows how the IPv4 notation maps to a binary representation of the IP address:

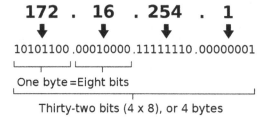

Figure 9-2. IPv4 addressing

A 32-bit value has 4.3 billion unique combinations. A few are lost to overheads that are needed for network management. Find out about those on the Wikipedia page for IPv4. Careful design of the network architecture allows separate sub-networks to be connected together with a router. That expands the range of addressable endpoint nodes, but it is a more complex solution than just increasing the size of the addressing space. Find out more about IPv4 here:

```
https://en.wikipedia.org/wiki/IPv4
https://tools.ietf.org/html/rfc791
```

You should be conversant enough with your network and the way it works to interact with other ARTIK modules or remote systems properly. You cannot simply make up addresses and randomly assign them. Every device on a network must have a unique address. Duplicate addresses cause an address collision. Network nodes with the same address are unreachable at best and may render your network inoperative at worst.

IPv4 uses a sub-net mask to map the nodes on your local network to the wider world. The router keeps track of this mapping. Net masks are defined in classes, and unless you are a very big organization, you will likely have a class C network. Your net mask will probably be 255.255.255.0. This allows 256 separate nodes on your local network. A few of these addresses are reserved, so you should plan on allocating no more than 250. Other workstations and devices such as printers and file servers in your lab will use some addresses on your network.

Keeping track of IP address allocations is very important. By default, your ARTIK will acquire a network address using Dynamic Host Configuration Protocol (DHCP). This depends on the router having a pool of addresses that it can vend to requesting nodes when they start up. When that pool of addresses runs out, any subsequent DHCP configurable nodes will not be able to get on the net, as an address cannot be granted to them until one is freed up by another node's relinquishing of it. The DHCP service can do more than just define an IP address; there is more information about how it works here:

```
https://en.wikipedia.org/wiki/Dynamic_Host_Configuration_Protocol
```

Your router will define a prefix for the sub-net. Typically, this might be 192.168.1.*** and you then add your selected node number as the last number in the quad to define a specific IP address. Some addresses are reserved. Table 9-2 summarizes a few important addresses:

Table 9-2. *Reserved IP Addresses on Your Sub-net*

IP Address	Reserved for
255.255.255.0	Not strictly an IP address, this is the net mask for a class C IP address.
192.168.0.0	Base address for the local area network
192.168.1.1	Reserved as the IP address for the router
192.168.1.255	Broadcast a message to all nodes on the sub-net.
127.0.0.0	Local host. Used for processes to communicate with network ports on the machine they are running on.

Find out more about reserved addresses here:

```
https://en.wikipedia.org/wiki/Reserved_IP_addresses
```

IPv6 Addressing Notation

Internet Protocol version 6 became necessary in order to solve the problem of the IPv4 addresses running out. There are very few free IPv4 addresses available now. IPv6 provides a massive increase in the number of addressable endpoints mapped onto the Internet. IPv6 also simplifies some of the complexities of IPv4 addressing, routing, and packet delivery as fragments.

The address space is extended to 128 bits instead of the earlier 32. This allows for many billions of addresses. Consequently, a new notation scheme is used to describe the 3.4×10^{38} possible endpoints. Typical IPv6 addresses look like this:

```
2001:0db8:0000:0000:0000:ff00:0042:8329
```

Shorten IPv6 address descriptions by applying simple rules. Omit leading zeros from any of the colon-separated groups. Then replace runs of zeros with a double colon, although you can only do this once. The preceding example can be shortened to this value with no loss of addressing granularity with the zero rule:

```
2001:db8:0:0:0:ff00:42:8329
```

And by applying the colon rule it can be shortened to this:

```
2001:db8::ff00:42:8329
```

Figure 9-3 shows how the IPv6 address notation maps to the binary representation:

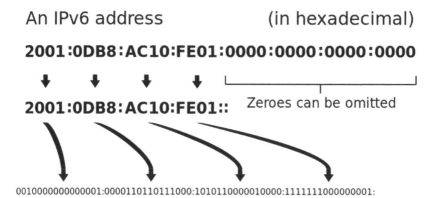

Figure 9-3. IP v6 addressing

Internet Protocol version 6 is gradually taking over from IPv4, but it is not yet a direct replacement. They cannot coexist together on the same wire, but there are mechanisms for tunneling IPv4 protocol on IPv6 networks and vice versa.

IPv6 is also in use on the smart grid where smart meters for measurement of utility supplies and other nodes are managed as a micro-mesh network before sending the data back to the billing system using the IPv6 backbone. Some of these networks run over IEEE 802.15.4 wireless networks for part of their journey. Find out more about IPv6 here:

```
https://en.wikipedia.org/wiki/IPv6
https://en.wikipedia.org/wiki/IPv6_address
https://tools.ietf.org/html/rfc2460
https://en.wikipedia.org/wiki/6to4
```

Port Numbers

At each IP address, there are 65536 separate ports with which to open a connection. Separate the port number from the IP address with a colon character (:) in IPv4. With IPv6, the same delimiter is used, but because the IPv6 address itself uses colons, you should encapsulate the IPv6 address in square brackets ([...])and then append the colon and port number.

Port 80 is reserved for connecting a web server. The full IPv4 address for such a web server on your local sub-net is 192.168.1.54:80 although web servers can often be moved to an alternative port. In that case, the address might be 192.168.1.54:8080 instead. The equivalent IPv6 address would be described with this notation:

```
[fe80::21e:6ff:fe61:7a39]:8080
```

Processes that are already running on your ARTIK can listen for incoming messages on particular port numbers and respond to the requests. Alternatively, you can also register processes as network services. This is how Telnet and FTP work. The service manager listens for new connections on their behalf. A new process is then started up when a connection is initiated on its service port number. The incoming messages arriving via that connection are directed to the process that is bound to the port. Any output it generates is transmitted back to the requesting client. The process exits when it is done. The major benefit here is that you do not waste CPU resources on running processes that are not needed and resources are freedup when the work is completed. Find out more about port numbers here:

```
https://en.wikipedia.org/wiki/Port_(computer_networking)
https://en.wikipedia.org/wiki/List_of_TCP_and_UDP_port_numbers
```

Creating UNIX services is an interesting technique because your ARTIK could have listeners set up without consuming compute resources until they are needed. This would help conserve the battery, because unnecessary processes will only run when they are needed. Ports 0 to 1023 are reserved for well-known services and are secured against intrusion. Ports 1024 to 49151 are reserved for vendor applications and managed via a registry. Use these port numbers if you know that the registered application is not installed and will not be using them, but really it is better to avoid them. Ports 49152 to 65535 are available for you to use for your own processes on a first come, first served basis. These are called ephemeral or dynamic ports. You should design your software without hard coding the specific port number because there is no guarantee you will always have the same one allocated.

Using ports intelligently on multiple ARTIK modules and communicating between them via raw BSD socket protocols would be a neat way to build an ARTIK mesh- or grid-based architecture. Knowing what ports are available in other network nodes that are reachable from your ARTIK lets you leverage all kind of processes and resources that can save you from re-inventing lots of wheels.

The Switchover

Switching to IPv6 offers many benefits and extends the potential lifetime of your product, and it will be necessary as the IPv4 infrastructure is gradually deprecated. Even though your ARTIK can use IPv6 when you deploy it, your development system might live on an IPv4 sub-net connected to an IPv6 network via a router for some time to come.

IP Address Configuration in Your ARTIK

The IP address of the ARTIK module is set automatically via DHCP. This will work fine, provided your router is already configured to vend IP addresses for DHCP clients to lease. When you are developing software, it helps to eliminate variability in your setup. To make things more predictable, a statically defined address known to the hosting development workstation is a good idea. This removes the potential uncertainty that DHCP-vended addresses have.

Inspecting the IP Addresses

Inspect the current network configuration with the ifconfig command. Just type it without any additional options at the command-line prompt after you have logged in:

```
ifconfig
```

You should see a network configuration listed on the screen similar to the one shown in Listing 9-1.

Listing 9-1. IP Network Configuration Report

```
eth0: flags=4163<UP,BROADCAST,RUNNING,MULTICAST>  mtu 1500
        inet 192.168.1.200 netmask 255.255.255.0 broadcast 192.168.1.255
        inet6 fe80::21e:6ff:fe61:7a39  prefixlen 64  scopeid 0x20<link>
        ether 00:1e:06:61:7a:39  txqueuelen 1000  (Ethernet)
        RX packets 5  bytes 689 (689.0 B)
        RX errors 0  dropped 0  overruns 0  frame 0
        TX packets 37  bytes 6537 (6.3 KiB)
        TX errors 0  dropped 0 overruns 0  carrier 0  collisions 0
```

```
lo: flags=73<UP,LOOPBACK,RUNNING>  mtu 65536
        inet 127.0.0.1  netmask 255.0.0.0
        inet6 ::1  prefixlen 128  scopeid 0x10<host>
        loop  txqueuelen 0  (Local Loopback)
        RX packets 320  bytes 27840 (27.1 KiB)
        RX errors 0  dropped 0  overruns 0  frame 0
        TX packets 320  bytes 27840 (27.1 KiB)
        TX errors 0  dropped 0 overruns 0  carrier 0  collisions 0

p2p0: flags=4163<UP,BROADCAST,RUNNING,MULTICAST>  mtu 1500
        inet6 fe80::290:4cff:fe33:2211  prefixlen 64  scopeid 0x20<link>
        ether 00:90:4c:33:22:11  txqueuelen 1000  (Ethernet)
        RX packets 0  bytes 0 (0.0 B)
        RX errors 0  dropped 0  overruns 0  frame 0
        TX packets 0  bytes 0 (0.0 B)
        TX errors 0  dropped 0 overruns 0  carrier 0  collisions 0

wlan0: flags=4099<UP,BROADCAST,MULTICAST>  mtu 1500
        inet6 fe80::f609:d8ff:fe55:347b  prefixlen 64  scopeid 0x20<link>
        ether f4:09:d8:55:34:7b  txqueuelen 1000  (Ethernet)
        RX packets 0  bytes 0 (0.0 B)
        RX errors 0  dropped 1  overruns 0  frame 0
        TX packets 6  bytes 468 (468.0 B)
        TX errors 0  dropped 0 overruns 0  carrier 0  collisions 0
```

Note the IP address from your listing and keep that record updated if you statically define the IP address. You will need this value later if you plan to use the Temboo library.

Setting a Temporary IP Address on the Ethernet Interface

The Ethernet IP interface brought out to the RJ45 connector on the developer reference board is called eth0:.

If you want to change the IP address temporarily, use the ifconfig command. Changing the IP address temporarily allows access to different networks in the same location without changing the default settings of the board. Rebooting the ARTIK will undo this change, and it will revert to the default IP address next time it is booted up. Use this command to change the IP address:

```
ifconfig eth0 192.168.1.210
```

Use the ifconfig command again with no options to show that the interface now has a new IP address.

Setting a Default Persistent Static IP Address

Change the IP address to a static (unchanging) value that is effective even after rebooting the ARTIK module by editing the configuration file for that interface. Do that inside the ARTIK with the vi text editor. This defines the IP address of your ARTIK by default.

123

Be careful to use a new, unused, and unique IP address. Be careful not to collide with IP values that are reserved for the DHCP pool of addresses. That would prevent DHCP devices from connecting. If you are not already managing your collection of IP addresses on the sub-net, take a few minutes to create an Excel spreadsheet or just a text file to note all the IP addresses you have available and annotate the ones that are allocated to particular nodes. Getting into good habits with your documentation from the start will save you a lot of trouble later on. Follow these steps to configure the static IP address:

1. Open the etho: configuration script with this command:

    ```
    vi /etc/sysconfig/network-scripts/ifcfg-eth0
    ```

2. Change the BOOTPROTO parameter setting from dhcp to static.

3. Add the IPADDR variable and set the value to the IP address you want to use.

4. Add the NETMASK variable and set the value to the class of net mask that is appropriate for your sub-net. Most likely this is 255.255.255.0 for a class-C sub-net.

5. Add the BROADCAST variable and set the value to the IP address for your sub-net.

6. Add the NETWORK variable and set the value to the base IP address for your sub-net.

7. Add the GATEWAY variable and set the value to the IP address of the router that manages your sub-net.

8. The finished configuration should look something like this (with your network IP values substituted in place of the ones shown here):

    ```
    DEVICE="eth0"
    TYPE="Ethernet"
    ONBOOT="yes"
    BOOTPROTO="static"
    USERCTL="no"
    IPADDR=192.168.1.210
    NETMASK=255.255.255.0
    BROADCAST=192.168.1.255
    NETWORK=192.168.1.0
    GATEWAY=192.168.1.1
    ```

9. Type these keystrokes to exit from vi and save the changes to disk:

    ```
    [Escape] [:] [w] [q] [Return]
    ```

Configuring Your ARTIK for IPv6 Operation

If you want to activate IPv6 networking, follow these steps to turn it on and add the addresses to the Ethernet configuration. Remember that this cannot co-exist on a network that is running IPv4 protocols:

1. Open the networking configuration file with the vi editor:

    ```
    vi /etc/sysconfig/network
    ```

2. Find this line in the configuration file:

    ```
    NETWORKING_IPV6=no
    ```

3. Modify it to turn on the IPv6 protocol support:

    ```
    NETWORKING_IPV6=yes
    ```

4. Type these keystrokes to exit from vi and save the changes to disk:

    ```
    [Escape] [:] [w] [q] [Return]
    ```

5. Now open the eth0: configuration script with this command:

    ```
    vi /etc/sysconfig/network-scripts/ifcfg-eth0
    ```

6. Add the IPV6INIT variable and set the value to yes.

7. Add the IPV6ADDR variable and set the value to the colon-delimited IPv6 address you want to use.

8. Add the IPV6_DEFAULTGW variable and set the value to the IPv6 address for your router/gateway.

9. Type these keystrokes to exit from vi and save the changes to disk:

    ```
    [Escape] [:] [w] [q] [Return]
    ```

10. Restart the networking services in your ARTIK with this command to use the new configuration:

    ```
    service network restart
    ```

11. You should see this message while the network services restart:

    ```
    Restarting network (via systemctl):  [  OK  ]
    ```

12. Check it is all working with the IPv6 version of the ping command:

    ```
    ping6 ipv6.google.com
    ```

DNS Configurations

The DNS servers convert human-readable domain names to IP addresses. This process is called *resolving*. The opposite of resolving is performing a lookup to see what DNS entries correspond to an IP address. Look in the Utilities folder on your Macintosh and find the Network Utility app. This is useful for debugging this sort of thing. Use command-line tools on Linux. Windows users will have similar GUI network-management tools available. If they are not already part of your system, they should be available as downloads. Alternatively use the command-line tools from the Cygwin console. Use IPv4 or IPv6 addresses for the name servers.

By default, Linux will track a maximum of three DNS servers. The value is defined in the /usr/include/resolv.h file, but to alter it you would need to recompile at least some parts of the operating system. Having three nameservers should be sufficient for most scenarios.

Introducing systemd

Traditionally the services and processes have been managed by the inetd control daemon. This was the first process to start in a UNIX operating system and it managed the startup of all subsequent processes and services. In Fedora 22, this is all swept away and replaced by systemd, which is still in a state of evolution and not yet complete. This change has impacted the way that network services such as DNS are configured and has added a degree of complexity. Instead of simply editing a configuration file and restarting a process, the systemctl command needs to be used to communicate your changes to systemd so it can manage the configurations for you. Some systems administrators have mixed views on whether this is a good approach. It has now become the de facto standard. Find out more about systemd here:

```
https://fedoraproject.org/wiki/Systemd
https://en.wikipedia.org/wiki/Systemd
https://wiki.archlinux.org/index.php/systemd
https://www.freedesktop.org/software/systemd/man/systemd.html
https://www.freedesktop.org/software/systemd/man/resolved.conf.html
http://www.dynacont.net/documentation/linux/Useful_SystemD_commands/
```

The Impact of systemd on DNS Configuration

Traditionally, the DNS configuration is described in the /etc/resolv.conf file. In Fedora 22 on the ARTIK modules, this is now a symbolic link to /run/systemd/resolve/resolv.conf, where it is managed by the system resolve daemon. You should not edit that file directly, but rather should use the systemctl command to manage changes that you make to an alternative file (/etc/systemd/resolved.conf) if you want to benefit from the dynamic configuration mechanisms. Read about the parameters you can define in that configuration file here:

```
https://www.freedesktop.org/software/systemd/man/resolved.conf.html
```

Statically Configuring Your DNS Servers

The DNS resolve configuration file maintained by `systemctl` contains comments that suggest you can return to a manually edited static configuration. You need to make your own judgment call about whether that is a good idea. Guidance for creating a static DNS configuration is taken from here:

```
http://www.linuxfromscratch.org/lfs/view/systemd/chapter07/network.html
https://wiki.archlinux.org/index.php/resolv.conf
```

Follow these instructions to revert to a static configuration and add your DNS servers to the /etc/resolv.conf file:

1. Replace the symbolic link with a real file using these commands:

    ```
    mv /etc/resolv.conf /etc/resolv.conf_orig
    echo "" > /etc/resolv.conf
    ```

2. Open the resolver configuration file for editing with the vi editor:

    ```
    vi /etc/resolv.conf
    ```

3. Add your domain name as the first line:

    ```
    domain {your_domain_name}
    ```

4. Add your primary nameserver as the next line. Your Internet service provider most likely provides this:

    ```
    nameserver {IP_address_of_your_primary_nameserver}
    ```

5. Add your secondary (backup) nameserver:

    ```
    nameserver {IP_address_of_your_secondary_nameserver}
    ```

6. Because by default Linux only tracks three nameservers, you can only optionally add one more. Any additional nameservers after that might be ignored.

7. When you have added all the nameservers you want, type these keystrokes to exit from vi and save the changes to disk:

    ```
    [Escape] [:] [w] [q] [Return]
    ```

8. My Alpha test system needed to be rebooted for these changes to take effect. After rebooting and logging in again, this command worked fine. The Commercial Beta systems should work without a reboot:

    ```
    ping gnu.org
    ```

9. The following results were displayed:

```
PING gnu.org (208.118.235.148) 56(84) bytes of data.
64 bytes from wildebeest.gnu.org (208.118.235.148): icmp_seq=1 ttl=49 time=95.1 ms
64 bytes from wildebeest.gnu.org (208.118.235.148): icmp_seq=2 ttl=49 time=94.3 ms
64 bytes from wildebeest.gnu.org (208.118.235.148): icmp_seq=3 ttl=49 time=93.8 ms
64 bytes from wildebeest.gnu.org (208.118.235.148): icmp_seq=4 ttl=49 time=93.0 ms
```

You can optionally add the IP address of your router as an extra nameserver if it caches DNS lookups. It saves time if a nearby device can resolve the lookup. The router is the nearest device and the best place to look first. Google provides nameservers at these addresses. You can use these in place of others as your primary and secondary nameservers. There are privacy implications here, however:

- 8.8.8.8

- 8.8.8.4

This blog describes how to set up the systemd mechanisms and may be useful if you want to revert back to systemd after experimenting with static DNS configurations:

```
http://lukeluo.blogspot.co.uk/2015/04/the-best-way-to-configure-network.html
```

Getting State of Your IP Links

Use the ip network utility to list the currently configured interfaces:

```
ip link
```

Typical configuration report from the ip link command on an ARTIK 5 is shown in Listing 9-2:

Listing 9-2. IP Link Report

```
1: lo: <LOOPBACK,UP,LOWER_UP>
    mtu 65536
    qdisc noqueue
    state UNKNOWN
    mode DEFAULT
    group default
    link/loopback 00:00:00:00:00:00
    brd 00:00:00:00:00:00

2: sit0: <NOARP>
    mtu 1480
    qdisc noop
    state DOWN
    mode DEFAULT
    group default
    link/sit 0.0.0.0
    brd 0.0.0.0
```

```
3: ip6tnl0: <NOARP>
    mtu 1452
    qdisc noop
    state DOWN
    mode DEFAULT
    group default
    link/tunnel6 ::
    brd ::

4: p2p0: <BROADCAST,MULTICAST,UP,LOWER_UP>
    mtu 1500
    qdisc pfifo_fast
    state UNKNOWN
    mode DEFAULT
    group default
    qlen 1000
    link/ether 00:90:4c:33:22:11
    brd ff:ff:ff:ff:ff:ff

5: wlan0: <NO-CARRIER,BROADCAST,MULTICAST,UP,LOWER_UP>
    mtu 1500
    qdisc pfifo_fast
    state DORMANT
    mode DORMANT
    group default
    qlen 1000
    link/ether f4:09:d8:55:34:7b
    brd ff:ff:ff:ff:ff:ff
```

The IP links use interfaces with these names. The devices listed in your ARTIK module may be different than the list in Table 9-3 depending on how you configure your network settings.

Table 9-3. *Network Device Names*

Interface	Description
eth0:	The Ethernet cable connected to the RJ45 socket on the developer reference board
lo:	Loopback connections to this host
p2p0:	Peer-to-peer networking. Used by Virtualbox and Apple AirDrop, among other things.
wlan0:	Wireless local area network connection via Wi-Fi. Depending on your hardware, you may not be able to use p2p0: and wlan0: at the same time.
sit0:	This is for carrying IPv6 traffic on an IPv4 network.
ip6tnl0:	This is for carrying IPv4 traffic on an IPv6 network.

Find out more about the ip networking tool here:

```
http://linux-ip.net/html/tools-ip-link.html
```

Configure the Wi-Fi Networking

Your ARTIK 5 and 10 modules support Wi-Fi networking communications. They implement communications with the IEEE 802.11 protocol using the b, g, & n variants. The newer ac and ah variants are not yet supported but may be added later via an operating system upgrade.

If you want to know more about wireless communications, Kevin Sharp has posted a great article on the ARTIK blog:

```
https://www.artik.io/blog/2015/iot-101-connectivity
```

Setting Up Wi-Fi Communications

These instructions will show you how to bring up the Wi-Fi connectivity and register on your local Wi-Fi network. Log in to your ARTIK first, because the Wi-Fi configuration happens inside the ARTIK module. If an Ethernet connection is not yet configured, use the serial connection to open a command-line session with your ARTIK. After this is configured and working you will be able to connect using IP protocols and log in remotely with a wireless connection instead of using an Ethernet or serial wired connection. Follow these steps to set up your Wi-Fi communications:

1. Attach an antenna to the CPU WIFI ANT SMA antenna connector.

2. Open a terminal window and log in to your ARTIK.

3. Scan for wireless access points with this command:

   ```
   wpa_cli scan_results
   ```

4. If you have configured your wlan0 interface, you should see a list of Wi-Fi access points like this:

   ```
   bssid / frequency / signal level / flags / ssid
   00:1b:19:27:c4:7a      2412     -90     [WPA2-PSK-CCMP][WPS]
                                           [ESS]        BTHub5-K8H2
   78:ca:19:22:b5:55      2412     -91     [WPA2-PSK-CCMP][ESS]
   b8:c7:1d:18:8a:47      2412     -76     [WPA2-PSK-CCMP][ESS]
   ```

5. If the interface is not configured, the list will be empty. However, this could indicate your antenna is attached to the wrong SMA connector.

6. The interface name might be displayed as p2p-dev-wlan0 on some systems.

7. If you plan to edit your wpa_supplicant.conf file, make a safe copy with this command (the example should be typed on one line–it is split for readability):

```
cp /etc/wpa_supplicant/wpa_supplicant.conf ↵
    /etc/wpa_supplicant/wpa_supplicant.conf_backup
```

8. Decide the parameters you are going to need based on what you know about your own Wi-Fi network settings. You will need the network name and its password.

9. Use the wpa_passphrase command like this to write your router SSID and password into wpa_supplicant.conf (the example should be typed on one line–it is split for readability):

```
wpa_passphrase {your_wi_fi_network_SSID_name} ↵
    {your_wi_fi_network_password} >> ↵
    /etc/wpa_supplicant/wpa_supplicant.conf
```

10. Here is an example:

```
wpa_passphrase MyAP abcd1234 >> ↵
    /etc/wpa_supplicant/wpa_supplicant.conf
```

11. This will append these lines to the configuration file:

```
network={
        ssid=" MyAP"
        #psk=" abcd1234"
        psk=35512e2a988f53d57a3abf2302cab785f731e94c3895e ↵
            88a8eaa56bfe4f74979
}
```

12. Display the modified configuration file with this command:

```
cat /etc/wpa_supplicant/wpa_supplicant.conf
```

13. You should see something like this:

```
ctrl_interface=/var/run/wpa_supplicant
ctrl_interface_group=wheel
network={
        ssid="MyAP"
        #psk="abcd1234"
        psk=35512e2a988f53d57a3abf2302cab785f731e94c3895e ↵
            88a8eaa56bfe4f74979
}
```

14. Restart the wpa_supplicant service with this command to acquire your new configuration:

    ```
    systemctl restart wpa_supplicant
    ```

15. Configure a DHCP-vended IP address with the dhclient command. This may take a while, as your Wi-Fi router needs to respond. If it does not, then the command will time out. This will only work if your Wi-Fi router is compatible:

    ```
    dhclient wlan0
    ```

16. Now check that your wlan0 network has an IP address granted to it. Use this command:

    ```
    ifconfig wlan0
    ```

17. You should see something like this:

    ```
    wlan0: flags=4099<UP,BROADCAST,MULTICAST>  mtu 1500
            inet6 fe80::f609:d8ff:fe55:347b  prefixlen 64
    #x00A0; scopeid 0x20<link>
            ether f4:09:d8:55:34:7b
    txqueuelen 1000  (Ethernet)

    RX packets 0  bytes 0 (0.0 B)
            RX errors 0  dropped 2  overruns 0  frame 0
            TX packets 15  bytes 2778 (2.7 KiB)
            TX errors 0  dropped 0 overruns 0  carrier 0  collisions 0
    ```

18. Run this command to see the new status of your Wi-Fi connections:

    ```
    wpa_cli scan_results
    ```

19. Here is the result:

    ```
    Selected interface 'wlan0'
    bssid / frequency / signal level / flags / ssid
    00:1b:19:27:c4:7a    2412  -75   [WPA2-PSK-CCMP][ESS]
    78:ca:19:22:b5:55    2412  -92   [WPA2-PSK-CCMP][ESS]
    b8:c7:1d:18:8a:47    2412  -90   [WPA-EAP-CCMP+TKIP]
    [WPA2-EAP-CCMP+TKIP-preauth][ESS]    BTWifi-X
    ```

20. Verify the network connectivity with a ping command:

    ```
    ping gnu.org
    ```

Setting up the networking configuration is challenging because there are so many things that are different from one installation to another. Wireless networking is even more difficult if you follow good practice and secure your Wi-Fi router so it runs in stealth mode. This may stop your ARTIK from being able to connect to it because the SSID is not visible when scanning for available networks.

Another Way to Configure Your Wi-Fi

The nmcli command is a convenient way to interact with the Wi-Fi and other networking capabilities of your ARTIK. It is a much simpler way to configure your wireless connections. Find out more about nmcli here:

```
https://wiki.archlinux.org/index.php/NetworkManager
http://www.linux-commands-examples.com/nmcli
```

Martin Kronberg documents a different way to set up your ARTIK Wi-Fi using the nmcli command in his excellent blog article. The instructions are repeated here with a few additional illustrations and comments to support the example:

```
https://www.hackster.io/martinkronberg/artik10-sami-eab8f7
```

1. Attach an antenna to the **CPU WIFI ANT** SMA antenna connector (labelled J23 on the Commercial Beta developer boards).

2. Open a terminal window and log in to your ARTIK.

3. Get a list of Wi-Fi networks with this command:

    nmcli dev wifi list

4. This yields the results that look like the following. Note the entry with two dashes in the SSID column. This is an Apple Airport Express running in hidden network mode, which does not advertise its SSID. The other networks are from neighbors' dwellings nearby. Their networks are completely visible:

```
* SSID              MODE   CHAN  RATE       SIGNAL  BARS  SECURITY
  --                Infra  1     54 Mbit/s  44      ▬▬__  WPA2
  BTWifi-X          Infra  1     54 Mbit/s  14      ▬___  WPA1 WPA2 802.1X
  BTWifi-X          Infra  1     54 Mbit/s  12      ▬___  WPA1 WPA2 802.1X
  BTHub5-3N29       Infra  1     54 Mbit/s  14      ▬___  WPA2
  BTWifi-with-FON   Infra  1     54 Mbit/s  17      ▬___  --
  BTWifi-with-FON   Infra  1     54 Mbit/s  12      ▬___  --
  BTHub5-K9H6       Infra  1     54 Mbit/s  17      ▬___  WPA2
```

5. Add your Wi-Fi SSID, a static IP address, and the gateway IP (replace {your_ssid} with your own genuine SSID (Wi-Fi network name):

    ```
    nmcli con add con-name {your_ssid} ifname wlan0 type
    wifi ssid {your_ssid} \
    ip4 192.168.1.100/24 gw4 192.168.1.1
    ```

6. Set up the DNS. (Google provides the DNS in this example, but you can substitute your own):

    ```
    nmcli con mod {your_ssid} ipv4.dns "8.8.8.8 8.8.4.4"
    ```

7. Add the WPA password for your Wi-Fi network:

    ```
    nmcli con modify {your_ssid} wifi-sec.key-mgmt wpa-psk
    nmcli con modify {your_ssid} wifi-sec.psk {your_WPA_password}
    ```

8. Turn on the connection:

    ```
    nmcli con up {your_ssid}
    ```

9. If your Wi-Fi router is not compatible, you may see the following result. This will also happen if you are using an Apple Airport network configured into stealth (hidden network) mode so as to not advertise its SSID. The Wi-Fi service is visible, but it has no name. Use the Airport utility to turn off the hidden network setting, then reboot your Airport device and try again.

    ```
    Error: Connection activation failed: No suitable device
    found for this connection.
    ```

10. If it did work, you can now use your Wi-Fi connection with the ARTIK. You should see a message like this:

    ```
    Connection successfully activated (D-Bus active path:
    /org/freedesktop/NetworkManager/ActiveConnection/6)
    ```

11. Turn the Wi-Fi services off again with this command:

    ```
    nmcli r wifi off
    ```

■ **Note**   When you set up your Wi-Fi, you MUST enter an IP address that is on the same sub-net as your router/gateway. Also, it must not be in use by another device. Assume for example that the router is allocated with the IP address 192.168.1.1. All the devices on the network connected to that router must use an IP address of the form 192.168.1.XXX. The XXX corresponds to the zero bits in the class C netmask 255.255.255.0 that determines how the router converts addresses between each network it is integrating together.

Troubleshooting FAQ

There are many reasons why you might not get a Wi-Fi network going right away.
A simple mistake or a saturated network with no free capacity would prevent things from
working. In a very busy network, all of the DHCP addresses could be allocated already.
Let's review a few other possibilities.

No Suitable Device Found for This Connection

This might be because you are running an Apple Airport wireless network and you have it
set up for stealth mode. In stealth mode the SSID is not advertised, so the ARTIK cannot
identify the router from the scanned list. Arguably, this is a fault with the Broadcom driver
that manages Wi-Fi interfaces. Try turning off the hidden-network stealth mode while
you configure the ARTIK for Wi-Fi networking to see if that solves the problem. You may
need to run the network in this marginally less secure configuration when testing ARTIK
Wi-Fi operations.

No Network Configuration Set Up

If this configuration did not succeed, reboot your ARTIK and try the dhclient step again. If that
does not work, go back and check all of the steps again to see if you mistyped something.

"Failed to Connect" Message

When I scan for nearby detectable Wi-Fi networks, with the wpa_cli scan_results
command, I get this error message:

```
Failed to connect to non-global ctrl_ifname: (null) error: No such
file or directory
```

1. Try adding this line to the /etc/wpa_supplicant/
   wpa_supplicant.conf file to see if it corrects the problem:

   ```
   ctrl_interface=/var/run/wpa_supplicant
   ```

2. If you already have networks defined in your wpa_
   supplicant.conf, it should look something like this:

   ```
   ctrl_interface=/var/run/wpa_supplicant
   ctrl_interface_group=wheel

   network={
           ssid="MyAP"
           #psk="abcd1234"
           psk=35512e2a988f53d57a3abf230
   2cab785f731e99b58ea288a8eaa56bfe4f74979
   }
   ```

3. Restart the `wpa_supplicant` service with this command:

   ```
   systemctl restart wpa_supplicant
   ```

4. The `wpa_cli scan_result` command should work without showing the error now and you should see something like this:

```
Selected interface 'wlan0'
bssid / frequency / signal level / flags / ssid
b8:c7:5d:08:8a:97      2412    -92     [WPA2-PSK-CCMP][ESS]=
```

Advanced Wi-Fi Configuration

A sample configuration file is located in your ARTIK file system and contains examples of many other configurable parameters:

```
/usr/share/doc/wpa_supplicant/wpa_supplicant.conf
```

Edit this file to add the parameters you need for your live configuration. Only do this if you understand the technicalities of Wi-Fi networks. Make notes as you configure things and keep copies of the original file in case you need to undo your changes.

Manually edit your `wpa_supplicant.conf` file to include your advanced Wi-Fi router settings with this vi editor command to open it for updating:

```
vi /etc/wpa_supplicant/wpa_supplicant.conf
```

Automatically Reconnect Your Wi-Fi after Each Reboot

It is inconvenient to have to go through this reconfiguration every time you reboot your ARTIK. Follow these steps to edit your system initialization script and make the changes permanent:

1. Go to the `/etc/rc.d` directory with this command:

   ```
   cd /etc/rc.d
   ```

2. If there is an `rc.local` file, inspect it with this command:

   ```
   cat ./rc.local
   ```

3. You should see something like this:

```
#!/bin/sh
#
# This script will be executed *after* all the other init scripts.
# Put your own initialization stuff in here if you don't
# want to do the full Sys V style init stuff.
touch /var/lock/subsys/local
setterm -powersave off -blank 0
setterm -blank 0 >> /etc/issue
mkdir -p /var/run/swift
echo "Enable wifi"
depmod
modprobe dhd dhd_poll=1 dhd_intr=0 iface_name=wlan0
firmware_path=/etc/wifi/fw.bin nvram_path=/etc/wifi/nvram.txt
```

4. If there is not an rc.local file there, then we need to create one and set its file protections so it can be executed as the ARTIK starts up.

5. Open the rc.local file with this vi editor command:

```
vi ./rc.local
```

6. Add this line first. It will tell the startup code which shell to use to run the script:

```
#!/bin/sh
```

7. Add this line to the end of the Wi-Fi configuration instructions:

```
dhclient wlan0
```

8. Alternatively, this line may be more appropriate if you used nmcli to configure your Wi-Fi. Add it instead of the dhclient command:

```
nmcli con up {your_ssid}
```

9. Type these keystrokes to exit from vi and save the changes to disk:

```
[Escape] [:] [w] [q] [Return]
```

10. Now set the file permission flags to make the rc.local file executable if you needed to create a new file from scratch. Type this command:

```
chmod +x ./rc.local
```

11. Reboot your ARTIK module to test that it works.

Connecting with Telnet via SSH

You can log in to your ARTIK module across the network using the SSH protocol. Fedora 22 behaves differently to Fedora 20 and might require some configuration changes for this to work. The format for a connection is:

```
ssh {account_name}@{network_address}
```

Follow these steps from a terminal session on your developer workstation. You will need to know the IP address of your ARTIK, which may change if it is defined by DHCP:

1. Open a terminal window.

2. In our example, we know the IP address of the ARTIK is 192.168.1.202. Type this command:

    ```
    ssh root@192.168.1.202
    ```

3. You should see this message:

```
The authenticity of host '192.168.1.202 (192.168.1.202)' can't be established.
RSA key fingerprint is 0b:b5:38:b8:7d:20:69:a0:0b:a2:15:30:61:d7:cf:70.
Are you sure you want to continue connecting (yes/no)?
```

4. Type yes and press the [Return] key.

5. This confirms that you trust the remote node, and your security software (Mac OS in this example) presents this message:

    ```
    Warning: Permanently added '192.168.1.202' (RSA) to the list of
    known hosts.
    ```

6. You are then prompted to enter the password for the account you requested:

    ```
    root@192.168.1.202's password:
    ```

7. Enter the password, and you are logged in with a message telling you when the account was last used:

    ```
    Last login: Thu Mar  3 10:04:53 2016
    [root@dhcppc2 ~]#
    ```

    If your connection is rejected, then refer to the Fedora 22 system administrators guide. Chapter 7 describes how SSH works in detail.

    ```
    https://docs.fedoraproject.org/en-US/Fedora/22/html/
    System_Administrators_Guide/ch-OpenSSH.html
    ```

Configuring Your Bluetooth Wireless Interface

Your ARTIK modules all support Bluetooth communications. They implement a version called Bluetooth Low Energy (BLE) that consumes less power and helps make your battery last longer in a mobile situation. This configuration process is managed from the command line inside your ARTIK module. Log on there to start the configuration.

If you want to know more about wireless communications, Kevin Sharp has posted a great article on the ARTIK blog:

https://www.artik.io/blog/2015/iot-101-connectivity

Setting Up Bluetooth for an ARTIK 5 or 10

Here are the instructions for enabling Bluetooth on your ARTIK module and pairing it with another device for it to communicate with. You need download and install the Bluetooth software using a script that is already on your ARTIK module. Follow these steps to find the correct script and run it:

1. Attach an antenna to the Bluetooth SMA antenna connector (labelled J23 on the Commercial Beta developer boards).

2. Open a terminal window and log in to your ARTIK.

3. Change your working directory to the Bluetooth configuration directory:

   cd /etc/bluetooth

4. Now run a built-in script to download the firmware into the Broadcom Bluetooth hardware.

   ./fwdown.sh

5. Now enable the hci0 network interface:

   hciconfig hci0 up

6. Your Bluetooth network should now be running. Now it can pair with another device. Initiate the pairing from the ARTIK by running the Bluetooth control utility:

   bluetoothctl

7. Your command-line prompt should change to '[bluetooth]'. This indicates the utility is running. You should also see a message describing your Bluetooth controller. If this message does not appear, it is because the fwdown.sh script did not work or you executed the wrong one.

   [NEW] Controller F8:04:2E:EC:D8:A1 ARTIK5 [default]

8. Turn on the Bluetooth agent with this command:

    ```
    agent on
    ```

9. You should see this message:

    ```
    Agent registered
    ```

10. Now request access to the default agent with this command:

    ```
    default-agent
    ```

11. You should see this message on the screen:Default agent request successful

12. Start the Bluetooth scanner to see if there are any discoverable devices. To test this, turn on Bluetooth in a mobile phone and make it discoverable:

    ```
    scan on
    ```

13. The scanner tells you it has started looking for discoverable Bluetooth devices. It lists any devices that it finds. The line that follows that is tagged with the prefix string [CHG] describes this ARTIK. Discovered devices are tagged with the prefix string [NEW]. Note the device address, because the ARTIK will need that to pair with it:

    ```
    Discovery started
    [CHG] Controller 43:50:C0:00:00:00 Discovering: yes
    [NEW] Device B8:09:8A:6D:4A:74 XXXXXXX
    ```

14. Initiate the pairing request:

    ```
    pair B8:09:8A:6D:4A:74
    ```

15. The utility reports the progress as it connects to your other Bluetooth device:

    ```
    Attempting to pair with B8:09:8A:6D:4A:74
    [CHG] Device B8:09:8A:6D:4A:74 Connected: yes
    ```

16.   On the other device, you should see a message telling you a
       remote Bluetooth device is attempting to pair. Accept that
       pairing attempt there. When you do, the other device sends
       back a unique key value that needs to be confirmed by the
       agent in the ARTIK. Confirm the key by typing yes:

```
Request confirmation
[agent] Confirm passkey 622643 (yes/no): yes
```

17.   Connection-specific debugging messages are displayed.
       These tell you about the state of the connection:

```
[CHG] Device B8:09:8A:6D:4A:74 Modalias: bluetooth:v004Cp6D03d0830
[CHG] Device B8:09:8A:6D:4A:74 UUIDs:
00000000-deca-fade-deca-deafdecacafe
00001000-0000-1000-8000-00805f9b34fb
0000110a-0000-1000-8000-00805f9b34fb
0000110c-0000-1000-8000-00805f9b34fb
0000110e-0000-1000-8000-00805f9b34fb
00001116-0000-1000-8000-00805f9b34fb
00001200-0000-1000-8000-00805f9b34fb
```

18.   If the pairing worked, you should see this message:

```
[CHG] Device B8:09:8A:6D:4A:74 Paired: yes
Pairing successful
```

19.   Quit out of the Bluetooth utility with the exit command.

Summary

Now that you have configured your networking support in the ARTIK module, you have
some choice about how to connect to it. The software developer tools can cross compile
and deliver runnable applications directly to the ARTIK as part of the build process. Your
ARTIK can also communicate with the outside world and connect to online services such
as Temboo and SAMI when it needs to.

■ ■ ■

## CHAPTER 10

Configuring and Upgrading

Updating Your Operating System

From time to time, Samsung will release operating system upgrades–perhaps to introduce new features or if a security flaw has been discovered–and it is important to upgrade right away to prevent the ARTIK modules from being hacked by an intruder.

When you receive your new ARTIK development system, it should already have the latest version of the operating system installed. Sometimes manufacturers release updated operating systems after products have been shipped but before they have reached the customers. These products might not be intercepted and updated in transit before you receive them. There are rare occasions where an operating system update is called for right away. If you develop a new OS package yourself you will want to install it to test your product design. You might be manufacturing products on a large scale, and a vital step in that process is to image your product code onto the ARTIK modules as they pass through your production line.

Creating a bootable SD card with an operating system installer on it and then configuring the ARTIK so it can transfer that software into its secured operating system memory is the solution for all of these scenarios.

Writing Downloaded Images to an SD Card

After downloading or manufacturing a new software installation, you need to write the contents of a disk image file to the SD card you plan to use for updating your ARTIK OS. The process of doing so is slightly different if your development system is Windows based versus Apple Macintosh or Linux. Follow the instructions appropriate to your workstation type to prepare your SD card before installing an update into your ARTIK.

Writing Micro SD Card Images on Windows

Follow these instructions to acquire the SD card–writing software and load a firmware image onto an SD card with your Windows development workstation.

1. Download the SD image-writing program from SourceForge:

    `http://sourceforge.net/projects/win32diskimager/`

© Cliff Wootton 2016
C. Wootton, *Beginning Samsung ARTIK*, DOI 10.1007/978-1-4842-1952-2_10

2. Install the SD image-writing application.

3. Download the firmware image you want to use.

4. Plug an SD card reader into your development workstation.

5. Install the Micro SD card into your card reader. Currently, you must use a card with no more than 32GB capacity.

6. Start up the image-writing application. The required graphical user interface controls are labeled A, B & C in the following image:

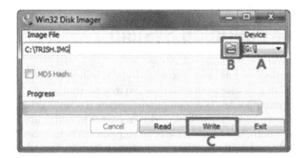

7. Select the drive where the Micro SD card is installed with the drop-down menu (A).

8. Choose the downloaded firmware image with the browse button (B).

9. Initiate the image copy by clicking on the Write button (C).

10. The progress indicator will indicate when the transfer is complete.

11. Quit the image-writing application when you are done.

Writing Micro SD Card Images on Linux

Follow these instructions to write your ARTIK firmware image on a Linux computer. These steps might be slightly different for you, depending on the version of Linux you are using. The biggest problem is reliably identifying the device name of your SD card. Try listing the available disks with the card not plugged in first and then try again with it plugged in to see what has changed. Here are the steps:

1. Download the firmware image you want to use and note where the downloaded file is so you can refer to it with the SD card loading command.

2. Plug an SD card reader into your development workstation. Your Linux installation should have all the drivers available for this already.

3. Install the Micro SD card into your card reader. Currently, you must use a card with no more than 32GB capacity.

4. Linux might automatically mount the SD card. Unmount it once you have discovered which device it is.

5. List the mounted disks with this command to identify exactly which one is the SD card:

    ```
    mount
    ```

6. This command also lists the disks to show how much space they have. Look for one that has the right capacity:

    ```
    df
    ```

7. You may see disk names with various partition suffixes. You want the raw disk number. This command lists all the disks in the /dev virtual file system on your development workstation:

    ```
    ls /dev | grep disk
    ```

8. Or perhaps the SD card has a different name or exists as a USB device. Inspect the whole list of logical devices with this command:

    ```
    ls /dev
    ```

9. Note the SD card device name carefully for use in the next command. It is very important that you correctly identify the SD card. You can seriously damage your system if you attempt to load ARTIK firmware onto the wrong device.

10. Unmount the SD card with this command. The SD device is called disk2 in this example, but it could be called sdb1 or a variety of other things. Make sure you are dismounting the correct device:

    ```
    sudo umount /dev/disk2
    ```

11. Use the cd command to go to the directory containing your downloaded ARTIK firmware image file.

12. Now use the dd block-copying command to physically duplicate the image file onto the SD drive. Explore the Linux documentation to establish the correct way to identify the target SD card. The command format is this:

    ```
    sudo dd if={downloaded_image_file_name} of=/dev/
    {your_sd_disk_name} bs=1m
    ```

If you make a mistake at this point and type in the device name of your boot disk instead of the SD card, the dd command will *completely* and *irrevocably* wipe out your operating system. Read the UNIX manual page for the dd command to understand what is happening here.

Writing Micro SD Card Images on Mac OS X

Use command-line tools to create the bootable SD card from a Samsung-generated disk image. You cannot use the GUI Disk Utility tool to clone the firmware image to the SD card. Mac OS X cannot read the format of the partitions on the image. Therefore, it cannot validate the image before restoring it.

If the SD card has been used before, it may have an Apple partition map. If it is a new SD card, it most likely has a Windows-compatible partition map and a DOS partition with the FAT16 or FAT32 format. The partition map on a new SD card is probably called FDisk_partition_scheme. Although it is not strictly necessary, you can reformat it and set the partition map to Master Boot Record (this is another name for the same partition scheme) and create a single partition. That single partition will get erased and replaced by the dd command that copies the image file to the SD card.

Use the GUI Disk Utility tool to alter the partition scheme on a recycled SD card. Then follow these instructions to write your ARTIK firmware image to an SD card on a Macintosh computer. Unless you are going to reconfigure the partition scheme on the SD card first, all of this happens in a terminal window at the Mac OS X command line:

1. Download the firmware image you want to use.

2. Plug an SD card reader into your development workstation.

3. Install the Micro SD card into your card reader. Currently, you must use a card with no more than 32GB storage capacity.

4. Mac OS X will automatically mount the SD card if it recognizes any compatible file-system partitions. Otherwise, you will see a dialog inviting you to initialize the SD card. It is safe to click on either the OK or Cancel buttons because the card will be completely erased when the new image is written onto it.

5. List the mounted disks with this command to identify exactly which one is the SD card:

   ```
   diskutil list
   ```

6. Make a note of the disk number of the SD card. It is very important that you identify the correct disk. You can seriously damage your system if you attempt to load ARTIK firmware onto the wrong one. You should see something like this:

```
/dev/disk0
   #:                        TYPE NAME              SIZE        IDENTIFIER
   0:     GUID_partition_scheme                  *750.2 GB     disk0
   1:                         EFI                 209.7 MB     disk0s1
   2:            Apple_HFS ADMN                   749.2 GB     disk0s2
   3:      Apple_Boot Recovery HD                 784.2 MB     disk0s3
/dev/disk1
   #:                        TYPE NAME              SIZE        IDENTIFIER
   0:     GUID_partition_scheme                  *750.2 GB     disk1
   1:                         EFI                 209.7 MB     disk1s1
   2:            Apple_HFS BACK                   749.8 GB     disk1s2
/dev/disk2
   #:                        TYPE NAME              SIZE        IDENTIFIER
   0:    FDisk_partition_scheme                   *1.0 GB      disk2
   1:            DOS_FAT_16 NO NAME                1.0 GB      disk2s1
```

7. Look at the sizes of the disks and figure out which one is the SD card. Note the disk reference carefully for use in the next command. The example system has some very large hard disks and one small one with a different partition scheme.

8. Note the partition scheme. It should be FDisk_partition_scheme but it might say Master Boot Record, which is also OK. If it says GUID or Apple partition scheme, erase the SD card and change the partition scheme to Master Boot Record with the Disk Utility tool before copying the image to it. See the instructions that follow if you need them.

9. Now use the command-line diskutil tool to unmount the SD card with this command. In this example, the SD card device is called disk2. Because this is allocated dynamically on a first come, first served basis, it might not be disk2 on your system. Check carefully and double check again to avoid accidentally damaging another disk drive:

    diskutil unmountDisk /dev/disk2

10. You should see this message:

    Unmount of all volumes on disk2 was successful

11. Use the cd command to go to the directory containing your downloaded ARTIK firmware image file.

12. Now use the dd block-copying command to physically duplicate the image file onto the SD drive. The command format is this:

    ```
    sudo dd if={downloaded_image_file} of=/dev/rdisk{sd_disk_number} bs=1m
    ```

13. Using disk2 as an example and a recent ARTIK 10 firmware image, you would have this:

    ```
    sudo dd if=artik10_20151109.img of=/dev/rdisk2 bs=1m
    ```

14. You should be prompted for an administrator password at this point.

15. While the dd command is executing, you should see a flashing activity light on your card reader. The copying may take a few minutes. The dd command will echo progress statistics to the screen:

    ```
    470+0 records in
    470+0 records out
    492830720 bytes transferred in 107.501932 secs (4584389 bytes/sec)
    ```

16. When the transfer has finished, Mac OS X may try to mount the disk and present an initialization-warning dialog. Just click on the Ignore button to dismiss it.

17. When the copying is finished, your SD card should have three new Linux partitions on it. You cannot mount these partitions on a Macintosh without installing additional disk drivers, because Mac OS does not understand Linux file-system partitions. List them to see that they are there:

    ```
    diskutil list
    ```

18. You should see the SD card with four new partitions looking something like this:

    ```
    /dev/disk2
       #:                       TYPE NAME        SIZE       IDENTIFIER
       0:     FDisk_partition_scheme           *1.0 GB      disk2
       1:                       Linux           33.6 MB     disk2s1
       2:                       Linux           33.6 MB     disk2s2
       3:                       Linux          424.7 MB     disk2s3
    ```

19. Take the SD card out of the reader.

20. Install the SD card in your target ARTIK developer reference board, and you are ready to update your ARTIK module.

When you use the dd command, the path to the target SD card in these examples is /dev/rdisk2 and not /dev/disk2. The r prefix is important. If you make a mistake at this point and type in the descriptor for your boot disk instead of the SD card, the dd command will wipe out your development system and render it un-bootable. You will also irretrievably lose all the documents, source code, and files that you had stored on that disk. This is worse than accidentally repartitioning the disk because it overwrites the disk contents. Be very careful, because recovery tools will be unable to repair your disk and bring your files back after that. Read the UNIX manual page for the dd command to understand what is happening here.

Ghost Disks on Mac OS X

You may see ghost disk drives listed on your Macintosh if you have previously mounted installer disk images. For example, Adobe Flash Player leaves behind a vestigial record of the installer disk even though it has been unmounted. This can offset the disk numbers. Any recommendation that you should use disk2 needs to be confirmed by locating a drive that has the expected size of your SD card. In this example it is disk2, but it might not be.

About Partition Maps on OS X

If you experience any problems when you try to boot the ARTIK module from this SD card after creating an image on a Macintosh workstation, you might not have created the SD card correctly. Run the Mac OS X Disk Utility tool and repartition the SD card to use a recognizable partitioning scheme that the ARTIK can understand.

Before you reconfigure the partitions with the Disk Utility, click on the Options button to set the partition map to Master Boot Record. This is a Windows-compatible partition map that the ARTIK understands. You cannot set the partition map to FDisk_partition_scheme with the Apple Disk Utility. The other two alternatives in the Disk Utility are for use only on Apple hardware systems. Do not set the partition map to one of the Apple-specific formats, because the ARTIK module will not be able to find the partitions on your SD card. Once the partition map is set correctly, create a single disk partition and repeat the image loading before attempting the update again. Follow these steps to repartition an SD card:

1. Fire up the GUI Disk Utility. It lives in the Utilities folder inside the Applications folder on your Macintosh desktop:

   {your_boot_disk} ➤ Applications ➤ Utilities ➤ Disk Utility app

2. Press the [Command] + [Shift] + [U] key combination.

3. Scroll down and double-click on the Disk Utility application icon to run it.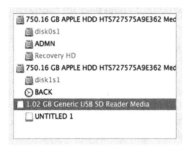

4. Make sure you choose the correct disk drive from the list of physical drives attached to your computer. The SD card should be easy to identify by its capacity. Be careful not to choose one of your hard disk drives inadvertently:

5. Choose the 1-partition setup:

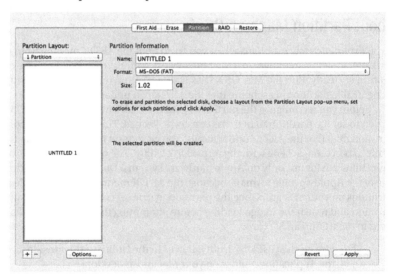

6. Click on the Options button to choose an appropriate
    partition scheme:

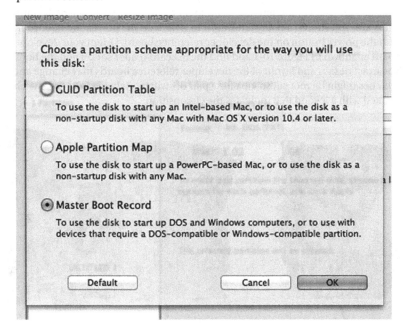

7. Choose the Master Boot Record partition scheme.

8. Click on the OK button to confirm the Master Boot Record
    partition scheme.

9. Click on the Apply button to rewrite the partition map and
    create a new partition.

10. Your SD card is now ready to resume the command-line
    image copy process.

Updating Your ARTIK 5 or 10

Look at your developer reference board to make sure you know where the important items are. You should already know how to switch on the power and boot your ARTIK with the power button on the developer reference board. Orient your developer reference board as shown in Figure 10-1 and find the SD card reader socket and the boot switches. The exact design and layout of the developer reference boards may change and the switches might be moved, so look for a pair of switches labeled SW2. The switches are marked with a legend that indicates the On position.

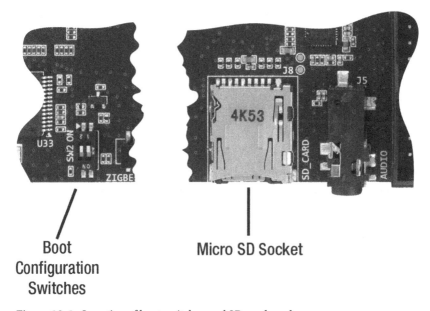

Boot
Configuration
Switches

Micro SD Socket

Figure 10-1. *Location of boot switches and SD card reader*

Follow these instructions to upgrade your operating system. This is described in the official documentation as updating the eMMC image.

1. Go to the developer downloads page. You will need to be signed in with your Samsung developer account to see this page:

    https://www.artik.io/developer/downloads

2. Read the notes about the firmware download. This is important, because your ARTIK module must be compatible before you upgrade. You should not attempt to install Beta firmware onto an Alpha developer reference board, as you may render your ARTIK module inoperative after that.

3. Observe the limitations on SD card capacity if the release notes describe them. Beta development systems can only recognize 32GB SD cards. A 64GB card is not compatible with Beta versions of the ARTIK. Earlier ARTIK models can only use 16GB SD cards.

4. Download an ARTIK operating system image to install. These are generally available in the "Downloads" section of the developer website, but they could be located elsewhere if Samsung create a special repository for eMMC images. Be careful to download the right firmware for your ARTIK. The model 5 and 10 firmware is different. Some versions are incompatible with hardware of a different vintage. This may be less of a problem once the product matures.

5. Plug an SD card reader into your development workstation.

6. Install the Micro SD card into your card reader. Currently, you must use a card with no more than 32GB capacity.

7. Write the image to the SD card. This is a slightly different process if your development system is Windows based versus Apple Macintosh based. Follow the instructions that are appropriate to your workstation type.

8. Eject/dismount the SD card from your development system.

9. Make sure your ARTIK developer reference board is powered off.

10. Remove the card from the SD card reader and install it into the Micro SD card slot on your ARTIK developer reference board.

11. Set the boot-mode switches on the developer reference board to boot the Micro SD card instead of the onboard operating system already installed on the ARTIK module.

12. Orient your developer reference board the other way up to see the switch depending on the vintage of your board and which way the switches are placed. The switches may be oriented upside down when viewed from the edge of the board. This can be confusing and make the On and Off positions ambiguous. Look closely, and you will see the switches have very small lettering on them, which indicates the correct orientation.

13. Set boot-mode switch 1 to the Off position.

14. Set boot-mode switch 2 to the On position.

15. Open your terminal window and connect via the serial interface.

16. Follow the update as it happens on the console screen.

17. Switch on the power supply to the developer reference board.

18. Press and hold the power (boot) button for a second to initiate a boot cycle.

19. You should see messages from the U-Boot loader as it starts up.

20. The boot loader should then display a message telling you it is booting from the SDMMC card instead of the internal operating system. You should see this message on the screen:

    ```
    Checking Boot Mode ... SDMMC
    ```

21. If you do not see this message, you probably have the boot mode switches set incorrectly. Check them again and reboot.

22. Booting the image on the SD card will automatically run an updater script to copy new software from the SD card into the main eMMC memory on your ARTIK module. Wait for this process to complete. Interrupting or powering off before it is finished may render your ARTIK unable to boot and it will be unrecoverable.

23. When the updating process is done, you should see this message on the screen:

    ```
    Upgrade completed!
    ```

24. Power off the ARTIK developer reference board.

25. Remove the SD card from the Micro SD socket on your developer reference board. You may want to keep it with your other ARTIK accessories in case you want to upgrade again.

26. Reset the boot-mode switches on the developer reference board to boot the eMMC memory inside the ARTIK module.

27. Set the boot-mode switch 1 to the Off position.

28. Set the boot-mode switch 2 to the Off position.

29. Switch on the power supply to the developer reference board.

30. Press and hold the power (boot) button down for a second to initiate a boot cycle.

31. You should see messages from the U-Boot loader again as it starts up.

32. The boot loader should then display a message telling you it is booting from the internal operating system in the ARTIK's eMMC memory. You should see this message on the screen:

```
Checking Boot Mode ... EMMC4.41
```

33. If you do not see this message, you probably have the boot-mode switches set incorrectly.

34. Check them again and reboot.

After upgrading the OS, you should always check the virtual file system to see whether any devices or hardware addresses have changed. Keeping a copy of the listing of the /dev and /sys virtual file systems and comparing that with one you capture after an upgrade will tell you if anything moved. If it did, your code may need to be altered to accommodate the change.

Known Firmware Versions

Table 10-1 lists the publicly available firmware versions that have been released via the Samsung developer downloads page. There may be others that you have been supplied with directly from Samsung. Download new firmware only from the Samsung developer downloads page to ensure you have an authoritative copy. You will need to be signed on with your developer account to reach the page and access the firmware:

```
https://www.artik.io/developer/downloads
```

Table 10-1. *ARTIK Firmware Release Versions History*

ARTIK	Date	Notes
5	2015-10-07	Only use this on Alpha boards. Alpha firmware is built with Yocto from Fedora 20. Ethernet driver support unavailable on this version.
5	2015-11-11	Only use this on 0.3 version (Beta) boards. Beta firmware is built with Yocto from Fedora 22. Adds support for Ethernet interface, Analog write, and I2C device access. Temboo library is not available on this version.
10	2015-10-07	Only use this on Alpha boards. Alpha firmware is built with Yocto from Fedora 20.
10	2015-11-09	Only use this on 0.3 version (Beta) boards. Beta firmware is built with Yocto from Fedora 22. Adds USB camera support via the Linux UVC driver, Analog write, and I2C device access. Temboo library is not available on this version.

Installing Software on Your ARTIK

Installation of new software utilities on Linux is managed via the Redhat Package Manager (RPM). Each software package consists of an archive of files along with information about the package. There is also an API framework with which advanced developers can create multiple installer packages with languages such as C or Python.

The package manager expects the installation archives to be constructed in a particular way and to have the .rpm file extension. These are more sophisticated than a simple Zip archive because they contain instructions for configuring the packages as they are installed. The archive packages also include descriptive text and version number details. Removing packages is facilitated by the uninstaller support that is built in to the archive. Find out more about the rpm tool here:

```
http://www.rpm.org/
https://en.wikipedia.org/wiki/RPM_Package_Manager
https://docs.fedoraproject.org/en-US/Fedora_Draft_Documentation/0.1/html/
RPM_Guide/
```

Using a package manager such as rpm makes the installation process consistent across a number of target platforms. After you have built and tested your ARTIK application code, use rpm as part of your deployment process to load your own software onto your ARTIK modules during your production workflow.

The rpm package manager is suitable for single stand-alone products with no knowledge of dependencies between multiple installed software packages. When you acquire software for your development environment, you often use an rpm front-end to work out dependencies on other installations. Two particularly well-known ones are yum and apt-get, but there are others that are summarized on the rpm Wikipedia page. Although the rpm tools are present on the ARTIK modules, Fedora version 22 replaces the yum toolkit with dnf which is functionally similar and has additional features. Find out more about dnf here:

```
https://fedoraproject.org/wiki/Dnf
```

Use the appropriate rpm commands to perform these operations on packaged software:

- Upgrade an already installed package

- Install a package from scratch

- Remove an installed package

- Query a package's contents

- Verify that a package has not been tampered with

- Check a package signature

Find out about the installed version of the rpm tool on your ARTIK by typing this command:

```
man rpm
```

Here is a very brief example of installing software directly with RPM:

1. Log in with the root account or use the su command to switch to the root account from your logged-in session.

2. Download the package that you want to install. It will have a name that describes the software and version number with the .rpm file extension. This example uses the MySoftware042b.rpm package name.

3. Type this command to install the software:

```
rpm -i MySoftware042b.rpm
```

4. Alternatively, type this command if the software is already installed and you want to update it:

```
rpm -U MySoftware042b.rpm
```

5. Log out of the root account when you are done.

Summary

Being able to install operating system updates or install additional software packages provides an upgrade path for you when you need it. Because the ARTIK OS is Linux based, most open-source packages can be installed. This can save you a great deal of development time and effort. Software features and functionality can be kept up to date with all the most recent developments. This also includes the software development tools that will be examined in the next chapter. These will be installed on your development workstation to cross-compile applications. Installing supporting tools directly on the ARTIK module is helpful for customizing how it works and deploying your own code. Now you know how to do it. In the fullness of time, other installer tools and options will become available. For now, these basic facilities should be sufficient.

## CHAPTER 11

Programming Your ARTIK

Everything Is the Same but Different

The ARTIK 5 and 10 modules are based on a Linux operating system. Your development platform might be Windows, Linux, or Mac OS X. They each have some subtly different characteristics that map onto your ARTIK in strange ways. This is likely to impact your programming more than any other aspect, so this chapter will discuss some topics that you need to be aware of when you are moving between different platforms. Sharing a folder from your development workstation and mounting it on your ARTIK or vice versa exposes you to the different ways that each operating system manages file names. These all cropped up during the investigative phase of this book-writing project.

Programming Your ARTIK

There are already several alternative ways to approach ARTIK programming. This is astonishing for a product so early in its lifecycle. It is reassuring as a developer, because the more people who embrace the ARTIK technology, the better it is for the whole community. It will encourage Samsung to take the platform further with new features, new module designs, and more support.

Plan your development process around what you expect to build and choose the best tools based on your goals. You have the choice to develop software in these fundamentally different ways:

- Natively inside the ARTIK as a compiled C language application

- Java running on a VM inside your ARTIK module

- Command-line shell scripts inside your ARTIK module

- Python scripts running inside your ARTIK module

- Arduino sketches running inside your ARTIK module

- JavaScript applications running as Node.js scripts inside your ARTIK module

- Compiled applications from source code generated via the Temboo toolkit online

© Cliff Wootton 2016
C. Wootton, *Beginning Samsung ARTIK*, DOI 10.1007/978-1-4842-1952-2_11

- Cross-compiled applications built on your development
  workstation and loaded into your ARTIK module

- Auto-generated code from the Temboo web-based code generator
  copied and compiled natively on your ARTIK module

Since the ARTIK is UNIX based, installing other tools and languages is also feasible if
you are prepared to do the extra work required to port them to the ARTIK environment.

Setting Up Your Software Development Environment

Maintaining and managing a project can become complicated. Having an integrated
development environment (IDE) that manages a collection of resources, configures a
compiler, and supports a graphical debugger can be a great help. Choose any of these
alternatives for creating your application source code:

- Raw C language source files with build scripts written as shell
  commands or for use with the make utility. Cross-compile these
  in your development workstation or natively compile with GCC
  inside your ARTIK.

- Eclipse IDE with the ARM cross-compilation tools installed and
  one of the debugging sub-systems configured to connect to the
  debugging stubs

- Arduino IDE on your development workstation with the
  libArduino cross-compiler for ARM installed

- Temboo online GUI developer tools

- Node.js, Python, and other scripts edited on your development
  workstation and copied to your ARTIK module for execution there

Code-Editing Tools

There are many alternative and inexpensive text editors to choose from. The most
popular ones are free, and there are very capable tools for all of the platforms you might
develop with:

- Edit directly in the UNIX environment by learning how to use the
  vi editing tools. There are books available to teach you all about it.
  There are many other editors (such as EMACS or PICO) but you
  may need to install them. The vi editor is always guaranteed to be
  available on a UNIX system.

- On Mac OS, there are two editors written by Bare Bones Software that are particularly good. Their premium editor is called BBEdit. It is inexpensive and powerful. From the same developer, the TextWrangler editor is free and provides many of the core code-editing tools you need.

- Windows-based developers can use Notepad+, which is similar to TextWrangler.

Folders vs. Directories

Because the command line and graphical user interface worlds have evolved independently, they use different terminology to describe the same thing. The constraints that GUI implementations place on end users to prevent their accessing important operating system components make this a quite sensible idea. Now that you are becoming familiar with the command-line interface (CLI), the UNIX nomenclature that describes the file containers may be unfamiliar.

In a graphical user environment, your file containers look like folders in a file cabinet, so we become used to describing them as folders. Traditional UNIX users call them directories. They are fundamentally the same thing, but in the UNIX environment you can see directories that are not mirrored as folders in your desktop environment. Anything whose name starts with a full stop (period) in the UNIX command-line environment is hidden when you view it from the desktop. Mac OS X uses extended file attributes to hide files without putting a prefixing full stop on their name. So in this book, the term *folder* is used in the context of a desktop user session where you can point and click on an item with a mouse or touch gesture. The term *directory* is used when describing a file container that you operate on from the command line via the terminal emulator and refer to directly by a name that you type.

File-System Path: Folder Separator Characters

There are three operating systems that you are likely to encounter: Windows, Macintosh, and Linux. They each have particular ways to separate folder or directory names when you are describing a fully qualified path to a file.

In Windows, the default separator for folders is a backslash character (\). This is usually hidden in the file explorer view but is very important in the command line. In Cygwin, the conversion to the UNIX form happens automatically if you enclose the path in single quotes. This command for example:

```
cd C:\windows\path
```

Should be typed with enclosing single quote characters (`'`):

```
cd 'C:\windows\path'
```

The single quotes are necessary to prevent the command-line shell from misinterpreting the backslashes as meta-character escape sequences.

On Mac OS X, the command line natively works like any other Linux. It uses POSIX-compatible paths with folder (directory) names separated by slash characters (/). If you use AppleScript or other utilities written for use with the Macintosh toolbox, you may see path names that are separated by colon characters (:) instead of slashes (/). Substitute a slash character wherever you see a colon in the file path.

Avoid creating a file name with a colon in it when you are working in the command line. You may be able to fix this from the command line, but sometimes you get a file that you cannot operate on to delete or rename. These are called "Files from hell." The only practical solution is to relocate the containing folder to a safe location out of the way and recreate it file by file (omitting the bad file, of course). Putting it in the trash will not work, because the trash-emptying logic is also unable to remove it. Some deeply complex code could edit the file-system database and fix things at the directory inode level or possibly access the disk and rewrite the directory by patching a physical disk block. Attempting that could lose your entire file system and potentially render the disk unreadable unless you know exactly what you are doing.

Linux users will never likely encounter any of these issues because they will always just use a slash character (/) as a folder name separator.

Spaces in File Names and Paths

Sometimes on Windows or Mac OS, you will use space characters in the GUI environment (File Explorer or Finder). These are preserved in the file and folder names at the command line, where they are called directories rather than folders. A space character is deemed to be an item separator for UNIX command-line arguments, which makes it awkward when the file names include a space. You should enclose a file path in double quote characters (") if you are using it as an argument to a UNIX command. The quotes are not necessary if there are no spaces in the name, but you may be passing the name in a variable. Encapsulate the reference to that variable in quotes to protect the file path when the variable value is rendered to replace the reference with its contents.

The paths with space characters can be described without the quotes if you use the backspace character to escape the embedded spaces. This is a bit more complex and prone to errors. These two paths are equivalent, but the quoted version is much easier to deal with:

- `"/users/cliff/desktop/my file name with spaces. txt"`
- `/users/cliff/desktop/my\ file\ name\ with\ spaces. txt`

Upper- and Lowercase Issues

Some file systems do not care about whether file and folder names are composed with upper- or lowercase letters. In others, the case is important. Some support a hybrid scenario where case is preserved but ignored. DOS just uses all uppercase letters. Mac OS X preserves the case when a file name or directory is created but ignores it thereafter.

The UNIX operating system (including Linux), preserves case and treats differently cased versions of file and folder names as strictly different entities so it is case sensitive. Consider this file name:

```
My_mixed_CASE_file_name. txt
```

Mac OS X will match the file with this description "my_mixed_case_file_name.txt" but UNIX will not. The underlying file system provides the case sensitivity. The HFS+ file system on Mac OS X is case insensitive, but if you mounted a case-sensitive file system, the command line in Mac OS X would honor that. Table 11-1 summarizes the case sensitivity for the operating systems we are interested in:

Table 11-1. *Case Preservation and Sensitivity on Operating Systems*

OS	Case Preservation	Case Sensitive
Windows Explorer	Yes	No
Cygwin on Windows	Yes	Yes
Windows Services for UNIX (POSIX)	Yes	Yes
Linux	Yes	Yes
Mac OS X Finder	Yes	No
Mac OS X Command Line	Yes	Yes
Mac OS X Command Line with HFS+	Yes	No
ARTIK 5 and 10	Yes	Yes

Read these articles for more information on this topic, especially if you intend to mount foreign file systems on your developer workstation or even on your ARTIK module:

```
https://en.wikipedia.org/wiki/Case_preservation
https://en.wikipedia.org/wiki/Case_sensitivity
https://www.dropbox.com/en/help/145
http://xahlee.info/UnixResource_dir/_/fileCaseSens.html
```

■ **Note** Moving folders full of files from case-sensitive file systems to case-insensitive file systems causes a collision between files that may have different file names on one but render as the same file name on the other. The copy may fail or it may silently replace two similarly named files with one. There is no guarantee which of the files will survive and which will be destroyed. Moving files from Windows or Mac OS X to an ARTIK will be fine, but moving files back from the ARTIK may not.

Of Camels and Underscores

Choosing a strategy that avoids space characters in file names suggests that using underscores in place of spaces is good. Some developers prefer to use Camel Case file names. This capitalizes each word but removes the spaces. Experience suggests that this is slightly more prone to typing mistakes in case-supporting operating systems whereas underscores are less likely to be mistyped.

- `my_underscore_separated_file_name. txt`
- `MyCamelCaseFileName. txt`

Let the Environment Do the Heavy Lifting

Finding the right separation between environment and file names is important. If the environment is going to change, possibly because the code is supported across multiple platforms, then defining the path to an important file can be done using environment variables in UNIX or registry entries in Windows. Mac OS X has a mechanism called the *defaults database*. Your application can query these definitions to construct a path to a folder containing the file you want to operate on. Then it can append the file name and extension. Manifest constants in the C pre-processor can be used to define the file-name portion so your code can be completely decoupled from the environment it is running in.

Considering all the possible file systems, apply the file-naming conventions that are the most limiting and use those to define the file-name portion. A totally portable file name can be constructed by limiting the file-name portion to eight characters, the file extension to three characters, and using only uppercase letters. This is the DOS 8.3 file-name convention. If you are not including DOS systems, you might relax these rules a little, but keeping file names short is good for compactness in an IoT scenario.

Links vs. Aliases

In the UNIX environment, you can create shortcuts using the symbolic link mechanism. These shortcuts behave like aliases in the Finder, but they are not the same thing.

UNIX also supports hard links to files that are indistinguishable from real files. So a file that has two hard links to it will not be removed and free up disk space when one of them is deleted. The second link must also be deleted to relinquish the space. This is sometimes useful as a way to avoid important files getting deleted accidentally. In UNIX, you can only make hard links to files that live on the same file system as the link itself. You cannot make hard links to directories. Symbolic links can cross between file-system boundaries without any problem and can reference a directory.

The Windows desktop also supports shortcuts that are managed differently than any symbolic links you create in Cygwin.

The Mac OS X Finder recognizes symbolic links and displays them as aliases, but it does not distinguish between two hard links pointing at the same file.

Mac OS Resource Forks

Classic Mac OS operating systems used to manage files quite differently than any other operating system. They had the normal file container that you could operate on as a data file to read and write the content. In addition, each file also had a separate container that was organized as an object-oriented database. This was where a structured collection of resources such as icons and localized texts would be stored. These two parts of the file were called the data fork and the resource fork.

Even before Mac OS X arrived, these two forks created some difficulties on non-Apple file systems. These were often hosted on Windows file servers. Usually, the Apple files were split into two separate normal files. For the Mac OS user the driver software reconstructed them as a single entity, but users of other platforms saw files with strange names often only copying one half for their own use or deleting what they thought was a spurious file, leading to corruption.

Later, these files were reconceived on Mac OS X as file bundles, which are simply nested folders that the Finder hides when you browse the contents of your disk. Thus, an application or a Keynote presentation is really a folder and not a single entity. Finder recognizes the .app or .key file extensions and does the right thing.

This is important for ARTIK developers because you might casually drag and drop a resource file from a Macintosh desktop and place it on your ARTIK. Because the ARTIK does not understand Mac OS naming conventions, it simply presents this as a folder containing various assets instead of as a single file. In the early Alpha builds of the ARTIK OS, some open-source material was distributed like this. Having removed the visible files, there were some hidden ones left behind because their file names had a dot prefix.

New-Line Characters

There are three kinds of new-line markers. Naturally, they are different for the three main operating system types. Although UNIX has been around longer than the other two, these differences came about for historical and proprietary reasons just like the different file-system separator characters.

If you use the wrong type of new-line markers, the UNIX command line in your ARTIK will not be able to distinguish one line of script from another. Table 11-2 summarizes the three different new-line character variations.

Table 11-2. *New-Line Characters*

New Line Terminator	Description
Single line-feed character (LF)	Used on UNIX systems by default. Set your editor preferences to this mode. This is the best kind of new-line marker to use for files inside the ARTIK.
Single carriage return (CR)	Used on classic Macintosh systems. Old legacy files from your archives may use this marker. UNIX will not see the line breaks and will get confused because everything will appear to be on one line.
Carriage return followed by line feed (CRLF)	Windows systems mark their line breaks by using both characters. Your UNIX command line will likely work OK but you may see listings with extra blank lines in some views.

Text editors such as TextWrangler and BBEdit on the Macintosh provide a mode switch at the bottom of every window to choose which of these alternatives to use. That gives you handy way to convert a file. Just open it in the editor, change the new-line mode, and save it again. Other editors on Windows and Linux probably have the same feature.

Drag and drop text-cleaning tools are available for use from your desktop. Install text-processing utilities in your development environment to clean blocks of text on the fly. Writing a text-cleaning function and using that as part of a file reader is also a neat work-around, although nothing is fixed permanently unless you rewrite the original source-file contents.

Typographers Quotes

Make sure you remove any curly quotes from your source files and replace them with straight ASCII quotes. Use either the single straight quote characters (') or double straight quote characters ("). Remove any of these curly quotes (' ' " ") from the source code. This applies to both single and double quotes. Your compiler will complain if you leave the curly quotes in your source code, but at least it will tell you what lines they are on.

Being in Two Places at Once

When you develop code for an embedded OS on an ARTIK module, sometimes you will be working on your hosting system and sending things to the ARTIK. At other times, you will be logged in directly to the ARTIK module, working natively in a command-line environment there. Because the ARTIK uses UNIX, it helps to keep your head straight if you also work in a UNIX-like environment on your hosting workstation.

It is also a good idea to configure the working setup to clearly style the window appearances differently or you will inevitably type a command intended for one environment into the other. Any visual cues you can give yourself will help you avoid silly mistakes.

Try color-coding your terminal windows. Then when you open a command-line interface on your workstation, it will look different than when you are logged on to your ARTIK. On Windows, use PuTTY for talking to your ARTIK and Cygwin for command-line work on your PC. Those applications already have different appearances. On Mac OS X, use iTerm for ARTIK work and the default Terminal application for command-line work on the Macintosh.

Another possibility would be to edit the .profile login configuration on the ARTIK and on your hosting workstation to set the command-line prompt. The login configuration file is named differently depending on the command-line shell you are using. Table 11-3 lists the initialization files that configure the shell command-line environment when you log in. The tilde character (~) denotes the home folder/directory path for your account:

Table 11-3. Command-Line Shells

Path	Shell	Description
/etc/profile	sh, bash, csh, ksh	Used by the standard Bourne shell or the improved bash (Bourne Again) shell to configure all user login sessions. Affects both kinds of shell environments.
/etc/bashrc	bash	Used by the Bourne Again (bash) shell to configure all user login sessions. Only used by bash shells. Not seen by sh shells.
~/.bash_profile	bash	Your own private settings for bash sessions. Used when you spawn sub-shells as well.
~/.bash_login	bash	Your own private settings used only when you login
~/.bashrc	bash	Your own private settings to initialize a bash shell or sub-shell
~/.profile	bash, csh, ksh	Use this generically for setting up your session, but beware that if you put bash-specific syntax in it, other shells may misunderstand the syntax.
~/.cshrc	csh	Your own private initialization settings for a C shell session.
~/.kshrc	ksh	Your own private initialization settings for a Korn shell session.
~/.bash_logout	bash	Shell commands to execute when you log out of a bash session. What you do here could indicate the difference between an orderly logout and a system crash that shuts everything down without warning.

Choose the scope (global or private) and then open the appropriate initialization file in your editor. Add this line to create an environment variable assignment that defines what your command-line prompt is going to be:

```
export PS1=" "
```

Start with an empty text string and construct a new prompt piece by piece. Aside from any arbitrary string of literal characters, add the following meta-characters to define your own custom command-line prompt. Type your custom string between the quotation marks that define the PS1 value. Be careful not to construct a new prompt that is too long or you will be coping with lines wrapping when you type long command-line strings. Use the meta-characters listed in Table 11-4 to construct a custom prompt according to your needs.

Table 11-4. *Shell Command Prompt-Formatting Meta-characters*

Meta-character	Meaning
\d	Current date
\t	Current time
\h	Host name
\#	Command number
\u	User name
\W	Current working directory
\w	Current working directory with full path

Newer versions of Mac OS X allow the use of an Emoji character since the terminal application is fully Unicode compliant. Make space for the Emoji in your PS1 string and drag the Emoji symbol from the special characters browser to the Terminal window and drop it there.

Add color instructions to your prompt text by incorporating their escape sequences. This is a good idea in order to distinguish between a root account and normal, unprivileged one. This example defines the prompt as a green dollar sign. Make sure that you reset the color to black at the end of the prompt or everything else you type will be green as well:

```
export PS1="\[\e[1;32m\]\$ \[\e[0m\]"
```

This part is the green color-control escape sequence:

```
\[\e[1;32m\]
```

This part is the escape sequence to set the color back to black for the rest of the command line. Without this all the text you type will be green too:

```
\[\e[0m\]
```

Remember to reset things when you change them or the color change will persist. Messing with the color settings is fun but generally not necessary. The more complex you make the prompt string, the harder it will be to capture a command-line history to a log file and convert it to a script. You will have to edit out all the color escape sequences first. Here are some helpful guides to defining prompt strings:

```
http://osxdaily.com/2006/12/11/how-to-customize-your-terminal-prompt/
http://osxdaily.com/2013/04/08/add-emoji-command-line-bash-prompt/
http://www.cyberciti.biz/tips/howto-linux-unix-bash-shell-setup-prompt.html
https://beginlinux.wordpress.com/2008/09/12/modify-your-command-prompt/
https://wiki.archlinux.org/index.php/Color_Bash_Prompt
```

Developing Your Code

You need an integrated development environment (IDE) to develop code in. This manages the complexity of building applications for multiple target platforms and switching debugging support in and out.

One of the biggest advantages of using an IDE to develop your applications is the way it brings together a collection of tools that were previously hard to integrate manually. This makes tasks such as refactoring (reorganizing the code in your project) much easier. Suppose you had a hundred source files and wanted to change the name of a variable throughout. If the variable is only used in ten of those files, finding it without an IDE takes a while because you would have to open all one hundred files and then search each of them one at a time and only edit one when you find a match. Your chances of missing one are very high, and you waste a lot of time checking files that you do not need to open. A global (project-wide) search/replace within an IDE solves this sort of problem in an elegant and efficient way.

The Eclipse IDE is available across all platforms and is easier to set up than modifying proprietary, platform-specific development environments such as Xcode. You could use the Arduino IDE with suitable plugin SDK libraries to support the ARTIK. Another interesting possibility is the cloud-based Temboo software development tool.

Make your own value judgment and choose the best solution for your development needs. More tools can be introduced later if your needs change.

What Is Cross-Compiling?

When you develop software with an IDE running on your development workstation, the code it produces needs to run on your ARTIK module. This is not the same kind of hardware as your development workstation. An IDE, by default, will build applications for the computer it is running on. Building applications for a different kind of computer is called cross-compiling. That computer is referred to as the target system and your development system is described as the host.

Your target platform in this case is one of the ARTIK 1, 5, or 10 modules. Your target module needs to be reachable by a network connection from your development workstation in order for the IDE to automatically deliver new applications as they are built. In that scenario, the development workstation is called the hosting computer.

Write code using an editor that is running inside the target platform and compile the code to build an application there. That is called *native compiling* because the work takes place on the same hardware system that the code will execute on.

The terms *target* and *client* are often used to describe the same thing, but there are subtle differences. A client would connect to a hosting system and treat it as a server and then request things from it. A target is where a process running on a hosting system will put things or send messages. The subtle difference is which device initiated the communication.

Building Code for the Correct Target CPU

Make sure you build executable applications that are compatible with the correct CPU in your ARTIK. ARM processors come in a variety of configurations, and each has a different instruction set. If you build for the wrong CPU, your executable most likely has some invalid instructions in it. The CPU will crash your application when it encounters an unknown instruction. This may be very hard to diagnose because it fails at the assembly-code level and you will not see anything wrong with your source code. Run your application in a debugger to examine the internal memory and variable usage. Table 11-5 summarizes the CPU types for which to compile your application.

Table 11-5. ARTIK Module CPU Architectures

Module	CPU Architecture
ARTIK 1	Dual MIPS®S32 processors
ARTIK 5	Dual ARM A7 processors
ARTIK 10	Quad ARM A7 + Quad ARM A15 processors

Debug vs. Release

Debugging software can be made easier by running the code inside an emulator on the development workstation to see if it works properly. An emulator is similar to the way that a computer system can be virtualized to create multiple virtual hosts or run Windows and Linux within an application such as VMWare or Parallels on a Macintosh. The emulator provides connections for a debugger to monitor the ARM application as it runs. This will not reveal every possible bug, and eventually the code will need to be tested on the target ARTIK module. This does give a lot of assurances that the application is fundamentally working properly though.

The next step is to debug natively within the target ARTIK with the application controlled remotely from the IDE. First, compile a debug version of the application with additional code embedded to support the debugger. When the application is running properly, build it again with the debugging support turned off and only ship production builds that are tagged with the Release status. Never ship a Debug version of an application, as this provides opportunities for intrusion and cyber attacks.

Managing Your Code

Manage the gradual evolution of your code so you can revert back to earlier versions and rework things. This ability to undo and start over goes way beyond what the undo function provides in your code editor. At best, you can only go back to the beginning of the editing session. Closing the file results in the loss of all of the undo history. Manually cloning working backups each time you start working is a simplistic solution. That approach wastes disk space, because lots of unchanged static items are cloned too.

We get around this by using a source code–management/control tool. Currently, the most favored tool is Git, which was developed by Linus Torvalds and his colleagues in 2005. Linus was the original developer of Linux.

Code management is well suited to collaboration on shared projects, but it is also useful if you are working on your own. It is good for managing website code and even book manuscripts. Any kind of text-based digital media can be version controlled with Git.

Git and other code-management repositories store the changes between the version you check in and the previous one. Git also has powerful branch-management tools. It helps you go off and fix a bug based on an earlier release without altering your main development source code. Fold that change back into your development work later when it is convenient. Git also manages conflicts where two opposing changes affect the same source file.

Before Git, the Apache Subversion (SVN) tools were popular. If you use a code-management application (such as Tower for the Macintosh), managing your code with Git is very easy. Tower for Mac OS X is an example of a very well-designed application that supports Git on your local machine and SVN on the remote repository. There are other tools available, and your choice of code repository is not constrained. Windows and Linux workstations are well supported with other GUI-based Git client apps. Find out more about code management here:

```
https://en.wikipedia.org/wiki/Git_(software)
https://en.wikipedia.org/wiki/Apache_Subversion
```

I recommend that you install a copy of Git on your workstation and then install a client tool to help you manage it more easily. That is, unless you want to do it all from the command line. Modern IDE tools have support for Git and SVN built in, or they can be extended to support code management. As you add features, commit the changes to the master repository with details of what you did. Try and stick to a discipline of only checking in a complete and working build. People who check in busted source code are not hugely popular with their peers because it breaks everyone else's workflow.

Later on, revert your changes if you installed a bug fix that turned out not to be right after all. Keeping things managed feature by feature also makes it easier to repurpose the new code into other projects, because the changes needed to add just that feature can be isolated by inspecting the code differences (we call them *deltas*).

Why Do You Need Java?

If you plan to use the Eclipse or Arduino IDE tools to develop your ARTIK software, or if you want to write Java code yourself, you will first need a working Java installation on your development workstation. Only install the software you require to get the job done. Installing too much software is inefficient, because unnecessary software processes may be started automatically. They will waste your available CPU and memory capacity.

Current practice in the industry is to not install a Java runtime environment (JRE) by default. You should be aware of the security implications and risk factors of installing Java and make sure you keep the installation up to date. You should upgrade to at least Java version 8 and consider all older versions to be deprecated.

It is a good idea to install the developer tools for Java. These are delivered as the standard edition Java development kit (JDK). This installs a JRE for you. However, be careful not to include the developer tools in your shipping production version, because this increases the risk of intrusion.

Checking the Java Version on Windows

Windows usually has a JRE installed. To find out if you have Java installed already on Windows and to see what version it is, follow these steps:

1. Launch the Windows Start menu.

2. Click on the Programs item.

3. Find the Java program listing.

4. Click on the About Java item to see the Java version.

Checking the Java Version on Mac OS X

Mac OS does not have Java installed by default. To check whether you have installed Java as a byproduct of using other tools, open a Terminal window and type these commands to see what version of Java is used for browser plugins:

```
cd /Library/Internet\ Plug-Ins/JavaAppletPlugin. plugin
. /Contents/Home/bin/java -version
```

This will echo the following information about the JRE if it is installed:

```
java version "1. 8. 0_60"
Java(TM) SE Runtime Environment (build 1. 8. 0_60-b27)
Java HotSpot(TM) 64-Bit Server VM (build 25. 60-b23, mixed mode)
```

Type the following command to check on the default version of the Java development kit (JDK), if you have one installed. This is also good for Linux operating systems:

```
java -version
```

The output is similar, but it may not be the same version as the browser plugin.

Checking the Java Version on Linux

Type the following command to check the default version of the JDK installed on your workstation:

```
java -version
```

This command should also work inside your ARTIK, because there are scenarios where having Java installed in an ARTIK are also helpful.

Installing Java

Java was originally developed by Sun Microsystems but is now owned and maintained by Oracle (that's the big database company). They provide installation guidelines for all the supported platforms. The goal of Java is to create a common platform for software to run on, regardless of the underlying operating system. The code you write is converted into tokens (bytecode) and interpreted by a virtual machine (the JVM) when you run the application. Find all the download links and installation instructions for Windows, Mac OS, and Linux versions of Java here:

```
http://docs.oracle.com/javase/8/docs/technotes/guides/install/install_
overview.html
```

Go to the following link on the Java website for additional details about installing and upgrading Java. Choose an operating system with the drop-down menu:

```
https://www.java.com/en/download/help/index_installing.xml
```

A JDK is recommended when you plan to develop software with Eclipse IDE. A JRE takes up much less space but lacks some of the tools you need when you are using Eclipse. JDK downloads are available from this page:

```
http://www.oracle.com/technetwork/java/javase/downloads/jdk8-
downloads-2133151.html
```

Check that you install the correct 32- or 64-bit version of Java that matches the version of Eclipse you plan to use. Both Java and Eclipse must be either 32- or 64-bit versions. A 64-bit Eclipse cannot run on top of a 32-bit Java virtual machine (JVM). Mac OS X is now always 64-bits.

You may see more than one version of the JDK available for installation. Usually, the later one is a better choice. Read through the release notes to understand any limitations or special considerations for your operating system. Keep a copy of the release notes in case you hit any snags later. A work-around for your problem is often described in the notes if it is well known.

Do You Need Java on Your ARTIK?

You only need the run-time environment (JRE) to run Java applications, and you certainly should not ship a production version of your project with a JDK installed. With the memory footprint limitations inside the ARTIK, it is probably a good idea to compile outside of the module and load the binary in from your development workstation.

Log in to your ARTIK and type the following command to see which version of Java is installed:

```
java -version
```

You should see a message like this echoed back:

```
java version "1. 8. 0_33"
Java(TM) SE Runtime Environment (build 1. 8. 0_33-b05)
Java HotSpot(TM) Client VM (build 25. 33-b05, mixed mode)
```

Check that this is the version you need and run an update if necessary. You should prioritize updates of the JRE on your ARTIK to keep it secure. Any unfixed intrusion vectors will compromise the security of your product. Robust security protection comes from good design and efficient support in the field. Consider designing a reliable support mechanism for deploying updates once people have purchased your product. Designing security into your product from the start is vital, or you could be faced with much pain and grief later, not to mention expense.

Summary

Getting the right combination of tools installed on your development workstation and the necessary client-side support for running your applications on the ARTIK might take you some time. Instead of installing everything, consider all of the alternatives and install just the software development tools you need on an as-needed basis.

Java is slightly different in that it is an enabling technology. Because it makes all platforms look very similar (the original goal was to make them all look the same), some software tool builders choose to write the software tool applications in Java. This allows them to maintain just a single version with some confidence that it will work on all the available operating systems.

It is worth investing some effort to use Java as a supporting tool for your development workstation. This depends on Java being available at the same version on all platforms. A consistent release strategy for all supported devices and platforms is well managed by Oracle these days.

Installing a Java development kit (JDK) in your ARTIK module is possible, but avoid running applications in a Java virtual machine (JVM) in your ARTIK unless it is mandated by your product design. Cross-compiled applications will yield a much better performance. They will be more efficient and use less memory.

CHAPTER 12

Using Eclipse IDE

Installing, Configuring, and Using Eclipse IDE

The Eclipse IDE tool is a versatile platform for developing applications for a variety of target platforms using different languages. Cross-compiling from C language to an executable that runs in the ARM processors in an ARTIK module is well supported. Cross-compiling from other languages is possible with some additional work setting your systems up. Anything that the GNU Compiler Collection (GCC) compiler can process is viable to start with.

The ARTIK 5 and 10 modules share a similar ARM CPU architecture for which there is already a plugin support kit that equips Eclipse with the tools for cross-compiling the applications. Use the Eclipse IDE on your development workstation to create applications for the ARTIK modules. Build the applications there and install the finished executable image across the network onto your target ARTIK module.

Before You Install Eclipse IDE

The Eclipse Integrated Development Environment (IDE) is built on a Java foundation platform. Therefore, Eclipse will work on any operating system that supports a viable Java virtual machine (JVM) and has a user interface. Install a JVM if it is not already present by installing a Java runtime environment (JRE). If you plan to develop software, a Java development kit (JDK) is better.

Use a JVM that is compatible with the version of Eclipse you plan to install. If you plan to install a 64-bit version of Eclipse, you should have a 64-bit version of the JVM to run it on. You may have multiple versions of the JVM installed on your workstation for different tasks. Knowing which one you are using is important. Keep notes and document everything you do, step by step.

Getting Help

The Eclipse IDE has been available for a long time. There are plenty of books available that will help you with every aspect of it. Start with these web pages if you want to read the online help provided by the Eclipse developers:

```
https://eclipse.org/users/
http://help.eclipse.org/mars/index.jsp
```

© Cliff Wootton 2016

C. Wootton, *Beginning Samsung ARTIK*, DOI 10.1007/978-1-4842-1952-2_12

If this does not solve your problem and you cannot find a book that covers it, use a search engine to find out what other Eclipse users have posted online. Often they will post exactly the question you want answered, and one of the more expert users will have explained how to solve the problem. Be sure to read all the comments and replies in case the best answer is at the end of the discussion. This is one of the better aspects of the Internet–the community helps one another. Be nice and ask your questions politely. If you find a better solution, give something back and help the rest of the community by posting it online for everyone else to enjoy.

Installing Eclipse IDE

If you install a version of Eclipse that lacks any specific tools, they can be added later from within the IDE. If you installed a Java-only development-oriented version, add the C/C++ tools later on when you need them. Study the Eclipse installation guide for more detailed help with installing Eclipse IDE tools:

```
https://wiki.eclipse.org/Eclipse/Installation
```

The online Samsung developer documentation for supporting Eclipse on Windows is comprehensive. There are subtle differences when installing on Mac OS X that are covered here as a supplement to that help.

Linux users are well supported by the Eclipse organization. A development workstation running Linux is a great foundation for building an Eclipse-based toolkit, but it will work on Windows or Mac OS X too.

Eclipse on Mac OS X

The Samsung developer web pages describe how to install Eclipse and build a toolchain on a Windows workstation. If you use a Macintosh workstation for development, there are some details of the installation and deployment of ARM cross-compiling tools that need special attention. The guidelines hosted by the Eclipse developers provide additional detailed help for installing Eclipse IDE on Mac OS X. A summary walkthrough for OS X is described here, but if you want to understand it more thoroughly, the Eclipse documentation will provide more insights. The installation steps are summarized as follows:

1. Decide whether to run 32-bit or 64-bit Eclipse IDE. The 64-bit option is optimal, and on a Macintosh it is the preferred solution because Mac OS X is fundamentally 64-bit throughout.

2. Install a compatible JDK with an embedded JVM.

3. A Java Runtime Environment (JRE) is installed with your JDK.

4. Check the versions to make sure everything was updated.

5. Download the Eclipse IDE installer from the following URL. Choose Eclipse IDE for C/C++ Developers to start with:

   `http://www.eclipse.org/downloads/packages/eclipse-ide-cc-developers/mars1`

6. The download is delivered in a compressed archive. Extract the files from the archive and install the package in the right place for your operating system.

7. Configure your Eclipse IDE application to use the right JVM. Choose the correct one if you have several versions installed. Inspect the `Eclipse.ini` document description for guidance:

   `https://wiki.eclipse.org/Eclipse.ini`

8. Start up your Eclipse IDE application. You should see a window telling you what version it is. The appearance of this window will change with each release of Eclipse IDE:

9. Eclipse will then ask you to choose a location for the workspace folder. This is where Eclipse maintains all your projects. If you are using source code–management software such as Git or SVN, you may already have a workspace set up.

10. Eclipse then presents the Welcome screen:

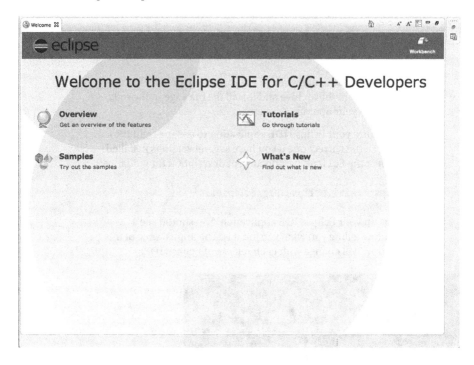

11. Read the "Getting Started" documentation here:

https://eclipse.org/users/

Workspace Preferences

The IDE can also be configured around your needs. This is all done via Workspace Preferences. When you install plugins or add tools for new languages, the preferences panel will inherit extra panes and tabs for you to configure options specific to those tools. Always take a look after adding new tools in order to tune the new behavior to your needs. There are some helpful guidelines in the GNU ARM for Eclipse IDE web pages:

http://gnuarmeclipse.github.io/eclipse/workspace/preferences/

Here are the configuration options for the base install:

- Auto-saving control
- Text-file encoding format
- Text editor presentation

- Line numbers

- Editor folding

- Code formatting

- Build configurations

- The build console appearance and behavior

- Documentation management with Doxygen

- Debugging

- Previous application persistence (auto open/debug)

Adding New Tools to Your Eclipse IDE

Follow these steps to add new tools to your Eclipse IDE:

1. Locate the Help menu and click on it.

2. Choose the "Install New Software..." option.

3. Choose one of the predefined sites or enter the details of one that is not listed by default.

4. Set any options relating to the way that tools are listed to filter the sub-set you want to see.

5. Eclipse now searches that repository for additional tools that are compatible with the version you have installed.

6. Choose the tools you want to add.

7. Click on the Next> button.

8. Eclipse builds an installation plan and downloads the components it needs to install the selected tool or tools you chose.

9. Click on the Next> button.

10. Accept the terms of the software license for the chosen tools.

11. Click on the Finish button to run the installation.

12. You can elect to run the installation in the background if you wish to carry on working while the installation takes place.

13. Eclipse presents a Restart dialog to complete the installation.

14. Click on the Yes button.

15. Eclipse then closes and restarts itself automatically to load the new tools so they are ready for you to access them.

What Is a Toolchain?

The toolchain is a collection of small utilities and command-line tools that help your build process. They are invoked one by one as needed by the IDE when you run a project build. The IDE expects them to be there, but for ARM development some of the components are missing. A manual installation is necessary, because the ARM-specific tools are not installed on operating systems by default.

Installing Support for ARTIK Development

The Eclipse IDE is not yet available in a pre-packaged format ready for ARM development. Solve that by installing the GNU ARM Eclipse plugin to cross-compile for the ARTIK CPU and add toolchain support to bind it to the Eclipse IDE application-building support.

Work carefully through this process and take plenty of notes at each step. Some tools require the location of things you installed earlier, and taking careful notes on what you configured will pay dividends later. The main steps are:

- Install the GNU plugins that support compiling for ARM-based computers. This tells the GCC compiler about the ARM chips. It can use the plugins to compile the source code appropriately.

- Install a toolchain that can be invoked to gather the component parts of your application together and create an executable.

- Install debugging support. Working through your application to isolate problems is much easier with a debugger.

- Configure your IDE to make remote connections to the target ARTIK module you are working on. This needs an ARTIK module that can be reached via your local area network (LAN).

Samsung provides detailed instructions for adding ARM cross-compiling tools to your Windows- or Linux-based Eclipse IDE. Configuring your Eclipse IDE for ARM cross development on a Mac OS platform is different than for Windows because some of the tools that the Windows-based approach uses are just not available on Mac OS. This developer guide web page has more details:

```
https://www.artik.io/developer/documentation/developer-guide/setting-up-
eclipse.html
```

Getting this to work on a Macintosh requires a few different steps, mainly because the Linaro toolchain is not available for Mac OS X. The installation process cannot be completed without installing an alternative to Linaro. In addition, the user interface is organized slightly differently. The guidance in the Samsung instructions for Windows is still helpful as an illustration of what you need to replace.

Follow the steps carefully if this is the first time you have done this sort of installation. If you change something and it is not done properly, you might run into trouble with subtle problems later on.

Why Build Tools Are Needed

This information is specific to a Windows installation only. The Windows build tools are necessary because they are provided by default on a UNIX workstation such as Linux or Mac OS but not on Windows. The IDE needs to have the make tools available in order to build your app. The GNU ARM Eclipse Windows build tools are recommended because they integrate your cross-compiling tools better than the external make.exe utilities that might process file-name paths incorrectly. A helpful description and installation guidelines are available on the GNU ARM Eclipse IDE support pages here:

http://gnuarmeclipse.github.io/windows-build-tools/
http://gnuarmeclipse.github.io/windows-build-tools/install/

Ensure the corresponding build tools are available on a Macintosh by installing Xcode first. Xcode is offered free of charge from the Apple Macintosh App Store. We will not be using Xcode directly as an IDE, but it includes some very useful stand-alone tools for controlling project builds and comparing different versions of the source code.

Installing the GNU ARM Eclipse Plugin on Mac OS X

Although the installation steps are covered briefly here, there is a very useful reference page in the GNU ARM Eclipse support website. That page describes the inner workings of the cross-compiler and what to do if anything goes wrong:

http://gnuarmeclipse.github.io/plugins/install/

Use the Eclipse New Software Installer configuration tool in the IDE to configure a toolchain that creates an ARM executable for the correct architecture. The remote system connections and secure copy tools are fine though. Follow these steps to add the necessary plugins to your Eclipse IDE:

1. Start up your Eclipse IDE as normal.

2. Locate the Help menu and click on it.

3. Choose the "Install New Software..." option from the Help menu.

4. Click on the Add button.

5. Type this text into the Name textbox:

   GNU ARM Eclipse Plug-ins

6. Type this URL into the Location textbox:

   http://gnuarmeclipse.sourceforge.net/updates

7. Click on the OK button.

8. Eclipse now searches that location for the plugin you described.

9. Set any options relating to the way that tools are listed to filter the sub-set you want to see.

10. Choose the GNU ARM Cross-Development tools.

11. Click on the Next> button.

12. Eclipse builds an installation plan and downloads the components it needs to install the selected tool or tools you chose.

13. Click on the Next> button.

14. Accept the terms of the software license for the chosen tools.

15. Click on the Finish button to run the installation.

16. On Mac OS X, you may get a warning about installing unsigned software. Click on the OK button if you trust the source that the code was downloaded from.

17. Eclipse then presents a Restart dialog to complete the installation.

18. Click on the Yes button.

19. Eclipse then closes and restarts itself automatically to load the ARM cross-development tools so they are ready for you to use.

Installing an ARM Toolchain on Mac OS

There are some generic UNIX build tools that you will need for your ARM toolchain. Installing Xcode adds some of these for you. The Xcode IDE cannot be used on its own for developing ARM applications that run in an ARTIK module. Installing an Eclipse toolchain in addition to Xcode is a good alternative. Adding the GNU ARM Toolchain to your Eclipse IDE is described on this web page:

http://gnuarmeclipse.github.io/toolchain/install/

Note carefully where you install this toolchain so as to be able to enter the details into projects that need to use it later. Read the Samsung developer documentation for instructions on installing toolchains on Windows or Linux to get some insights into what we are about to do. Follow these steps to install the toolchain on your Macintosh:

1. Download the toolchain installer from this URL:

   ```
   https://launchpad.net/gcc-arm-embedded/+download
   ```

2. The installer file name will look like this (although the version numbers may be different):

   ```
   gcc-arm-none-eabi-4_9-2015q3-20150921-mac.tar.bz2
   ```

3. Open a Terminal window on your Macintosh with the Terminal application in the utilities folder:

   ```
   {your_boot_disk} ➤ Applications ➤ Utilities ➤ Terminal app
   ```

4. Locate the downloaded file.

5. Change the working directory in your Terminal window to the same directory as the downloaded file. The location depends on where you normally put downloads.

6. There is a trick for going to a shortcut. Type cd followed by a Space character, but do not press the [Return] key yet.

7. Now look in the title bar of the window for the folder containing your download.

8. Click and hold for a moment until the icon is highlighted. Then drag and drop it onto your Terminal window. Magically, the Finder and the Terminal application will collaborate to work out the fully qualified path to that folder. They automatically convert it to a directory reference and fill it in for you.

9. Now press the [Return] key, and your terminal session will go to the correct working directory.

10. Type the following command and press the [Return] key to check that the downloaded file is visible. Copy and paste the name into a temporary clippings text file to use later:

    ```
    ls -la
    ```

11. Type the following command to display the download location and copy it to your clippings file later:

    ```
    pwd
    ```

12. You should see a path displayed in a conventional UNIX fashion like this:

```
/Users/cliff/Downloads
```

13. Check that the recommended location for installing these tools already exists. This command will create it if it does not exist:

```
sudo mkdir -p /usr/local
```

14. You will be prompted for your administrator account password at this point unless you are already logged on as a super user. The password privilege will persist for a short while. You may not be asked a second time if you use the sudo command again right away, as there is a timeout built into the authentication support:

15. Now go to the destination directory where you plan to install the toolchain:

```
cd /usr/local
```

16. Unpack the previously downloaded archive file and place the contents into the destination directory. The command format is illustrated here, followed by an example:

```
sudo tar xjf {path_to_download_directory}/{name_of_
downloaded_file}
sudo tar xjf /MyDownloads/gcc-arm-none-eabi-4_9-2015q3-
20150921-mac.tar.bz2
```

17. Check that the unpacking step worked with this command:

```
ls -la
```

18. You should see a listing like this:

```
drwxr-xr-x    8 root   wheel  272 19 Nov 15:02 .
drwxr-xr-x@ 13 root   wheel  442 31 Jan  2013 ..
drwxr-xr-x    6 root   wheel  204 19 Nov 15:02 gcc-arm-
none-eabi-4_9-2015q3
```

19. There may be other items listed if your /usr/local directory was already there.

20. Run a quick test to see that the compiler is functional with this command. Make sure that the path matches the name of the unpacked directory. As time goes on, version numbers will change. The name of this package will evolve as a consequence:

```
/usr/local/gcc-arm-none-eabi-4_9-2015q3/bin/arm-none-
eabi-gcc --version
```

21. You should see a message from the compiler that looks like this:

```
arm-none-eabi-gcc (GNU Tools for ARM Embedded
Processors) 4.9.3 20150529 (release)
[ARM/embedded-4_9-branch revision 227977]
Copyright (C) 2014 Free Software Foundation, Inc.
This is free software; see the source for copying
conditions. There is NO
warranty; not even for MERCHANTABILITY or FITNESS FOR A
PARTICULAR PURPOSE.
```

22. If you look inside this package you will find a collection of Read-Me text files, license messages, and PDF documentation files. Explore this from the Finder or unpack a separate copy of the archive there. Inspect that copy or dismantle it without damaging anything in your installed toolkit. Keeping an extra copy of the PDF documentation nearby for quick reference is also a good idea.

23. Your toolchain is now installed. You may want to install other toolchains for different building processes. Make sure you note the correct path to this one so you can call it up to configure a development project later.

Read about semi-hosting stubs later in this chapter to resolve warning messages that the linker throws when it discovers that low-level input/output functions are not present. Further coverage of debugging is covered in Chapter 20 where you can find out about the GNU Debugger (GDB) and the Quick Emulator (QEMU) for simulating the ARM environment for testing your applications.

Configuring Your IDE for Remote Exploring

Development will proceed more quickly if you can easily copy files from your development workstation to the ARTIK module and execute commands to run scripts and applications there. If you cross-compile applications on your development system, just copy them across. Or alternatively copy the source files to your ARTIK and compile them there. Tell Eclipse to set up a Remote System Explorer and configure the connection to your target ARTIK module. This will only work if you have a viable network connection that reaches your ARTIK. The setup instructions for Windows are covered in the Samsung Eclipse Setup Guide. Execute the following instructions to set this up on the Eclipse IDE running on your Macintosh:

1. In Eclipse, click on this menu item to open a list of perspective tools:

   Window ➤ Perspective ➤ Open Perspective ➤ Other

2. Choose the Remote System Explorer item.

3. Click on the OK button. Once you have already opened the Remote System Explorer, it will be listed above the Other item in the main menu bar. Choose it directly without needing to navigate these panels.

4. Click on the New Connection icon to create a connection to your ARTIK.

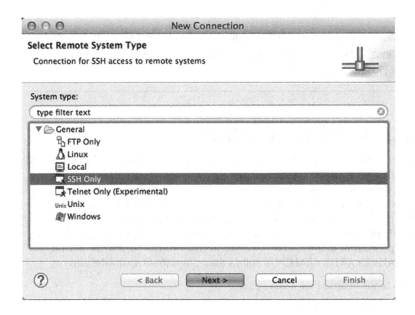

5.   Select SSH Only and enter the Host name or IP address for your ARTIK to create a new connection.

6.   Specify a name for this connection.

7.   Add descriptive text so you know what it is later.

8.   Verify the existence of the remote host.

9.   Click on the Finish button.

10. The connection is added.

11. Open the Sftp Files item to explore the remote file system.

12. Open the Ssh Shells item to execute remote commands on the system.

▼ ARTIK
   ▶ Sftp Files
   ▶ Ssh Shells

■ **Note** This is only going to work reliably if your ARTIK has a statically defined IP address or if you have a local DNS that is smart enough to know what the IP address is for a DHCP-configured node on your network.

Setting Up a Default Toolchain

You should only do this if you plan to use your Eclipse IDE just for making ARM executable images to install on your ARTIK. If you need to build apps for different platforms, the default setup is different for every project, and you can skip this altogether. These values will be populated by default into new projects when you create them. Override these settings within the project. If you plan to work on lots of different architectures with your Eclipse IDE, this might not save you any time. It could even lead to subtle problems with building applications that will slow you down because you forgot that the default application build is for ARTIK ARM CPUs. Follow these steps to set up the defaults:

1. Go to the Eclipse Preferences panel.

2. Unfold the C/C++ item.

3. Unfold the Build item.

4. Click on the Global Tools Paths item.

5. On a Macintosh the Xcode command-line build tools are used. Set the Build Tools folder to be empty.

6. Set the Toolchain folder to the top level /bin directory inside the Toolchain folder that was installed earlier.

7. Close the Preferences panel.

8. Now any new projects will inherit these settings by default. Existing projects will not be altered and will need to be edited to use these new settings.

■ **Note** There is a small caveat to using the Xcode command-line build tools. Apple is prone to completely revising the way that Xcode works and how its internals are organized. Be very careful to check all this after upgrading Xcode when a new version is released. You might inadvertently break your ARTIK toolchain and have to diagnose why it cannot find the tools it needs because the path has changed.

Semi-hosting Stubs

When you build an embedded application with Eclipse IDE, the low-level handling of input and output has nowhere to go because the library omits the API endpoints. The runtime environment inside the ARTIK needs to provide them instead. You may need to write kernel level drivers or add new devices that map the standard input/output to the hardware you attach to the ARTIK.

Semi-hosting configurations attach external hardware or software to these points to exercise the application at runtime and capture any output it generates and feed input to it. Temporarily resolve broken links by installing debugging tools. Ultimately they should be resolved permanently with your own code that interacts with the hardware your ARTIK is embedded into. You should not put the debugging support into a shipped product design.

To get your application to compile, provide a set of stubs as part of your source code. The linker can use these to resolve any references to the missing functions. Append the code shown in Listing 12-1 to the end of your main.c and add the _ansi.h header as a #include at the top. Alternatively, create a new source file in your project and put these items there so you can resolve the broken linker references and enhance the code later.

Listing 12-1. Semi-hosting Stub Placeholders

```
... Your headers here ...

#include <_ansi.h>

... Your code here ...

int _isatty(void) { return 1; }
int _fstat(void)  { return 1; }
int _read(void)   { return 1; }
int _lseek(void)  { return 1; }
int _close(void)  { return 1; }
int _write(void)  { return 1; }
int _sbrk(void)   { return 1; }

void _exit (int status) { while(1 == 1); }
```

■ **Note** Replace these stubs with other functional code that interacts with the hardware your embedded application is running in.

Your hardware design dictates whether additional libraries of code need to be linked. The semi-hosting function calls can call debugging log functions when you test in the development workstation. When the application is moved to the ARTIK, your engineering team must write supporting code (possibly as kernel extensions) that resolves these endpoints. For example, standard output may be presented on an LCD display rather than on the serial console.

Research the installation of these open-source libraries, which are all somewhat related to one another. Then you can make an informed choice about the best one to use for your project:

- newlib
- newlib-nano
- gloss
- nosys

The newlib library is maintained by the RedHat organization. Download the source and build it first. The newlib-nano library is part of Eclipse by default and should be selectable with a checkbox in the linker properties. This version of newlib is designed to be very fast and efficient in an embedded scenario. The gloss and nosys libraries are related to newlib as sub-sets or super-sets of functionality. Experiment with them to find the optimum solution for your design, which may require custom code to interact with your own hardware.

Support for the MIPS Architecture

The ARTIK 1 module has a MIPS®32 CPU, unlike the ARTIK 5 and 10, which use ARM processors. The Eclipse IDE will need additional toolchain support for the MIPS CPU compilations.

Support for Eclipse Smart Home

The OpenHAB2 project is being built on top of the Eclipse Smart Home project. Therefore, you may want to investigate this in more detail and install additional tools to support your experiments. Go to the Git repositories for the OpenHAB project source code if you want to download and build your own installation:

https://github.com/openhab/openhab
https://github.com/openhab/openhab2
http://www.eclipse.org/smarthome/

Note that OpenHAB support is built into ARTIK 10 modules but not ARTIK 5 modules.

Making a New ARM Project

Now you are ready to create a new project and build it. Windows and Linux users can follow the instructions in the Samsung guidelines. Here is the build process based on those guidelines, but modified for Macintosh-based development workstations:

1. In your Eclipse IDE, create a new C language project. You will get offered a choice of the available project types.

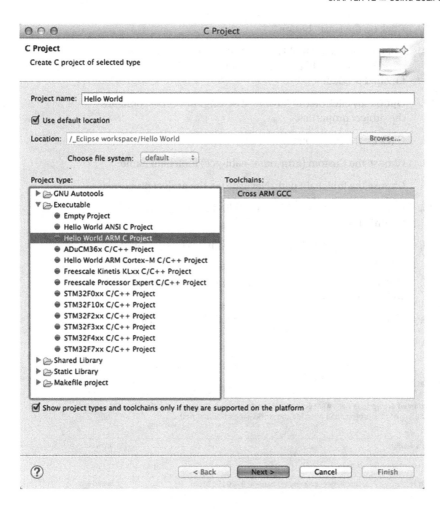

2. Enter the project name.

3. Choose the Hello World ARM C Project type.

4. Click on the Next> button.

5. Put your name as the author.

6. Add your copyright message.

7. Modify the "Hello, world" greeting text if you want to.

8. Change the "Linker semi-hosting option" textbox to the
    following string of options. Note especially the pairs of dash
    characters (--) on the start and end options:

    ```
    -Wl,--start-group -lgcc -lc -lc -lm -Wl,--end-group
    ```

9. Click on the Next> button.

10. Choose whether to build a Debug, Release, or both types of executable result. Do not ship a debug version in your finished product.

11. Optionally click on the Advanced Settings button to configure the project properties.

12. Click on the Next> button.

13. Choose the Custom (arm-none-eabi-gcc) toolchain name.

14. Choose the toolchain path. Navigate via the project properties.

15. Browse the projects collection and find the project you want to configure.

16. Select the Hello World project (for example) in the project explorer panel.

17. Open the project properties by pressing the [Command] + [I] key combination.

18. Unfold the disclosure arrow beside the C/C++ Build item.

19. Click on the Tools Paths item.

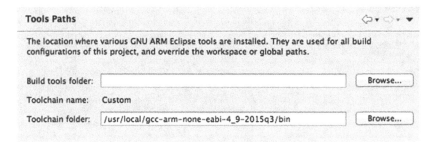

20. Click on the Browse button for the Toolchain folder.

21. Navigate to the /usr/local directory and select the top-level /bin directory within the toolchain that was installed earlier. This is why it is so helpful to keep plenty of notes about what you do.

22. Now click on the Settings item to view the tool settings.

23. Choose the target processor type with which to display the CPU architecture settings.

24. Set the ARM family value to one of the following depending on which ARTIK processor you are building your application for:

cortex-a7
cortex-a15

25. Set the Instruction Set value to ARM (-marm).

26. Now choose the Toolchains tab in the same panel.

27. Set the Name value to Custom (arm-none-eabi-gcc).

28. Set the Architecture value to one of the following depending on whether you want a 32-bit or 64-bit compatible application to load into your ARTIK:

ARM (AArch32)
ARM (AArch64)

29. Set the Prefix value to match the toolchain. This is used to construct paths to run toolchain items. Use the value arm-none-eabi- to define your prefix.

30. Click on the Apply button.

31. Click on the OK button to close the properties panel.

32. The project is now configured and ready to build.

33. Press the [Command] + [B] key combination to execute this menu item:

Project ➤ Build all

34. You should see some compiler output on the console panel that looks like this:

```
01:49:58 **** Incremental Build of configuration Debug for project
Hello World ****
make all
Building file: ../src/main.c
Invoking: Cross ARM C Compiler
arm-none-eabi-gcc -mcpu=cortex-a15 -marm -O0 -fmessage-length=0
-fsigned-char -ffunction-sections -fdata-sections -g3 -std=gnu11
-MMD -MP -MF"src/main.d" -MT"src/main.o" -c -o "src/main.o"
"../src/main.c"
Finished building: ../src/main.c
Building target: Hello World.elf
Invoking: Cross ARM C Linker
arm-none-eabi-gcc -mcpu=cortex-a15 -marm -O0 -fmessage-length=0
-fsigned-char -ffunction-sections -fdata-sections -g3 -Xlinker
```

```
--gc-sections -Wl,-Map,"Hello World.map" -Wl,--start-group -lgcc
-lc -lc -lm -Wl,--end-group -o "Hello World.elf" ./src/main.o
Finished building target: Hello World.elf

Invoking: Cross ARM GNU Create Flash Image
arm-none-eabi-objcopy -O ihex "Hello World.elf"  "Hello World.hex"
Finished building: Hello World.hex

Invoking: Cross ARM GNU Print Size
arm-none-eabi-size --format=berkeley "Hello World.elf"
   text    data     bss     dec     hex filename
   8344    2124      84   10552    2938 Hello World.elf
Finished building: Hello World.siz

01:49:59 Build Finished (took 172ms)
```

Deploy the Binary to Your ARTIK

Deploying your compiled application to your target ARTIK module is straightforward. Just open the remote shell and execute this command:

```
{project_location}/Debug/HelloWorld.elf
```

Summary

The Eclipse IDE can build applications for a variety of platforms. Today the ARTIK is the most important to you, but you can also build applications for other devices. Eclipse can use the network connectivity to deliver applications directly to the target ARTIK module. When the applications are installed, they can be run in debug mode and tethered to the GDB running on your development workstation inside Eclipse IDE. This should create a rapid cyclic development environment where you will Run ➤ Debug ➤ Fix ➤ Deploy very quickly. This will not make a fundamentally bad application design into a good one, but it will help you debug your intended behavior. Then you can turn off the debugging support and build a release version of your application for deployment to production.

The next chapter will examine an alternative to using Eclipse. The Arduino IDE is smaller and much less complex than the Eclipse IDE, but it is well suited for application designs that are architecturally similar to an Arduino project.

■ ■ ■

## CHAPTER 13

Using Arduino IDE

Installing, Configuring, and Using Arduino IDE

If your development needs are less sophisticated and do not merit the power of the Eclipse IDE, the Arduino IDE might be sufficient. This would be appropriate if you want to use the ARTIK to emulate an Arduino with its simple initialization and loop application paradigm.

Use the same Arduino IDE on your development workstation to develop applications for both your Arduino boards and the ARTIK 5 and 10 modules. These ARTIK modules share a similar ARM CPU architecture. The libArduino plugin support kit equips the Arduino IDE with the tools needed to cross-compile applications for installation on your ARTIK. The ARTIK will then emulate an Arduino as it runs the sketches.

An Arduino sketch is not the same as a native compiled ARTIK/ARM application. The sketch is loaded into an Arduino emulator and run via an interpreter. The benefits are that there are already many example Arduino sketches for you to use as a starting point. The downside that that performance may not be quite as fast and extending the functionality is limited to what you could do with an Arduino.

Move the source code for the sketches to the ARTIK module and run them there in a native mode to avoid the need to cross-compile.

Although the screenshots in this chapter show the Arduino IDE running in the Macintosh user interface, the guidance is applicable to Arduino IDE running on other platforms because it works the same everywhere.

Before You Install Arduino IDE

Because the Arduino integrated development environment (IDE) is built on a Java foundation platform, Arduino IDE will work on any operating system that supports a viable Java virtual machine (JVM) and a user interface. Add a JVM if it is not already present by installing a Java runtime environment (JRE). If you intend to develop Java applications then install a Java development kit (JDK) instead.

How To

Because the ARTIK is now registered as a certified partner with the Arduino organization, the recommended source for IDE tools and advice is here:

http://www.arduino.cc/

© Cliff Wootton 2016
C. Wootton, *Beginning Samsung ARTIK*, DOI 10.1007/978-1-4842-1952-2_13

Follow these steps to install the IDE and commence developing your Arduino code:

1. Go to the Arduino website and find the downloadable software page. Version 1.6.6 or later is recommended because that can be extended to cross-compile code for the ARTIK 5 and 10 modules:

   https://www.arduino.cc/en/Main/Software

2. Choose the installer you need and download it. There are alternatives for Windows, Macintosh, and Linux. For your Linux workstation, choose a 32-bit or 64-bit version. On Mac OS X, the 64-bit version is preferred.

3. Go to the "Getting Started" page for advice on how to install the Arduino IDE. There is a section for each of the operating systems:

   https://www.arduino.cc/en/Guide/HomePage

   a. Follow these instructions to install your IDE on Windows. The Windows 7, Vista, and XP versions of Windows are covered. Windows 8 and 10 will be similar, but the names of some items in the user interface may be different:

      https://www.arduino.cc/en/Guide/Windows

   b. Installing on a Macintosh is a little easier because there are default drivers already installed and the installation process is somewhat automated. The installation process is the same for all supported versions of Mac OS X. Nevertheless, you may have an unrecognized serial connector. Refer to chapter 6 for details on the serial interface setup that establishes a connection from your development workstation to the ARTIK developer reference board. The process is similar for connecting an Arduino:

      https://www.arduino.cc/en/Guide/MacOSX

   c. Installing on Linux is only a little bit more complicated because there are so many different Linux distributions. Choose the right one and follow the instructions appropriate to your variant of Linux. There is a catch-all manually configured set of instructions for any other versions of Linux that do not have a pre-baked installer guide:

      http://playground.arduino.cc/Learning/Linux
      http://playground.arduino.cc/Linux/All

4. Now you are ready to build sketches to load into an Arduino that can be controlled from your ARTIK, or to load them directly into your ARTIK and run them there.

■ **Note** There is a competing Arduino website at http://www.arduino.org/, which is run by another organization. This also has an Arduino IDE, but it is not compatible with the libArduino from Samsung. The http://www.arduino.cc/ website is the official and authoritative source for certified Arduino resources.

Recommended Settings for Your Arduino IDE

It is worth spending a few moments adjusting the preferences in your Arduino IDE for optimum performance. Follow these steps to alter the IDE preferences:

1. Start up your Arduino IDE application.

2. Open the Preferences panel.

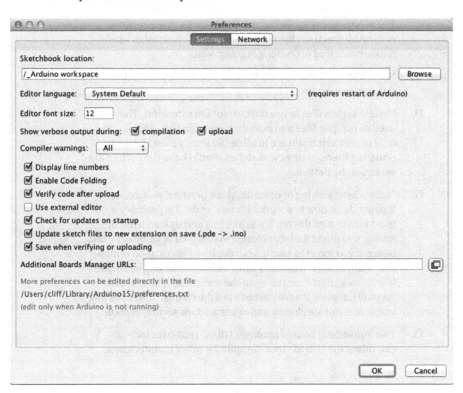

3.   Define a more appropriate location for your Arduino workspace if you prefer not to have it buried inside your Home folder.

4.   Turn on verbose messages when compiling. This is great help when debugging.

5.   Turn on verbose messages when uploading. You will immediately see whether there is a problem with installing your application if this is active. With this turned off, you may only see that an error happened but very little information about its context and detail.

6.   Set compiler warnings to all. Aim to eliminate all errors and warnings to ensure a clean application build.

7.   Turn on line-number displays. Often you will get warnings with line numbers. This helps you find the bad line of code right away.

8.   Enable code folding. This helps to de-clutter your screen by hiding blocks of code that you are not currently looking at.

9.   Turn on the option to verify code after it has been uploaded. These tests come for free at the expense of a few moments while Arduino IDE checks things for you. It is another useful reassurance that everything is going well.

10. "Check for updates on startup" tells you when your Arduino IDE application needs to be upgraded.

11. Update sketch files to use the current file extension. They used to be .pde files and now they are .ino files. This is only of concern if you are loading old legacy sketches and updating them. Your new sketches should have the correct file extension by default.

12. "Save when verifying or uploading" is a personal preference. It depends on how you work with your code. It is probably a good idea to turn this on. If you fix a bug and upload without saving, you might find that change makes your application work better. If you forget to save it, your deployed application is then one change newer than the source code, and the bug will regress (come back) next time you open the source file. The only time you will not want to save your edit is if the change makes the bug worse or if you are clumsy and delete a whole section of code.

13. The "Additional boards manager URLs" textbox is for extending the IDE to cross-compile for other architectures.

14. If you consider yourself a power user, the Preferences panel provides a link to where the preferences are stored so you can manually edit them. This is living dangerously if you do not make copies before you change things, and you should make sure that the Arduino IDE is not running when you edit the preferences.

▪ **Note** Maintain your source files via a Git repository. Alternatively, make a cloned copy to work on each time you start. Reverting to a previous version to undo some work is much easier if you planned that from the outset. Manually undoing changes is very unreliable and impossible to do once an edited file has been closed.

Installing and Configuring libArduino

The ARTIK Beta program introduces an additional library you can install into your Arduino IDE to cross-compile applications so as to run them directly in your ARTIK. If you feel that the Eclipse IDE is more than you need, the Arduino IDE is a simpler development environment to use, although it is not as flexible and powerful as Eclipse is.

To install the libArduino library, you must be running version 1.6.6 of the Arduino IDE obtained from the http://arduino.cc/ website. Do not download the IDE from the http://arduino.org/ website because it is not compatible, and the ARTIK libArduino library will not be available there. Here is the best download location:

https://www.arduino.cc/en/Main/Software

Follow these instructions to add the cross-compiler tools. This will install an ARTIK library into the Arduino IDE on our development workstation:

1. Start up your Arduino IDE.

2. Open the Preferences panel.

3. Edit the "Additional Board Manager URLs" textbox. If it is empty, just add the URL for the JSON manifest file. If there are other board managers there, click on the small icon to the right and add this one to the list:

   http://downloads.arduino.cc/libArduino/package_arduino.
   cc_linux_index.json

4. Quit and restart your Arduino IDE to read the new manifests into the board manager.

5. Open the board manager. It is located on a sub-menu in the tools menu:

```
Tools ➤ Board "{currently_chosen_Arduino}" ➤ Boards
manager...
```

6. Scroll down until you see the Samsung ARTIK modules listed.

7. Choose the Contributed items filter to reduce the size of the list:

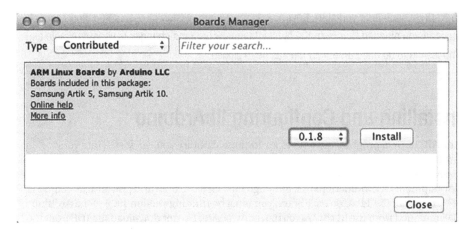

8. Select the version of the library you want to install from the pop-up menu list. The latest version is always selected by default.

9. Click on the Install button to download and install the selected version of the library.

10. The appropriate platform library is downloaded and installed into the Arduino IDE on your development workstation.

11. The board manager status is updated to reflect the version currently installed. If you want to change versions, a new pop-up list is available. Alternatively, you can replace the currently installed version of libArduino.

12. The ARTIK 5 and 10 modules will be listed in the Tools/Boards menu. Choose the one you want, and then all subsequent sketches will be compiled for that kind of ARTIK module.

▓ **Note** The Arduino IDE refers to these as ARTIK boards, but Samsung calls them ARTIK modules. It is a fine point but likely inherited because Arduino describes their products as boards.

Configuring Your ARTIK for Uploads (Board Setup)

The next step is to install software onto your ARTIK module for the Arduino IDE to communicate with. To do this "board setup" the `curl` command-line tool downloads an instruction script from `http://arduino.cc/` and passes it to the command-line shell in your ARTIK module for execution. That script will install the tools on your ARTIK automatically. Follow these steps to configure your ARTIK module:

1. Open a terminal window and connect to your ARTIK either via the serial interface or using the SSH telnet technique. Your ARTIK will need to be able to reach the Internet via your network.

2. Log in as normal with the system administrator account.

3. Type this command exactly as it appears here:

   ```
   curl -s downloads.arduino.cc/libArduino/install_artik_
   prereq.sh | sh
   ```

4. A confirmation prompt will be presented.

5. Press the [Y] key and then press the [Return] key to confirm that you want to continue.

6. The script then starts to set up various services and auto-start configurations.

7. The script will set up a port of the Android Debug Bridge Daemon (ADBD). The Arduino IDE in your development workstation understands how to communicate with this for uploading sketches.

8. The script sets up the ARTIK module to run the `avahi-daemon` process. This provides zero-configuration auto-discovery. Other nodes on your local area network can see the ARTIK module using the Apple Rendezvous/Bonjour protocols.

9. If the script is able to establish a connection to the Internet, it will then download and install the Arduino build tools, a local copy of `libArduino`, and platform configuration files.

10. When this is all complete, your ARTIK should show up in the IDE Tools/Ports menu courtesy of the auto-discovery protocols.

Uploading a Sketch to Your ARTIK with Arduino IDE

Upload sketches to your ARTIK module with a network connection or via the serial connection. The Arduino IDE can use either.

Network Upload Method

Follow these steps to upload a sketch to your ARTIK module after you have configured it successfully for an ADBD connection:

1. Make sure that both the ARTIK module and your development workstation are on the same network.

2. Open the sketch you want to upload in the Arduino IDE.

3. Open the Tools/Ports menu to reveal the list of connectible ports.

4. Choose your target ARTIK module.

5. Click on the Upload button in the Arduino IDE user interface.

6. Arduino IDE connects to the ARTIK.

7. The ARTIK module then challenges the IDE for a password.

8. Since it is logging in via the root account, the usual credentials will apply. Enter the normal password (root) and press the [Return] key.

9. Arduino IDE will upload the sketch to the ARTIK module.

10. The ARTIK module will then execute the sketch automatically.

11. If the ARTIK module does not show up in the Tools/Ports menu, check to see if it is configured for the same network.

12. Use the following command on both the development workstation and the ARTIK module and compare the results to see whether the network connectivity is consistent:

    ```
    ifconfig -a
    ```

13. The sub-net part of the address should be the same, but the last item in the IP address quad should be different. They should both have the same net mask, and the router/gateway should be the same on both.

14. If the network configuration is OK, restart the avahi daemon:

    ```
    avahi-daemon -r
    ```

Serial Upload Method

This is an experimental upload technique that is only available on Linux or Mac OS X (UNIX-based) development workstations. The necessary tools are installed via the board setup process you just executed on your ARTIK module. Follow these instructions to upload a sketch to your ARTIK:

1. Make sure your ARTIK module is connected to your development workstation with the mini USB cable. This is how you get a serial connection.

2. Log in to your ARTIK module with the root account:

    root

3. Enter the normal password and press the [Return] key.

4. Execute the following command on the ARTIK module. If it does not work, run the board setup again to ensure it is installed:

    ./watcher

5. Now open the Arduino IDE on your development workstation.

6. Open the sketch you want to upload in the Arduino IDE.

7. Open the Tools/Ports menu to reveal the list of connectible ports.

8. If the watcher is running and your development workstation is connected via a serial interface through the USB cable, your Arduino IDE should list it in the Port/Serial Ports menu.

9. Choose your target ARTIK module.

10. Click on the Upload button in the Arduino IDE user interface.

11. Arduino IDE will upload the sketch to the ARTIK module.

12. The ARTIK module will then execute the sketch automatically.

Native Sketch Compilation

Although you can create C or C++ software and compile it natively on your ARTIK, you can also create Arduino sketches and compile those natively. The script that sets up the ADBD and avahi-daemon also installs an Arduino sketch compiler. Use this command to compile a sketch and run it:

/root/compile_sketch_native {your_sketch_name}.ino

Refer to the libArduino manual for more information about the availability of this support.

Recommended Update Cycle

The libArduino kit for cross-compiling to ARTIK 5 and 10 executable images is at a very early stage of development. The developers are working on all the underlying Arduino IDE, the library code, and the toolkit. You should regularly update your IDE using the hourly build version and then check the board manager to see if a newer version of the cross-compiler kit is available.

Developing with libArduino SDK

This chapter is compatible with Beta versions of the ARTIK developer reference boards and version 3 of the *How To Guide* for libArduino. If your developer reference board is a later revision your pinouts might be different, and if your libArduino documentation is a later version, the instructions in that manual may have different steps.

Arduino Pins: Type 1 Developer Reference Board

The Type 1 developer reference board is only used for developing code for an ARTIK 1 module. This has fewer Arduino-compatible pins than the other ARTIK modules have. The Arduino-compatible pins for a Type 1 board are illustrated in Figure 13-1.

Figure 13-1. *Type 1 Arduino pins*

Table 13-1 lists the available Arduino-compatible pin connections on a Type 1 developer reference board.

Table 13-1. *Arduino-Compatible Pins on a Type 1 Developer Reference Board*

Pin Name	Description
0	Arduino serial Rx data input via the Serial object. This is the pin nearest the mounting hole in the corner of the board.
1	Arduino serial Tx data output via the Serial object
2	Arduino-compatible pin 2
3~	Use for PWM output with the analogWrite() function
4	Arduino-compatible pin 4
5~	Use for PWM output with the analogWrite() function
6~	Use for PWM output with the analogWrite() function
7	Arduino-compatible pin 7
8	Arduino-compatible pin 8
9~	Use for PWM output with the analogWrite() function. This is the pin nearest to the LCD connector.

Arduino Pins: Type 5 and Type 10 Developer Reference Boards

The Type 5 and Type 10 developer reference boards are used for developing code for ARTIK 5 or ARTIK 10, respectively. They were introduced as part of the Beta release. Although the pins are arranged in the same physical layout, the pin addresses are mapped to different locations in the virtual file system. The application source will need to be modified slightly to cope with that. Figure 13-2 illustrates the pin layout for both boards based on Beta versions. The complete set of pinouts for the other peripheral connections are examined in much more detail in the companion Apress *ARTIK Reference Guide*.

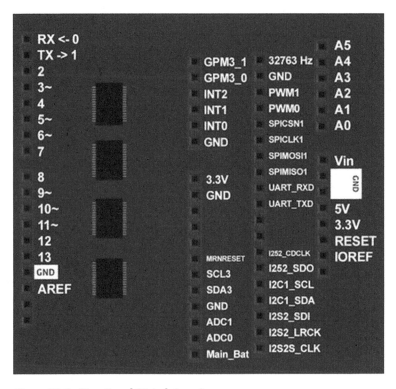

Figure 13-2. *Type 5 and 10 Arduino pins*

Table 13-2 lists the available Arduino pin connections on a Type 5 or 10 developer reference board.

Table 13-2. *Arduino-Compatible Pins on a Type 5 or Type 10 Developer Reference Board*

Header	Pin Name	Description
J26-8	RX <- 0	Arduino serial Rx data input via the Serial object
J26-7	TX -> 1	Arduino serial Tx data output via the Serial object
J26-6	2	Arduino-compatible pin 2
J26-5	3~	Use for PWM output with the analogWrite() function
J26-4	4	Arduino-compatible pin 4
J26-3	5~	Use for PWM output with the analogWrite() function
J26-2	6~	Use for PWM output with the analogWrite() function
J26-1	7	Arduino-compatible pin 7
J27-10	8	Arduino-compatible pin 8
J27-9	9~	Use for PWM output with the analogWrite() function
J27-8	10~	Use for PWM output with the analogWrite() function
J27-7	11~	Use for PWM output with the analogWrite() function
J27-6	12	Arduino-compatible pin 12
J27-5	13	Arduino-compatible pin 13
J27-4	GND	Additional grounding pin
J27-3	AREF	Reference voltage for ADC converters
J24-1	A0	Analog input 0
J24-2	A1	Analog input 1
J24-3	A2	Analog input 2
J24-4	A3	Analog input 3
J24-5	A4	Analog input 4
J24-6	A5	Analog input 5
J25-8	Vin	Reference voltage for analog inputs

System Commands

Use the systemCommand() function to execute a command-line script or run an application from within your ARTIK sketch. The function returns whatever the command outputs as a string. The syntax of the systemCommand() function is:

```
String myResult = systemCommand({command_line_instruction});
```

Detecting the Board Version

Use the systemCommand() function to examine the /proc file system and find out things about the running process. Here is an example that checks for a particular CPU type:

```
String cpu_type = systemCommand("cat /proc/cpuinfo | grep -i EXYNOS5");
```

If the result is empty, then assume you have an ARTIK 5. If there is any text in the result, it is an ARTIK 10. The conditional block of code shown in Listing 13-1 will set your board-version variable accordingly.

Listing 13-1. Setting a Board Version

```
if(cpu_type == "")
{
    cpu_type = "Artik5";
}
else
{
    cpu_type = "Artik10";
}
```

In the future, the ARTIK may be so successful in the marketplace that Samsung introduces more models. Then you will need to make this test more specific. The currently known hardware strings are summarized in Table 13-3.

Table 13-3. ARTIK Processor Hardware Identifiers

Hardware Name	ARTIK Module Type
Exynos3	ARTIK 5
Exynos5	ARTIK 10

The Serial Object

The Serial object provides an API for the serial port exported on pins 0 and 1. Arduino-compatible systems conventionally label these pins as Rx and Tx. Every message printed using the Serial object will be redirected to those pins. Interact with the Serial object by using an FTDI 3.3V TTL adapter (or similar) in your hardware.

Connect the Rx on your ARTIK module to the Tx on the other device and vice versa for a return path. Refer to Figure 13-3 to see how this is connected. This establishes a bi-directional communication channel over two wires. A simple protocol exchanges data between the connected devices.

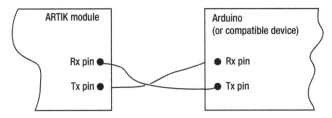

Figure 13-3. *Cross-coupled Rx and Tx pins*

Call this method first from your setup() function to initialize the Serial object with the right communications baud rate:

```
Serial.begin(9600);
```

Send a message via the Serial object line. The second example adds a new line automatically:

```
Serial.print("My text");
Serial.println("My text");
```

This is typically used to communicate between two Arduino boards, but it can talk to any compatible serial interface. This is a way to communicate with legacy broadcast equipment via an RS232 or RS485 interface. Old semi-redundant hardware can be given a new lease on life in a modern broadcast or recording studio if only your master control system can tell it what to do.

The Serial1 Object

This is a useful debugging output if you logged in to the ARTIK command line via a network connection. The Serial1 object manages the serial port where you usually perform a login. Using this serial port will wipe out the login shell. Make sure your command line is connected over a network connection via ssh before launching a sketch that uses the Serial1 object. The Serial1 object is mapped to different logical devices on the ARTIK 5 and 10 modules. Table 13-4 summarizes the devices for each ARTIK module type.

Table 13-4. *Serial1 Object TTY Addresses*

Model	TTY Device
ARTIK 5	/dev/ttySAC2
ARTIK 10	/dev/ttySAC3

The DebugSerial Object

Printing output to the DebugSerial object uses the /dev/console virtual device. Call this method first from your setup() function to initialize the DebugSerial object with the right communications baud rate:

```
DebugSerial.begin(115200);
```

Interact with the DebugSerial object to send a message with this method:

```
DebugSerial.println("My text message");
```

Pin Modes

There are two sets of pins in the Arduino design, and these are carried over to the ARTIK modules. The digital pins (labelled 0 to 13) can be set for input or output. Some of the pins can be driven with a pulse-width modulated (PWM) square wave to create a pseudo-analog output. The analog pins (labelled A0 to A5) are always used for input, and the pin-mode setting is unnecessary.

When you write code for the ARTIK with the Arduino IDE, it follows the tradition of the Arduino when you interact with the digital input/output pins. Use the pinMode() function to control whether the digital pins are connected to drivers (output) or sensors (input). The pinMode() function syntax is as follows:

```
pinMode({pin_number}, {pin_mode});
```

Where {pin_number} is in the range 0 to 13 and {pin_mode} can be INPUT or OUTPUT.
Both of these values are defined as manifest constants. The internal value these symbols represent is irrelevant provided you use the manifest constant names in your source code. The correct value will be inserted automatically when you compile your application. It is important that you use the manifest constants consistently everywhere. For example:

```
pinMode(13, OUTPUT);
```

■ **Note** The pulse-width modulation (PWM) should be described as pulse-width strobing when it is used to drive an LED to control the apparent brightness. The human eye has persistence of vision that this PWM approach exploits. If the retina worked instantly and humans had no persistence of vision, the individual flashes would be visible. Persistence of vision aggregates the LED illumination and averages it out over time so humans perceive an apparent dimming effect at lower duty cycles.

Reading Digital Input Pin Values

If a digital pin mode is set to INPUT, read the incoming values that are controlled by a switch or sensor. Use the digitalRead() function to acquire the value, like this:

```
myValue = digitalRead({pin_number});
```

Where {pin_number} is in the range 0 to 13. For example:

```
buttonState = digitalRead(2);
```

Setting Digital Output Pin Values

After you have set the pin mode to OUTPUT, set the value of a digital pin to HIGH or LOW. You do this with the digitalWrite() function. If you are driving a low-current circuit such as a single LED indicator, the ARTIK should be able to provide enough current to illuminate the LED provided you current-limit the circuit with an appropriate resistance. The correct resistance depends on the supply voltage and the LED being used. In the Samsung tutorial a 220Ω resistor is used, but LED indicators come in a variety of voltage and current configurations, and that resistor may not be correct for your device. Here is a useful calculator and another page with some theory for working out an appropriate value:

```
http://led.linear1.org/1led.wiz
http://electronics.stackexchange.com/questions/17179/
```

Drive a higher-current device by amplifying the switching value with a power transistor, or use it to operate a relay, solenoid, or thyristor. If you are trying to control mains-powered equipment then you should include an opto-isolator to keep you or your ARTIK from being fried. The digitalWrite() function syntax for this is:

```
digitalWrite({pin_number}, {pin_value});
```

Where {pin_number} is in the range 0 to 13 and {pin_value} can be HIGH or LOW.

Both of these values are defined as manifest constants. The constants will substitute the correct values when you compile the application. For example:

```
digitalWrite(13, HIGH);
```

■ **Note** On the early Alpha release ARTIK developer reference boards, the voltage of the HIGH and LOW values are reversed when compared with the Beta boards, which set the levels correctly. Setting a digital pin to HIGH on an Alpha developer reference board is the equivalent of setting it to LOW on a Beta board and vice versa for setting it LOW. If in doubt, check with a voltage meter.

Setting Analog Output Pin Values

After you have set the digital pin mode to OUTPUT, set the value of that pin to an analog value. Similar to an Arduino, the ARTIK is not actually setting a continuously variable analog value, but rather is defining the duty cycle of a pulse-width modulated square wave. This is still, strictly speaking, a digital output.

Set the pin value with the analogWrite() function. The pulse train runs at a constant rate, but the width of the pulses is adjusted to a value proportional to the input value. This pulse train operates at different frequencies according to the kind of device it runs on. The implementation of the ARTIK module hardware is different than that for the Arduino. Clocks and timers in an ARTIK module run at a different frequency, which you should check if it is important to your implementation. The same current-limiting concepts that would apply in the Arduino environment also apply here. The analogWrite() function syntax is:

```
analogWrite({pin_number}, {pin_value});
```

Where {pin_number} is in the range 0 to 13 and {pin_value} is between 0 (always off) and 255 (always on). For example:

```
analogWrite(13, HIGH);
```

The pulse width varies according to the value, as shown in Figure 13-4, while the frequency remains constant.

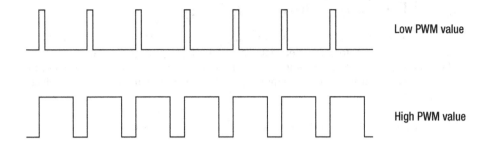

Figure 13-4. Pulse-width modulation

Once you set the value, the pin will output a continuous stream of pulses whose width is proportional to the value. Subsequently calling analogWrite(), digitalRead(), or digitalWrite() on that pin will halt the output of the PWM pulse train.

If you want a genuinely analog varying-voltage output, use the digital pins to control the inputs to a digital-to-analog converter (DAC). Adjust the DC voltage output precisely or generate other waveform shapes by converting a stream of digital sample values to voltages.

Reading the Analog Inputs

When you interact with sensors, everything comes down to measuring a value. Physical sensors are often based around changes in electrical resistance. The modern sensor components have a lot of input intelligence and present meaningful values mapped into a range the Arduino and ARTIK can understand.

Read the incoming values on the analog inputs, which can be controlled by a valuator or sensor. These inputs are completely separate from the digital pins. The input is connected to an analog-to-digital converter (ADC) that yields a numeric value between 0 and 1023. Use the analogRead() function to acquire the value, like this:

myValue = analogRead({pin_number});

Where {pin_number} is between 0 and 7. For example:

sensorValue = analogRead(2);

Serial Peripheral Interface (SPI)

The ARTIK emulates an SPI connection on pins 11, 12, and 13. The companion *ARTIK Reference Guide* goes into much more detail about these peripherals. Read the following Wikipedia article to find out more about SPI. This implementation emulates the Arduino UNO outputs. The Arduino UNO is popular and widely used with many example projects you can study and repurpose to work on the ARTIK:

```
https://en.wikipedia.org/wiki/Serial_Peripheral_Interface_Bus
```

Detecting Interrupts

One way of triggering an action based on a button press is to register an interrupt handler. A suitable interrupt-handling function must be declared first. Use the following function to set one up:

```
attachInterrupt(13, interruptHandler, FALLING);
```

Now, when the value on digital input pin 13 goes from HIGH to LOW, the interruptHandler() function will be called automatically.

Pausing for Breath

You may notice that your ARTIK module heats up when it is running. If the CPU is running at 100 percent utilization, you may be working it harder than is necessary. Keeping your ARTIK running continuously may not be needed, and it could just be "busy-waiting." If you are driving indicators, strobe the LEDs to conserve power. This works because the human eye has persistence of vision and perceives the light as if it were on all the time. You should also think in eco-friendly terms when designing your code. Your ARTIK is likely to be running from a limited battery supply when it is in a mobile situation. Eke out that battery capacity by adding delay() functions after you do some useful work if it is not necessary to repeat the task again immediately. This is appropriate when you are checking for user input, but not in the middle of an audio-sampling loop. The syntax for the delay() function is as follows:

```
delay({millisecond_time_value});
```

For example:

```
delay(1000);
```

Powersaving Mode

Control whether your CPU is running in powersave or performance mode with these two function calls:

```
goPowerSave();
goPerformance();
```

Track the powersaving state by storing a flag value inside the application. Switch states based on the flag value. Then manage the flag value by assigning a TRUE value to it according to the needs of your application. You should define the type of the powersave variable to get an unambiguous Boolean test. See the example in Listing 13-2:

Listing 13-2. Powersave Example

```
// Test this variable later on in your application code with a conditional
branch
// Define the type and set the default value to TRUE
// Change the value when your application needs to switch the powersave mode

Binary powersave = TRUE;

... more code here ...
... powersave value might be set or cleared when needed ...

if(powersave)
{
    goPowerSave();
}
else
{
    goPerformance();
}
```

Compiling and Running Sketches Natively

When you install the Arduino support into your ARTIK, you also make available the Arduino sketch compiler. Invoke that directly on a sketch inside your ARTIK and run it natively from the command line. Follow these steps to create and run a sketch directly in your ARTIK:

1. Log in to your ARTIK from a terminal app.

2. Use the cd command to go to a safe working directory.

3. Use the vi editor to create a sketch file with the code you want to run, or import one from your development system. The file will have an .ino file extension. The example calls it my_sketch.ino for now.

4. Compile and run your sketch with this command:

```
/root/compile_sketch_native my_sketch.ino
```

Where to Find Out More

The Samsung ARTIK developer documentation has a few interesting tutorials that explain how to connect up switches and LED indicators and then interact with them from your code. The libArduino How-To Guide also has useful information about programming your ARTIK in a similar way to an Arduino. Check out the documentation pages here:

```
https://www.artik.io/developer/documentation/tutorials/
```

Elsewhere on the Internet there are many IoT resources coming online. The Hackster·IO blog is also another useful resource. If you want to study Arduino projects and adapt them, the Adafruit tutorials are very helpful. There are good examples on the Instructables blog. The Temboo cloud-based development environment generates code that you can copy and paste into your own projects. See the following:

```
https://learn.adafruit.com/
https://www.hackster.io/
http://www.instructables.com/
http://www.temboo.com/
```

The Arduino reference library is a good source of knowledge about API calls. Since the ARTIK sets out to be Arduino compatible, the API should be the same, although there may be a few small differences. There are features that the ARTIK modules have that are not part of the standard Arduino design. The ARTIK module functionality should be considered a super-set of this Arduino reference. Consult the Arduino reference Home page here:

```
https://www.arduino.cc/en/Reference/HomePage
```

Troubleshooting

There are many ways that software can go wrong. Nobody can possibly predict every problem you will encounter, but here are a few that cropped up during the research for this book.

Managing the Type 5 vs. Type 10 Pin-Number Differences

The pin numbering on the developer reference boards is different for each board type. Be especially careful with the Type 5 and Type 10 boards released as Beta products, because although the pins are presented in a similar way, the mapping of the pin numbers is not identical. Code that works on an ARTIK 10 running in a Type 10 developer reference board will not work on an ARTIK 5 without recompiling.

You can detect the kind of ARTIK you are using from inside your application by inspecting the /proc/cpuinfo virtual file-system location and making the appropriate changes dynamically.

A static approach would create a manifest constant with a #define pre-processor directive and give it a symbolic name. Create an include file on your ARTIK 5 and your ARTIK 10 with the symbolic name mapped to the correct pin for each module type. This abstracts the problem out of your main source code.

Dynamic software detection of the type of ARTIK your code is running in is a better approach. Then you can create a single instance of the source code that will compile and run on different types of ARTIK modules.

CPU Utilization at 100 Percent

If you notice that your ARTIK gets very hot and the CPU usage is always 100 percent, then your sketch is running with a very high priority to simulate real-time operations. Fix this by adding delay() function calls when your code needs to be inactive. Pay particular attention to this if you migrate code from projects on other platforms.

Another source of concern is processes that reach an end point and use a while(1) {} call to lock the process from continuing execution. In this case, use an exit() function instead. Your code will stop until it is called for again.

Digital Read Only Ever Reports a 1 Value

This function call should return a 1 or 0 depending on the state of what is connected to it. The pins are pulled up to a 3.3v level with a 10KΩ resistance. Your hardware needs to defeat this and ground the pin to ensure that it returns a zero value. Then the digitalRead() function should return the correct result.

Porting Projects from Other Architectures

Almost every example and library from the Arduino resources is usable, apart from anything that is tagged as architecture or as being Arduino-board specific. Modify anything that uses SPI/I2C/PWM interfaces to make the pin mapping and values you use in your repurposed code compatible with their virtual file system locations in your target ARTIK module.

Logic Levels

Earlier Alpha prototype developer reference boards had an active low output on their Arduino pins. Setting the pin value to HIGH forced the output voltage to zero instead, and setting it to LOW raised the pin voltage to 3.3v.

This is corrected on the Beta version of the ARTIK developer reference boards. If you plan to use the same code on both vintages of the reference board, your software needs to change the values you set on the pins depending on which kind of board it is running in. Measure the voltages with a multi-meter to check you are seeing the value you expect to see when you set a pin as HIGH or LOW.

Work around the difference by defining this value as a manifest constant that maps the HIGH and LOW constants and then use different header files in each developer reference board. A more complex solution would be to detect whether you are running in an Alpha prototype or Beta prototype board. You may have to infer that by inspecting the ARTIK CPU and then manually modifying an include file.

Summary

Now you have a simple alternative to using Eclipse IDE. This Arduino development tool is great for creating Arduino sketches that run directly in your ARTIK. This is one of the benefits of Samsung being a fully qualified partner of the Arduino organization. Support for the ARTIK is likely to grow in sophistication as developers get to know the libArduino library capabilities and then start to enhance them. The Arduino is one of the great success stories in open software and open hardware. The ARTIK modules can enjoy all of the upsides of that community spirit while simultaneously creating their own ARTIK community alongside.

■ ■ ■

## CHAPTER 14

Using the Command Line

Command-Line ARM Toolchains

Sometimes a command line is sufficient, instead of using the Eclipse or Arduino IDE with their sophisticated project management tools. Construct your own application-building workflow in your development workstation and create custom build scripts to compile and link your applications in whatever way you need to.

Building a working toolchain from scratch is not a trivial job. This is not something you want to attempt unless you are comfortable with systems administration on a UNIX platform. This is complex enough to merit a complete book about it.

If you build the ARM toolchain carefully, item by item, from the raw source code, you stand a better chance of success than if you just randomly pick what looks like a viable binary image. Compiling and building the toolkit on your development workstation makes it immediately more compatible with your system. Work through the process step by step and check that everything is working properly as you go.

Ubuntu Linux

A compiler package that contains a set of useful related tools is available from this website:

http://packages.ubuntu.com/precise/devel/gcc-arm-linux-gnueabihf

Toolkits are available for AMD or Intel CPU architectures. Install the correct one for your development system hardware. Use these commands on your development machine to install the cross-compilers for C and C++:

```
get install gcc-arm-linux-gnueabihf
get install g++-arm-linux-gnueabihf
```

To test the installation, create a standard hello_world.c source file and compile using this command for the C code version:

```
arm-linux-gnueabihf-gcc -o hello hello_world.c
```

© Cliff Wootton 2016
C. Wootton, *Beginning Samsung ARTIK*, DOI 10.1007/978-1-4842-1952-2_14

Use this command for the C++ version, using an appropriate `hello_world.cpp` source file:

```
arm-linux-gnueabihf-g++ -o hello_cpp hello_world.cpp
```

Debian Linux

If your development workstation is of the Debian variety, the following is a good starting point. Find out about ARM toolchain alternatives here:

```
https://wiki.debian.org/CrossToolchains
```

Mac OS X

Cross-compiling ARM applications on a Macintosh is possible, but the experience in the developer community is less well evolved than that for Linux or Windows. Some effort is needed to bring your development environment up to an equivalent capability. The GNU toolchain expects a particular version of some command-line tools that are already installed on the Mac OS command line. The Mac OS X tools are derived from a Berkeley Software Distribution (BSD) heritage that lacks some critical command-line options that GNU expects to be there (although it adds others as well). For this to work correctly, you must install additional command-line tools and ensure the GNU toolkit finds those before it finds the default BSD versions. This article is a good starting point and also leads to another that describes the necessary configuration steps:

```
http://hackaday.com/2012/12/07/building-an-arm-cross-compiler-on-osx/
http://www.benmont.com/tech/crosscompiler.html
```

You need to become familiar with the open-source installation tools MacPorts and Brew, because some packages are easiest to install with the pre-packaged kits that are used by these installers.

It is vital that you back up your development system before starting any of these installations. Make sure that you are building this on a genuinely disposable machine that you can afford to crash and burn and then flatten and reinstall everything on. This not the kind of thing to do on a machine you use to run your business or keep the family photo archive on, because there are opportunities to completely trash the file system if you are not very careful.

The term GNU is a play on words which describes a recursive acronym. GNU stands for GNU's Not UNIX. The acronym contains the acronym itself which makes it recursive. This is somewhat of a tradition in the open source community. More details here:

```
http://www.gnu.org/fun/jokes/gnu-overflow.html
https://en.wikipedia.org/wiki/GNU
```

Adding a UNIX Command Line to Windows

The ARTIK modules all run a UNIX operating system internally. Developers who host their project tools on Windows will benefit from installing a UNIX command-line environment directly on their workstations. Try out some UNIX commands directly on your local desktop to familiarize yourself before using them on your ARTIK module. Download the Cygwin installation kit from the website here:

```
http://cygwin.com/install.html
```

Make sure you use the correct 32-bit or 64-bit executable depending on the version of Windows you are running. This will install the basic kit. Choose additional packages to install by selecting them when you run the setup application. Add more of the Cygwin modules later depending on what you are doing with it. Read the guidance notes on the installer page for more information. Check out the Cygwin documentation and FAQs here:

```
https://www.cygwin.com/
https://cygwin.com/cygwin-ug-net.html
https://www.cygwin.com/faq.html
https://en.wikipedia.org/wiki/Cygwin
```

If you are not already familiar with UNIX, check out these web articles for an introduction. Spend time learning more about it and practice with the tutorial exercises:

```
http://www.lemoda.net/windows/windows2unix/windows2unix.html
http://www.admin-magazine.com/Articles/Linux-Essentials-for-Windows-
Admins-Part-1
http://www.admin-magazine.com/Articles/Linux-Essentials-for-Windows-
Admins-Part-2
http://matt.might.net/articles/basic-unix/
http://math.sut.ac.th/surrey/tutorial.html
```

UNIX I/O Streams and Redirection

The UNIX operating system is a very flexible system when it comes to input/output redirection, and there are a variety of solutions. If you don't know much about it, search online for tutorials about the standard input, standard output, and standard error streams. Then learn how to redirect them. Here are some useful resources:

```
https://github.com/pkrumins/bash-redirections-cheat-sheet
http://www.tldp.org/LDP/abs/html/io-redirection.html
http://tldp.org/HOWTO/Bash-Prog-Intro-HOWTO-3.html
http://wiki.bash-hackers.org/syntax/redirection
```

What's Where?

Knowing what the top-level directories contain will help you to find things inside your ARTIK module from the command line. These file-system paths are used to access files and devices from inside your application source code. Listing 14-1 shows a summary of the top-level directory structure.

Listing 14-1. Top-level Directory Structure

```
[/]
 !
+- [bin]          - OS command-line tools
 !
+- [boot]         - Support for the boot process
 !
+- [dev]          - Device mirrored virtual file system
 !
+- [etc]          - System configuration files
 !
+- [home]         - Home folders for user accounts
 !
+- [lib]          - Libraries of code and kernel extensions
 !
+- [lost+found]   - Files recovered by a disk repair
 !
+- [media]        - Removable media mount points
 !
+- [mnt]          - File systems' and devices' mount points
 !
+- [opt]          - Optional add-on software not part of the default OS
 !
+- [proc]         - A virtual file system with mirrors of running processes
 !
+- [root]         - System administrator home folder
 !
+- [run]          - Information about the running system since it was last booted
 !
+- [sbin]         - System administrator tools
 !
+- [srv]          - Server- and service-related data
 !
+- [sys]          - A virtual file system that mirrors the system hardware
 !
+- [tmp]          - Temporary working data purged at shutdown/reboot.
                    Only removes your items.
 !
+- [usr]          - User-provided binaries, data, and applications
 !
+- [var]          - System-related variable data storage
```

Read more about the internals of your operating system here:

```
https://en.wikipedia.org/wiki/Filesystem_Hierarchy_Standard
http://www.tldp.org/guides.html
http://www.tldp.org/LDP/Linux-Filesystem-Hierarchy/html/
```

File System Mapped Properties Inside the ARTIK

Inside your ARTIK module, the Linux operating system does some clever things to help you interact with your system. It mirrors internal values from the kernel through virtual file systems. That makes it much easier to find and read various operating properties of the system and the processes running in it. Things that were hard to do before are easier now because you can access them like regular data files. The running processes are mirrored into the file system under the /proc virtual file system tree. The /sys and /dev virtual file system trees also provide information about the operating system and its devices. The companion Apress *ARTIK Reference Guide* will go into this in much more detail. Just to whet your appetite, a couple of simple examples here will show how to query these virtual file systems for information about your system. Read the online documentation and then explore.

■ **Note**   Make sure you only read things and be careful not to write data to places that you do not understand. This is a good proverb to keep in mind: "*Only take photos. Leave nothing behind except for footprints.*"

What CPU Is Available?

Find out about the current CPU configuration of your ARTIK module with this command:

```
cat /proc/cpuinfo
```

The example shown in Listing 14-2 was run on a Type 5 Beta prototype developer reference board with an ARTIK 5 mounted on it. Your output may be different, but it will contain similar information.

Listing 14-2. Processor Info Virtual File Listing

```
processor       : 0
model name      : ARMv7 Processor rev 3 (v7l)
BogoMIPS        : 13.71
Features        : swp half thumb fastmult vfp edsp neon vfpv3 tls vfpv4
                  idiva idivt
CPU implementer : 0x41
CPU architecture: 7
CPU variant     : 0x0
CPU part        : 0xc07
CPU revision    : 3
```

```
processor         : 1
model name        : ARMv7 Processor rev 3 (v7l)
BogoMIPS          : 13.71
Features          : swp half thumb fastmult vfp edsp neon vfpv3 tls vfpv4
                    idiva idivt
CPU implementer : 0x41
CPU architecture: 7
CPU variant       : 0x0
CPU part          : 0xc07
CPU revision      : 3

Hardware          : Exynos3
Revision          : 0000
Serial            : 0000000000000000
```

You should see something similar on your ARTIK. Type this command to see what else is accessible in the /proc virtual file system:

```
ls /proc
```

If you add the -la option (ls -la /proc), the listing will mark the sub-directory items. If the listed items are just files, you can use the cat command to send them to the screen unless they contain binary information. You will learn a lot about your ARTIK module by exploring, but be careful that you only *read* the files unless you know that it is safe to *write* to them.

Detecting Current Processor Speed

Use this command to detect the current processor speed for the primary CPU:

```
cat /sys/devices/system/cpu/cpu0/cpufreq/cpuinfo_cur_freq
```

This example refers to cpu0. The secondary CPU is identified as cpu1. It has a different set of properties. There is much more for you to learn about the internals of your ARTIK module by exploring it yourself.

Connecting to Remote Web Servers

There are two useful tools already included in your ARTIK operating system for interacting with a remote web server. The wget and curl tools both provide a way to make a request to a web server and process the response into usable output. Direct the response to a file–for example to make a downloader.

The wget tool is especially good for building web spiders that can recursively traverse a web page and seek out the child pages from the links embedded within it. The curl tool has a counterpart called libCurl that encapsulates it inside your compiled C-code application. Here is a useful comparison between the different download tools:

```
http://curl.haxx.se/docs/comparison-table.html
```

Install these download tools onto your ARTIK if they provide functionality you need in addition to what the curl and wget commands can already do. The curl tool operates in a GET and PUT context. The wget tool only pulls (downloads) content from a remote system. Optionally, use the wput tool to upload content to a remote destination. The curl command is probably powerful enough for most needs. Only install wput if you need it. The major advantage with wget is that it can be used to recursively download the contents of a website without needing to process the download and create supplementary commands. You need to add your own code to do that with the curl tool.

Examples with curl

Here are a few simple examples of curl commands. This is a very useful and easy-to-learn tool. View the result of a request on a web server with this command:

```
curl http://www.example.org/
```

The raw HTML of the web page content will be displayed on your screen. This is not the same as requesting a page for viewing in a web browser; you are seeing what the web browser would have captured before it formatted and presented it to you. This is extremely useful for debugging a remote service. Redirect the output into a temporary data file to do more work with it later like this:

```
curl http://www.example.org/ > /tmp/www_example_org.html
```

The curl command can write the output to a file rather than use redirection. Accomplish the same result like this:

```
curl -o /tmp/www_example_org.html http://www.example.org/
```

In this example, the command-line option is a lowercase letter (-o). An uppercase letter (-O) tells the curl command to derive the file name from the URL request. Then the filename parameter can be omitted.

Sometimes a web server will redirect an HTTP: request to another location when a file has moved. The curl command can automatically follow that redirection with an additional option. The new redirect-following curl command looks like this:

```
curl -L http://www.example.org/
```

Sometimes, a file will be protected with an authentication challenge and response. Provide a user name and password to access the remote resource. Add that authentication with -u option:

```
curl -u {my_username}:{my_password} http://www.example.org/
```

Not all remote assets are served via an HTTP: protocol on a web server. Use curl to access files on an FTP server too. Authentication details are needed to reach the FTP server and log on to access the contents. This command downloads a file called xss.php and stores it in the current directory:

```
curl -u {my_username}:{my_password} -O ftp://ftp_server/public/xss.php
```

Put files back on an FTP server using the -T option, like this:

```
curl -u {my_username}:{my_password} -T myfile.txt ftp://ftp_server/
```

With the ability to get and put files with curl, you have the means to upload data that can be shared with other mobile devices. With this design, you are in complete control of the security. If you need something more secure and also a means of delivering shared content to other devices, use the SAMI system to exchange your content. Find out more about curl here:

```
http://www.thegeekstuff.com/2012/04/curl-examples/
https://en.wikipedia.org/wiki/CURL
http://curl.haxx.se
```

Useful UNIX Commands Inside Your ARTIK

You are probably going to spend a significant amount of time logged in to your ARTIK and living in the UNIX command-line environment there. Here are some useful tricks and tips to make that process a little easier and more convenient.

Quitting and Aborting Processes

When you initiate UNIX commands, some of them will continue running until you explicitly tell them to stop. Sometimes you do that with a [Control] + [c] key combination or a [Control] + [d] combination. If the command spawns a sub-shell, try the exit command to leave that shell and bounce back up to the calling parent shell. Some utilities expect you to type quit or bye to exit. Kill a process by checking for the process ID (PID) and using the kill -9 command on it. This sends a signal to the process that halts it right away. This is not an ideal way to stop something, but it may be necessary. Here is how:

1. Find the process ID (PID):

    ```
    ps -ef | grep {your_application_name}
    ```

2. This should display a matching process, like this:

    ```
    501 1185 1 0 2:47pm xxxxxx 0:01.16 /xxx/yyyy
    ```

3. Note the second number (1185 in this example). That is the PID for your application process. The first number is the parent PID. This may refer to your command-line shell. You should see that value repeated a few times. The application PID you are interested in will only be listed once.

4. Now kill the screen process by sending a signal to the process identified by the correct PID value. Substitute the PID value you discovered in this command:

    ```
    kill -9 1185
    ```

5. Check that it has gone by listing the processes again.

■ **Note** **DO NOT ACCIDENTALLY KILL THE PARENT PROCESS**. If you do, your workstation session might be forcibly aborted. This is a bad thing because it can corrupt files, and in extreme cases it can blow away the partition map and destroy the main hard disk. Rebooting your workstation is now the only solution unless your application was running in a sub-shell. You should run a disk repair with the fsck tool immediately in case something was broken.

Inhibiting the Debugging Messages

In the earlier Alpha prototype version of the ARTIK OS, a background-scanning process displays a status message on the console every few seconds. This soon becomes an annoyance, because if you try to edit a file, the status text breaks up the display of the edited text. Refresh the screen to correct the appearance of the file you are editing when this happens. The default configuration has changed in the Beta release, and the messages are now suppressed.

If this causes problems, there are two ways to tell the ARTIK to turn off the debugging messages that the wl_escan_handler presents every few seconds.

The simplest solution is just to hide them. The scanner still outputs the messages, but the text is redirected into a sink where they disappear. UNIX developers describe that as redirecting the output to /dev/null. Long-time UNIX enthusiasts sometimes call it the Bit-Bucket.

The more difficult solution is to stop the scanner from running, but it is always a good idea to avoid using a sledgehammer to crack a nut if there is a simpler solution. Unless you know what that scanner is doing and why it is important for it to run, stopping it could have unwanted side effects. For example, other things you do need might stop running. If you do not need the messages, type this command to suppress them:

```
dmesg -n 3
```

This sets the level at which messages to the console are suppressed or allowed. If you want to see them again, set the debugging message level to make them visible again with this command:

```
dmesg -n 7
```

If the scanner is no longer running, they will not appear, even at dmesg level 7.

Setting the Correct Date

Your ARTIK module will almost certainly have the wrong date when you unpack it and boot it for the first time. You must set the date and time manually every time it boots, unless you provide a battery backup or configure your ARTIK to call a timeserver to set the time automatically.

Use the date command with the -s option to set the date. The command should look something like the following, but make sure you use the right date and time values when you type it on the ARTIK command line:

```
date -s '2015-M-D HH:MM:SS'
```

Checking Your Memory Usage

The memory footprint of the ARTIK operating system is designed to be very small. Your application code may use significantly more memory, depending on what you do with it. Configuring additional services in the OS core may increase this memory usage. Use this command when you are logged in to your ARTIK to see how much memory is being used:

```
free -m
```

The example in Listing 14-3 illustrates a list of the memory usage captured immediately after booting an ARTIK 5 module.

Listing 14-3. Free Memory Report

```
          total      used      free    shared   buff/cache   available
Mem:        490        33       388         0           68         442
Swap:         0         0         0
```

The vi Editor (Why vi?)

If you log in to your ARTIK and explore the file system with the command line you will soon want to edit or create files. Although there are a lot of different editors available for UNIX and you may already have a favorite, the only one that is guaranteed to always be there is vi. Occasionally, systems integrators will add other text editor applications for you, but you can never rely on that happening. The vi editor is guaranteed to always be present on a UNIX system.

These days, a newer version of vi is part of the standardized UNIX toolkit. This is called vi Improved and is called up by the vim command. Old habits die hard, and if you were in the habit of typing vi, that still works and calls the vim editor anyway. The vim editor is upwards compatible, and all the reference resources online that describe how vi works should be supported by vim as well.

How to Use vi

Here are some quick reference notes about how to use vi. If you want to get deeply involved with this, there are books available on how to preset your own special keys and write macros. You will not need those advanced features for simple editing jobs. If the debugging messages are being logged to the screen, tell the ARTIK to turn them off while you use vi or else the screen becomes cluttered with text you did not type. That gets confusing very quickly. Use this command to turn the messages off:

```
dmesg -n 3
```

Open a File for Editing or Create a New One

To open a file you just describe it as the last item after any options when you invoke the vi or vim commands. This command opens a file in the current working directory. The explicit reference to the current directory is not always necessary, but there are risks in being ambiguous about things in the UNIX operating system. Both of these commands do the same thing:

```
vi myfile.txt
vi ./myfile.txt
```

This command opens a file in the parent directory:

```
vi ../file_in_parent_directory.txt
```

This command opens a file at a specific location rooted at the top-level directory in the file system:

```
vi /home/specific_file.txt
```

Inside the vi Editor

There are two operating modes when you are in a vi editing session. By default you will be in command mode. Press the letter [I] key to go into insert mode and add new text or else your keystrokes will be interpreted as commands. Now any characters you type will push the existing text rightward as they are added. Leave insert mode by pressing the [Escape] key. This modal behavior takes a bit of getting used to if you normally use a text editor in a graphical user interface (GUI).

Saving and Exiting

This is how you exit and save the edited file. Extended command mode is initiated by pressing the [:] (colon) key. The most likely command you want right now is to quit and save the file. The [w] will write the file and the [q] key will exit from the vi editor. Type this sequence of keystrokes to save and quit:

```
[:] [w] [q] [Return]
```

This command will quit and discard any edits you have made:

```
[:] [q] [Return]
```

If you are inserting or appending text, press the [Escape] key first to go back to command mode.

Command Mode

In command mode, the letter keys perform editing actions. Like the rest of UNIX, the vi commands are case sensitive. Some commands are happy to accept a number preceding them to carry out the command multiple times. You can enter an extended command-line mode by pressing the [:] (colon) key. Very often in UNIX, there is more than one way to accomplish what you want to do. This is also true for the vi editor. Table 14-1 covers the commands you will find most useful at first. It is worth spending some time to learn the others to speed up your text-editing sessions.

Table 14-1. Command Mode Keystrokes in the vi Editor

Command	Description
0 (zero)	Position the cursor at the beginning of the current line.
$	Position the cursor at the end of the current line.
i	Insert new text before the current character.
I	Insert new text before the current line.
a	Insert new text after the current character.
A	Append text to the end of the current line.
r	Replace the character under the cursor with the next character you type.
o (lower case letter o)	Create a new empty line after the current one and move the cursor to start inserting new text there.
O (upper case letter O)	Create a new empty line before the current one and insert new text there.
dd	Delete the current line.
{number}dd	Delete {number} lines. Be careful here because it is easy to delete more than you intended.
D	Delete from the cursor to the end of the line.
x	Delete the current character.
(number)x	Delete {number} characters.
X	Delete previous character to the left of the cursor.

(continued)

Table 14-1. (*continued*)

Command	Description
J	Join current and next lines into one line.
u	Undo the most recent command just done on the current line. This is very limited and not like the continuous undo on a GUI editor.
yy	Yank the current line into a buffer. This is like a clipboard cut.
{number}yy	Yank {number} lines into the clipboard buffer.
p	Put the yanked buffer text after the cursor. This is like a clipboard paste.
P	Put the yanked buffer text before the cursor. This is like a clipboard paste.
:w	Write the changes back to the current file and continue editing.
:wq	Write the changes back to the current file and quit back to the command line.
:w {filename}	Write the changes to a different file.
:w!	Force-write the changes to the current file when the file protections would normally prohibit the change.
:w! {filename}	Force-write the changes to a different file when the file protections would normally prohibit the change.
:q	Quit the editing session and discard any changes made.
:f {filename}	Change the name of the current file. Subsequent writes will use the new name.
:r {filename}	Insert the contents of the named file at the current cursor position.
:! {command}	Execute a command in the shell without leaving the editor.
:r! {command}	Execute a command in the shell without leaving the editor and insert the resulting output from it at the current cursor position.
ZZ	Write the changes to the current file and exit.
:set number	Toggle line number display.
:set autoindent	Automatically indent following lines to the same depth.
/{pattern}	Search forward for {pattern} in the current file. There are many more things you can do with searches.
?{pattern}	Search backward.
n	Repeat previous search and find the next instance.
N	Find the previous instance.
~	Switch the case of the character under the cursor.
:%s/{old}/{new}/g	Replace all occurrences of old by new in file.

Here are some reference guides to more vi commands:

```
http://www.astrohandbook.com/ch20/vi_guide.html
http://hea-www.harvard.edu/~fine/Tech/vi.html
http://www.ibm.com/developerworks/aix/library/au-vitips.html
http://www.catswhocode.com/blog/100-vim-commands-every-programmer-should-know
```

The GCC Compiler

Every UNIX operating system can compile applications from source code by default. Because of its heritage as an open-source operating system, Linux naturally takes advantage of the GCC compiler. Your ARTIK module continues this tradition and GCC works just fine inside it for native compilations. The discussions here about the GCC compiler are mainly relevant to your ARTIK module but also apply to your development workstation if you have GCC and its supporting tools installed there.

Figure 14-1. *GCC logo*

The GNU Compiler Collection (GCC) has proven to be an excellent application-building tool for many years and formed the core of the NeXT Step developer workflow before being assimilated into Mac OS X. For a long time GCC was part of the Xcode tools on Mac OS X, but it has now been replaced by Apple's own Clang/LLVM compiler. Find out the latest information about GCC here:

```
https://gcc.gnu.org/
https://en.wikipedia.org/wiki/GNU_Compiler_Collection
```

> ■ **Note** There are two important aspects of GCC. First, it is built in as a native tool inside your ARTIK module. Second, it is available by default on Linux and can be installed on Mac OS X or Windows as well. This allows you to cross-compile on your development workstation or natively compile inside the ARTIK module.

Language Support

The GCC tools are not just for compiling C code. They also include other languages, such as Fortran, Objective-C, and C++. There are experimental projects to add Pascal and other similar languages. Developers can exploit this because the application-building process is managed in two phases. First, the source code is compiled down to an intermediate form called object code. Then the application is linked together by taking the object code that you have just made and binding it with libraries of previously compiled code. Understand the mechanisms for passing parameters and making calls to functions independent of any language. Then, part of your application can be composed in a different language and integrated by the linker.

Variable containers can be described as either values or references. Objective-C adds a third possibility of calling with a selector that connects to a named function handler at runtime. This allows Objective-C code to be modified and extended after the application has been compiled and linked. This is also useful for debugging.

If you have complex mathematics algorithms or statistics analyzers written in Fortran, it is feasible to compile and link to them from a C-language application and reuse the code.

This is an advanced technique, and we'll leave it there for now, but just knowing something is possible can save you from wasting a lot of time trying to do it another way.

Supporting Libraries

The ANSI Standard C development tools include a library of code that is powerful enough to accomplish most application-development goals. By adhering to the standards-based approach, code can be recycled from other projects. Some of the code might also run in the development workstation. Compiling it with GCC and debugging it there will be easier than downloading it to the ARTIK every time for testing. Your development environment may be able to emulate the internals of an ARTIK sufficiently well that your code behaves as if it were embedded inside the ARTIK module.

If you want to develop in an object-oriented fashion, consider the GNUStep library. This is an open-source project that emulates the NeXT Step functionality in an API-compatible way. Then you can write applications in Objective-C to exploit this library. The abstraction of Model-View-Controller (MVC) techniques and other object-oriented patterns in your design could be beneficial. Find out more about GNUStep here:

```
http://www.gnustep.org/
https://en.wikipedia.org/wiki/GNUstep
```

A server-side design that runs without a visible UI would be a good starting point for an ARTIK-based project. The ARTIK modules all have a video display output. Your application could incorporate a graphical user interface presented on that display.

The Temboo support libraries are all included in the ARTIK modules. Use them to communicate with a cloud-based IoT service. Temboo will be covered in Chapter 19.

Samsung also provides a distributed IoT system that that is securely integrated with the ARTIK modules. The SAMI ecosystem will be described in Chapter 18.

GCC ARM Compiler Support

With the right support, GCC on your development workstation can compile your source code into ARM-compatible executable images. To do this you need the GCC ARM EABI kits. The setup process is different for each operating system. On Windows, the Linaro toolkit might be sufficient and is designed to work on Linux too. The Linaro toolchain is not a viable solution for Mac OS X, however, because it has not been ported to the Macintosh platform. The installation of the toolchain is different for each Linux distribution. Here are some helpful guidelines for different operating systems so as to tailor the process for your needs. Download the PDF describing how to build the toolchain from scratch here. This web page has links to release notes, installation kits, technical guides and license documents. All of the downloads are presented in a menu on the right hand side of the page:

```
https://launchpad.net/gcc-arm-embedded
```

Once you have the toolchain working for ARM processors in ARTIK 5 and 10 modules, add the support for compiling MIPS®32 binaries if you intend to develop for your ARTIK 1 modules.

Getting GCC Up and Running

The GCC compiler in your ARTIK module or development workstation can be enhanced with additional libraries. They can be added now or later on to enhance the linker compatibility with open-source projects. Your GCC compiler command will normally have a format like this:

```
gcc -L{directory_to_search} -l{library} -I{source_file} -o {output_application}
```

The -L directory to search indicates where the compiler should look for libraries, which are specified with the -l option. Both of these options can be used multiple times in more complex builds. The -I source file is a description of your code that the compiler is going to build. The output application is the name of the executable that the compiler will create when it finishes linking all the pieces together.

Some of the command-line options are position sensitive. Adding them randomly to your compiler instructions may not work unless you are very lucky. This is why an integrated development environment (IDE) in your development workstation is particularly useful–it manages the construction of these command lines for you and assembles the options in the correct order. Get more help on the command-line options here:

```
https://gcc.gnu.org/onlinedocs/gcc/Option-Index.html
```

If you get an error about cdefs.h not being found, you should install the glibc-headers and try compiling your application again. Use the dnf or yum installer tools like this:

```
yum reinstall glibc-headers
dnf reinstall glibc-headers
```

Watch carefully for any errors in this installation. It should go smoothly, and once it is complete your application should compile correctly.

Writing a Simple Program (Hello World)

Here is the classic C-language Hello World program source code. It has a couple of small modifications so as to avoid generating compiler warnings. A main() function would normally return an integer value to indicate that it executed correctly or had a problem. A zero value indicates that everything was good. New-line markers are added to separate the lines and space out the output text. Follow these steps to create a source file you can compile with gcc:

1. Go to the temporary directory:

   ```
   cd /tmp
   ```

2. Open a new file with the vi editor:

   ```
   vi ./hello.c
   ```

3. Go into insert mode by pressing the letter [I] key.

4. Type the following source code into the vi editor. The #include line in the source file adds the standard I/O functions:

   ```
   #include<stdio.h>

   int main()
   {
       printf("\nARTIK says:\n\nHello World\n\n");
       return 0;
   }
   ```

5. Type these keystrokes to exit from vi and save the changes to disk:

   ```
   [Escape] [:] [w] [q] [Return]
   ```

6. Check that the previous steps worked by viewing the file that was created:

   ```
   cat hello.c
   ```

7. You should see the text you just edited listed on the screen.

235

8. Compile the Hello World program with a simple GCC command, as no additional libraries are needed:

```
gcc -Wall hello.c -o hello
```

9. Run the application you just built. Use the ./ prefix to indicate that it lives in the current working directory:

```
./hello
```

10. You should see this message echoed on the screen:

```
ARTIK says:
```

```
Hello World
```

This proves the ARTIK has a viable compiler. Move forward with your development plans and create more complex applications.

Compiler Warnings

It is a good idea to fully understand your application code and eliminate any error messages and warnings as early as possible. When you introduce a faulty line of code, it is immediately obvious that you broke something. It is hard to spot a genuine and important error message if you get 100 lines of warnings about trivial things that have not yet been optimized.

Adding the -Wall option turns on all warnings and error messages. Work down these systematically and eliminate them either by fixing code or by adding extra command-line options to control the compiler until there are no warnings left.

You should always use all of the help the compiler can give you and work to eliminate all errors. When you see a warning message, you know it is something you have just done when you last edited your source code. If you have hundreds of warnings, spotting a new one is hard, and the debugging process is more difficult. Zero warnings = good code. This is no guarantee that your application is perfectly conceived and well designed, but at least it builds successfully. That is a good first step.

Next Steps

Make use of the GCC compiler from an Eclipse IDE or transfer the output from a Temboo session to the ARTIK module and compile it there. The Temboo code is too long to retype again manually. Instead, just copy the code from the Temboo website and put it in a local file on the development workstation. Use a serial copy tool to transfer the code to your target ARTIK module. Log in to the ARTIK and compile it there.

SCP: Secure Copy

Once you have your ARTIK configured for IP networking, use the IP address to send files to it from your desktop workstation. The scp command is specifically designed for that task. You would use this from the UNIX command line on your desktop development system. For example, you can use this from the Cygwin terminal application on Windows.

File Upload to ARTIK Module

The source file to copy can be anywhere on your local workstation, but you need a UNIX path to reach it. The account name needs to have sufficient privileges to write to the destination directory where you are copying the files. In most ARTIK-based examples, the root account is used. The IP address is where your ARTIK is configured to exist on your local area network (LAN). The destination directory indicates where to deposit the file inside the ARTIK module. The format of an scp command is as follows:

```
scp {source_file_to_copy} {account_name}@{remote_IP_address}:/{destination_
directory}
```

Using scp to copy the hello.c source file from a development workstation to a target ARTIK module looks like this:

```
scp /my_files/hello.c root@192.168.1.57:/tmp
```

File Download from ARTIK Module

Use the scp tool to bring files back from an ARTIK module to your hosting development workstation. Just switch the parameters around the other way. The remote directory is described as a source rather than as a destination:

```
scp {account_name}@{remote_IP_address}:/{source_directory + file_path}
{local_directory}
```

Summary

This chapter is not just about building applications from the command line, although that is useful. Acquiring UNIX command-line skills is a valuable thing. It is career enhancing, because manipulating text files and lists is very easy to do from a command line. Automating the process by putting those commands in a shell script adds more leverage. These things are extraordinarily difficult to do with a GUI-based workstation. Organize scheduled automatic runs of your scripts so that data is collated regularly and without manual intervention and you will have your text processing available on an industrial scale. Incorporate the command-line programming inside AppleScripts or Automator workflows to create drag and drop tools you can use from the Finder on a Macintosh workstation. Then you will have a range of new abilities at your fingertips with which to amplify your productivity.

CHAPTER 15

Programming in C Language

Programming Your ARTIK Natively in C

This chapter will concentrate on the internals of the ARTIK modules. Accessing the internal logic and peripherals of the ARTIK from a natively coded C-language application is arguably the simplest approach to developing ARTIK solutions. Log on to your ARTIK module and do everything from the command line. You are working on the "bare metal" without the help of an IDE, and indeed without much help from your development workstation other than it being a place where you open a terminal window. You can work very effectively in this environment by editing your source files in vi and compiling and linking them directly with the GCC compiler. You can increase your leverage by using an IDE such as Eclipse or Arduino in your development workstation. Keep your source code on that computer. Archive and version-control it with Git or SVN.

Coding Strategies

Let's just spend a moment to recap the source code Edit ➤ Compile ➤ Link ➤ Run cycle. You will repeat this sequence many times to iterate your design from a concept to a finished application.

I like to type only a couple of lines of code and then test that right away so that if there are errors, it is really easy to find what caused them. I assert certain things about my application and use logging and printing often to check that the application is generating what I expect. I find this "debugging as I go" approach to be very productive because it imparts a level of confidence that the code written so far is functional and trustworthy; that is, providing my architectural design and concepts were sound to begin with. Consequently, I develop from the bottom up, ensuring working foundations are running properly before I build a superstructure on top. Skyscrapers are built like that, and it makes sense to build software that way too.

The goal is to create a working application with good performance and reliability. Everyone has a preferred creative style. You may have a completely different way of working, and that is just fine. If your technique works for you and leads to a satisfactory outcome, it completely vindicates your approach. The most important thing is to plan the design first. Only start to write code when you know what you want to build.

© Cliff Wootton 2016
C. Wootton, *Beginning Samsung ARTIK*, DOI 10.1007/978-1-4842-1952-2_15

Creating a Simple Application

Here is an example application that reads and displays the contents of the Fedora release-version file in the /etc directory:

1. Go to the temporary files directory:

    ```
    cd /tmp
    ```

2. Use the vi editor to create a file called file_reader.c:

    ```
    vi file_reader.c
    ```

3. Switch to the insert mode by pressing the uppercase letter [I] key and type this code into the editor:

    ```c
    #include <stdio.h>

    int main()
    {
       FILE *fp;
       char str[60];

       /* open a file for reading */
       fp = fopen("/etc/fedora-release" , "r");

       if(fp == NULL)
       {
          perror("Error opening file");
          return(-1);
       }
       if( fgets (str, 60, fp)!= NULL )
       {
          /* write the file content to stdout */
          puts(str);
       }
       fclose(fp);

       return(0);
    }
    ```

4. Type the following keystrokes to exit from vi and save the changes to disk:

    ```
    [Escape] [:] [w] [q] [Return]
    ```

5. Now compile the source code with GCC:

```
gcc -Wall file_reader.c -o file_reader
```

6. Run your compiled program with this command:

```
./file_reader
```

7. You should see the following text echoed on the screen. If your ARTIK operating system has been updated, you will see a different version number:

```
Fedora release 22 (Twenty Two)
```

Looking Deeper Inside Your ARTIK

The Linux kernel exports a lot of the internal values out to virtual file-system locations that are mapped into your user-accessible domain. From your point of view, these kernel parameters look just like regular files that you can open and read or write to. This makes it much easier to find and communicate with the kernel internals–if the file access is permitted–without needing to understand a lot about the mechanics of kernel messaging and its internals. Most of the time you will be reading the contents of these virtual file-system locations. Very occasionally you will write to them to configure something or to set a value of a pin. You should understand what you are doing if you attempt to alter anything with a write. Read about this virtual file-system mapping here:

```
https://en.wikipedia.org/wiki/Filesystem_Hierarchy_Standard
http://www.tldp.org/LDP/Linux-Filesystem-Hierarchy/html/
https://en.wikipedia.org/wiki/Sysfs
https://en.wikipedia.org/wiki/Procfs
https://en.wikipedia.org/wiki/Device_tree
https://en.wikipedia.org/wiki/Configfs
```

You will learn a lot by reading the documentation on how the kernel of your OS handles embedded hardware devices. This is not for the faint of heart. This is seriously deep and complex stuff. As much as possible, you should try to use libraries that encapsulate all of this complexity. They are there to help you.

However, the pins on your ARTIK may not have such mature library support, and you may only be able to access them directly through the /sys virtual file system. Logical devices are accessible via the /dev virtual file system. The allocated memory space and other properties of running processes can be accessed through the /proc virtual file system. All of these require that your account, and hence your running application, has sufficient privileges to access these locations in the file system. Find out more about the kernel here:

```
https://www.kernel.org/doc/Documentation/
```

About the /sys Virtual File System

This tree of virtual file-system entities provides direct access to the system hardware and attached peripherals. Explore this to find the locations of the SPI, PCI, I2C, and I2S hardware API endpoints. Consult the online documentation about those peripheral devices to work out how to interact with them. Listing 15-1 shows a map of the basic organization of the /sys directory:

Listing 15-1. The sys Virtual File System

```
[/sys]
  !
  +- [block]              - Block structured devices such as disks & memory
  !
  +- [bus]                - Registered buses (only two shown as examples)
  !   !
  !   +- [i2c]            - I2C bus
  !   !   !
  !   !   +- [devices]    - I2C devices with loaded drivers
  !   !
  !   +- [spi]            - SPI bus
  !
  +- [class]              - Devices organized into classes
  !
  +- [dev]                - Devices collated by type (block or
                            character access)
  !
  +- [devices]            - Devices known by the kernel
  !
  +- [firmware]           - Embedded firmware images
  !
  +- [fs]                 - User-accessible file systems
  !
  +- [kernel]             - Mount points for other virtual file systems
  !
  +- [module]             - Currently loaded kernel modules
  !
  +- [power]              - Power management sub-system
```

The peripherals are mapped into the ARTIK file system to allow your code to operate on them as if they were regular files. Just open the relevant virtual file to get a file descriptor. Read or write the value and close the file. This uses the file-system tree that starts at the /sys directory. This is the head of the sysfs virtual file system. These peripheral accessors are examined in much more detail in the companion Apress *ARTIK Reference Guide*.

> ■ **Note** Always carefully list the contents of the /sys virtual file system to explore the layout and determine the exact spelling of any peripheral device paths you intend to use. They might change as the OS is upgraded. Spending some time examining the layout of this file system for differences will save you a lot of debugging heartache later.

GPIO Pins

One way to access the General Purpose Input Output (GPIO) pins is to work in the Arduino domain, but that limits the complexity of the applications you can build. A better way to access the GPIO pins is by referencing them as a file in the /sys virtual file system. The operating system exports them from a secure, protected, kernel-controlled environment and presents them to you in a simple-to-use manner. Files have properties that control whether you can read or write to them. The existence of a virtual file tells you whether a feature is present on the board or not. Virtual file systems respond in ways that normal files do not. A value written to a virtual file is intercepted by the file-system manager, which sends a message to the kernel rather than storing the value in a physical file within the file system. Read this document first and then try experimenting:

https://www.kernel.org/doc/Documentation/gpio/sysfs.txt

Read it again to reinforce the learning experience. Each time you go through a read-and-experiment cycle, you build a more complete mental model of the technology you are learning about. Practice and repetition works for engineering just as effectively as for learning a musical instrument.

GPIO: Pin Mapping

To access the GPIO pins, set the direction of the pin first and then read or write a value to it. Some pin numbers are different between the ARTIK 5 and 10 modules. For example, GPIO 8 on an ARTIK 10 is equivalent to GPIO 121 on an ARTIK 5. Figure 15-1 shows the general arrangement of the pins on the developer reference boards.

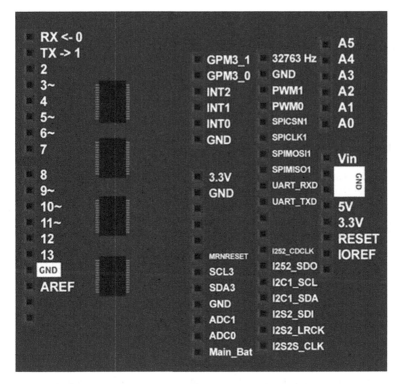

Figure 15-1. *Type 5 and Type 10 developer reference board GPIO pins*

Table 15-1 lists the available GPIO pin connections for a Type 5 or Type 10 developer reference board.

Table 15-1. *GPIO Pin Connections*

Header label	Logical name	ARTIK 5	ARTIK 10
J26-2	GPX0[0]	GPIO 121	GPIO 8
J26-3	GPX0[1]	GPIO 122	GPIO 9
J26-4	GPX0[2]	GPIO 123	GPIO 10
J26-7	GPX0[3]	GPIO 124	GPIO 11
J27-8	GPX0[4]	GPIO 125	GPIO 12
J27-9	GPX0[5]	GPIO 126	GPIO 13
J27-10	GPX0[6]	GPIO 127	GPIO 14
J27-11	GPX1[0]	GPIO 129	GPIO 16
J27-12	GPX1[5]	GPIO 134	GPIO 21
J27-13	GPX1[6]	GPIO 135	GPIO 22

GPIO: Pin Export to the User Domain

Because the GPIO interface is managed as a virtual file system and presents each entity as a regular file, the standard UNIX file-system permissions will conditionally allow you to perform these operations on the GPIO pins it manages. To make a GPIO available to your application, you need to export it first. While it is exported, your application owns that pin and another application cannot access it. Make sure you relinquish it when you are done. Open the /sys/class/gpio/export file and write a GPIO pin number to it. Listing 15-2 is an example code fragment that writes to a GPIO pin.

Listing 15-2. Writing to a GPIO Pin

```
// Define the target pin number
myGPIOPinNumber = 19;

// Open a messaging channel to the kernel
if((myGPIoExportFd = fopen("/sys/class/gpio/export", "w")) == NULL)
{
    printf("Error: unable to export GPIO pin\n");
    return false;
}

// Tell the kernel which pin to use
fprintf(myGPIoExportFd, "%d\n", myGPIOPinNumber);

// Close the kernel messaging channel
fclose(myGPIoExportFd);
```

The following code is the command-line equivalent that you must embed inside a shell script. Python and Node.js programmers can reproduce this by doing the same simple file access:

```
echo 19 > /sys/class/gpio/export
```

When you are done with this GPIO, release it for use by other applications by writing the pin number to the unexport file location. Here is the replacement line you need:

```
if((myGPIoExportFd = fopen("/sys/class/gpio/unexport", "w")) == NULL)
```

And from the command line or shell scripts you do this:

```
echo 19 > /sys/class/gpio/unexport
```

GPIO: Pin Direction Setting

When your application asks the kernel to export a GPIO into the user-accessible domain, the kernel creates a new node within the /sys virtual file system to represent that pin. After the kernel has created it for you, your application can read or write to that node as if it were a regular file. Ask the kernel to configure the pin direction. Then you can request the current value if it is configured for input or send a value to the pin if it is an output. The path to the new node representing the pin will be:

```
/sys/class/gpio/gpio{pin_number}
```

Give that GPIO pin instructions by writing to sub-directories within it. The pin mode or direction (for this node) is controlled by this virtual file-system location:

```
/sys/class/gpio/gpio{pin_number}/direction
```

Use the sprintf() function to manufacture a path name from the pin number, like this:

```
sprintf(myGPIOModeName, "/sys/class/gpio/gpio%d/direction",
myGPIOPinNumber);
```

Write the message "out" or "in" depending on whether the code controls something by setting its output level or reads a sensor value by treating the value as an input. Open the direction-configuration virtual file and set it to the required mode as shown in Listing 15-3.

Listing 15-3. Setting a GPIO Pin Mode

```
// Select one of these values to choose a mode
myGPIOMode = "out";
//myGPIOMode = "in";

// Open the direction configuration for the GPIO node
if((myGPIOModeFd = fopen(myGPIOModeName, "w")) == NULL)
{
   printf("Error: can't open pin direction\n");
   return false;
}

// Set the pin mode with the passed-in direction
fprintf(myGPIOModeFd, "%s\n", myGPIOMode);

// Close the direction configurator
fclose(myGPIOModeFd);
```

GPIO: Digital Value Setting

When you set the pin mode for a GPIO to be an output, writing to a special path within the GPIO node can set the value in the virtual file system:

```
/sys/class/gpio/gpio{pin_number}/value
```

Manufacture the path to that value-setting location with sprintf( ), like this:

```
sprintf(myGPIOValueName, "/sys/class/gpio/gpio%d/value", myGPIOPinNumber);
```

Listing 15-4 shows how to set the value on that GPIO having already synthesized the path to reach it.

Listing 15-4. Setting a GPIO Pin Value

```
// Select one of these values to set on the pin
myGPIOValue = 1;  // Represents HIGH
//myGPIOValue = 0; // Represents LOW

// Open the value configuration for the GPIO node
if((myGPIOValueFd = fopen(myGPIOValueName, "w")) == NULL)
{
    printf("Error: can't open pin value for writing\n");
    return false;
}

// Set the pin value with the passed-in setting
fprintf(myGPIOValueFd, "%d\n", myGPIOValue);

// Close the value configurator
fclose(myGPIOValueFd);
```

GPIO: Digital Value Reading

To read the value of the GPIO pin, just set the pin mode for input, then open the path to the value configurator and read in the value from the virtual file. The following values are available from an input GPIO pin:

```
0 - Low
1 - High
```

When you set the pin mode for a GPIO to be an input, the value can be acquired by reading from a special path within the GPIO node in the virtual file system:

```
/sys/class/gpio/gpio{pin_number}/value
```

Manufacture the path to that value-setting location with sprintf(), like this:

```
sprintf(myGPIOValueName, "/sys/class/gpio/gpio%d/value", myGPIOPinNumber);
```

Acquire the value from the GPIO pin with an fgets() function that is configured to read just two characters at a time. Listing 15-5 provides an example code fragment that reads a GPIO pin.

Listing 15-5. Reading a GPIO Pin Value

```
// Open the value configuration for the GPIO node
if((myGPIOValueFd = fopen(myGPIOValueName, "r")) == NULL)
{
   printf("Error: can't open pin value for reading\n");
   return false;
}

// Read the pin value
fgets(myResult, 2, myGPIOValueFd);

// Close the value configurator
fclose(myGPIOValueFd);
```

Convert the value to an integer before returning it to your application:

```
myInteger = atoi(myResult);
```

GPIO: Edge Detecting

By taking the value-reading example further, the virtual file edge can be used instead of a value to detect rising or falling edges. Detecting button press or button release actions becomes much easier because state management and button changes become atomic functions. Atomic functionality encapsulates things so only a single line of code is necessary where an entire function was required before.

This virtual file path will only exist if the driver for the GPIO supports this functionality. Inspect the file system embedded in your ARTIK to see if this feature is available. The read path for detecting an edge on the same example {pin_number} would be:

```
/sys/class/gpio/gpio{pin_number}/edge
```

The following values will be returned:

- none - No change detected
- rising - The value was low but has just gone high
- falling - The value was high but has just gone low

■ **Note** The GPIO documentation describes this feature, but it may not be implemented in all drivers to begin with and may show up as a feature addition later on.

Reading Analog Input Values

GPIO is only available for digital input and output. A different virtual file-system location accesses the analog voltage being imposed on a pin by a sensor. This example is good for an ARTIK 5 module. Here is the path to the analog-to-digital convertors (ADC) that are connected to the analog input pins A0 to A5:

```
/sys/devices/12d10000.adc/iio:device0/in_voltage{pin_number}_raw
```

Create your own suite of functions to manufacture a path to the virtual file-system location with a sprintf(), like this:

```
sprintf(myPinName, "/sys/devices/12d10000.adc/iio:device0/in_voltage%d_raw",
myPinNumber);
```

Acquire the value from the analog pin with an fgets() function that is configured to read eight characters at a time. The example code in Listing 15-6 shows how to read an analog pin value:

Listing 15-6. Reading Analog Pins

```
// Open the value configuration for the GPIO node
if((myFileDescriptor = fopen(myPinName, "r")) == NULL)
{
    printf("Error: can't open analog voltage value for reading\n");
    return false;
}

// Read the pin value
fgets(myResult, 8, myFileDescriptor);

// Close the value configurator
fclose(myFileDescriptor);
```

Convert the value to an integer before returning it to your application with the atoi() function:

```
myInteger = atoi(myResult);
```

You will get a value between 0 and 4096 that represents the voltage on that input pin. The value 4096 represents 5 volts. Scale the value accordingly like this:

```
myVoltage = (5 * myResult) / 4096;
```

You may want to apply different conversion factors depending on what your sensor is measuring and how it maps the values it detects to a voltage.

Analog Read Differences Between ARTIK 5 and 10

The sysfs virtual file-system base address for analog pins is different for the ARTIK 5 and 10 modules. Note the different hex-coded hardware addresses. Table 15-2 shows the alternative file-system locations.

Table 15-2. *Analog Pin Addresses*

Module	Virtual File-system Address
ARTIK 5	/sys/devices/12d10000.adc/iio:device0/in_voltageX_raw
ARTIK 10	/sys/devices/126c0000.adc/iio:device0/in_voltageX_raw

Get around this by defining a manifest constant to map the analog pins. An include file that is different for each ARTIK module type will decouple the reference to the hardware.

■ **Note** The organization of the sysfs virtual file system is prone to change as the ARTIK OS evolves. Predicting what the addresses within sysfs will be for later operating system versions is impossible to do. Therefore, you should apply some forensic inspection techniques to your ARTIK file system to determine the exact location of these addresses. If the addresses change after an OS upgrade or if you purchase later hardware, they should be quite easy to find because the format will be similar, but the specific hex-code portion of the address might change. The defined manifest constant will help you a lot.

Library Function Toolkit

Create a library of tools to make it easier to reuse common fragments of code multiple times. Listings 15-7 to 15-12 illustrate how to wrap GPIO configuration and value management within functions so they can be reused multiple times. Call these from your main application code. Define the INPUT, OUTPUT, HIGH, and LOW values as manifest constants in a file included at the start of the source code so that your applications can share values and be coded consistently.

Listing 15-7. Manifest Constant Definitions

```
#define INPUT 0
#define OUTPUT 1

#define LOW 0
#define HIGH 1
```

Listing 15-8. Main Application Code

```
myStatusResult = setDigitalPinMode(19, OUTPUT);
myStatusResult = setDigitalPinMode(20, INPUT);

myStatusResult = digitalWrite(19, HIGH);
myStatusResult = digitalWrite(19, LOW);

myValue = digitalRead(20);
myValue = analogRead(1);
```

Listing 15-9. The setDigitalPinMode() Function

```
bool setDigitalPinMode(int aPinNumber, int aPinMode)
{
    FILE * myFileDescriptor;
    char myNodeName[128];

    // Exporting the pin to be used
    if(( myFileDescriptor = fopen("/sys/class/gpio/export", "w")) == NULL)
    {
        printf("Error: unable to export pin number %d\n", aPinNumber);
        return false;
    }

    fprintf(myFileDescriptor, "%d\n", aPinNumber);

    fclose(myFileDescriptor);

    // Setting direction of the pin (pin mode)
    sprintf(myNodeName, "/sys/class/gpio/gpio%d/direction", aPinNumber);

    if((myFileDescriptor = fopen(myNodeName, "w")) == NULL)
    {
        printf("Error: can't open pin direction for node %s\n", myNodeName);
        return false;
    }

    if(aPinMode == OUTPUT)
    {
        fprintf(myFileDescriptor, "out\n");
    }
```

251

```
   else
   {
      fprintf(myFileDescriptor, "in\n");
   }

   fclose(myFileDescriptor);

   return true;
}
```

Listing 15-10. The digitalWrite() Function

```
bool digitalWrite(int aPinNumber, int aPinValue)
{
   FILE * myFileDescriptor;
   char myNodeName[128];

   // Open pin value file
   sprintf(myNodeName, "/sys/class/gpio/gpio%d/value", aPinNumber);

   if((myFileDescriptor = fopen(myNodeName, "w")) == NULL)
   {
      printf("Error: can't open pin value for node %s\n", myNodeName);
      return false;
   }
   if(aPinValue == HIGH)
   {
      fprintf(myFileDescriptor, "1\n");
   }
   else
   {
      fprintf(myFileDescriptor, "0\n");
   }

   fclose(myFileDescriptor);

   return true;
}
```

Listing 15-11. The digitalRead() Function

```
int digitalRead(int aPinNumber)
{
   FILE * myFileDescriptor;
   char myNodeName[128];
   char myResultValue[2];

   // Open pin value file
```

```
    sprintf(myNodeName, "/sys/class/gpio/gpio%d/value", aPinNumber);

    if((myFileDescriptor = fopen(myNodeName, "r")) == NULL)
    {
        printf("Error: can't open pin value for node %s\n", myNodeName);
        return false;
    }

    fgets(myResultValue, 2, myFileDescriptor);

    fclose(myFileDescriptor);

    return atoi(myResultValue);
}
```

Listing 15-12. The analogRead() Function

```
int analogRead(int aPinNumber)
{
    FILE * myFileDescriptor;
    char myNodeName[64];
    char myResultValue[8];

    // open value file
    sprintf(myNodeName, "/sys/devices/12d10000.adc/iio:device0/in_
    voltage%d_raw", aPinNumber);

    if((myFileDescriptor = fopen(myNodeName, "r")) == NULL)
    {
        printf("Error: can't open analog voltage value\n");
        return 0;
    }

    fgets(myResultValue, 8, myFileDescriptor);
    fclose(myFileDescriptor);

    return atoi(myResultValue);
}
```

It is possible to simplify this code by combining some of these different examples into one function to set the GPIO pin mode before writing and eliminate the need for a separate configuration function call. This would make the pins automatically configure each time they are used, but this is wasteful if you want to write a series of values out through the same GPIO pin.

An Example

Once you have a library of low-level functions with simple names with which to access the hardware, your high-level application code will become less complex. The example in Listing 15-13 is based on the tutorial for reading a temperature sensor and exploits the analogRead() function to do the hard work.

Listing 15-13. Read a Temperature Sensor

```
int inputPin = 7;

int currentRun = 0;
const int MAX_RUNS = 10;

int main(void)
{

    // Loop just 10 times
    while(currentRun < MAX_RUNS)
    {
        // Acquire the value
        int sensorVal = analogRead(inputPin);

        // Output a message
        printf("current sensor is %f\n", sensorVal);

        // Increment the run counter
        currentRun++;

        // Wait for a second
        sleep(1);
    }
}
```

Accessing Remote Systems with libCurl

Communicate with a remote system such as SAMI via an HTTP: or REST API interface. Use wget or curl commands from the command line. If you link your C language application with the libCurl library by adding it to your project build instructions, you can access the low-level curl functions directly from your source code. Binding the library directly to your application is more efficient than delegating to a command line and the equivalent functionality is identical. Both libCurl and the curl command line support are pre-installed by default.

The libCurl client-side library is thread-safe, fast, and IPv6 portable. Use the "easy" interface to make ARTIK applications communicate with SAMI programmatically.

Create a reference to the curl entity defined by libCurl and pass values to it. Ask it to execute the transaction with the remote system and dispose of it neatly at the end. Create a source file with the code shown in Listing 15-14 in it. Edit it with vi and save the code in the my_application.c file.

Listing 15-14. Calling libCurl

```
// --- Include the header file to use libCurl from your source code
//     or you will see compiler errors:
#include <curl/curl.h>

// --- Define a variable to act as a handle (or pointer) to reference
//     the curl entity.
//     Create another to store the result string when you send the
//     curl call to action.
   CURL *myCurlEntity;
   CURLcode myCurlResult;

// --- Initialize the curl entity
   myCurlEntity = curl_easy_init();

// --- Create a set of request headers
   struct curl_slist *requestHeader = NULL;

   char bearer[60]="";

   requestHeader = curl_slist_append(requestHeader,
                   "Content-Type: application/json");

   sprintf(bearer, "Authorization: Bearer %s", device_token);

   requestHeader = curl_slist_append(requestHeader, bearer);

// --- Create a request body to transmit to the remote system.
//     In this example, it is a SAMI transaction request
//     formatted with JSON data structures:

   char requestBody[256]="";

   sprintf(requestBody,"{\n
     \"sdid\": \"%s\",\n
     \"type\": \"message\",\n
     \"data\": {\n
          \"temperature\": %f                    \n
     }\n
   }", device_id, temperature);
```

```
// --- Now configure the options on the curl entity to make it ready:
   curl_easy_setopt(myCurlEntity, CURLOPT_URL, samiUrl);
   curl_easy_setopt(myCurlEntity, CURLOPT_HTTPHEADER, requestHeader);
   curl_easy_setopt(myCurlEntity, CURLOPT_POSTFIELDS, requestBody);
   curl_easy_setopt(myCurlEntity, CURLOPT_VERBOSE, 1L);

// --- Make the call and capture the result:
   myCurlResult = curl_easy_perform(myCurlEntity);

// --- Handle an error if there was one:
   if (myCurlResult != CURLE_OK)
   {
      fprintf(stderr, "curl_easy_perform() failed: %s\n",
      curl_easy_strerror(myCurlResult));
   }

// --- Free up the memory allocated to the headers when they were created
//      and clean up any other internal storage managed by the libCurl tools:
   curl_slist_free_all(requestHeader);

   curl_easy_cleanup(myCurlEntity);
```

Now your libCurl-based application is ready to be built. Compiling and linking your application to include the libCurl library is done by adding a library option to the linker command, like this:

```
gcc my_application.c -o my_application -lcurl
```

Summary

Although this chapter discusses the GPIO and other peripherals from the perspective of a C-language program, because they are presented through a virtual file system, they can be accessed by any language or programming tool that can operate on a file. Node.js, Python, shell scripts, or even raw command-line echo tools can be used to access the GPIO pins.

The closer you get to the "bare metal" when programming, the more efficiently your applications will run. Developing ARTIK applications natively in C language is almost the most efficient coding method. Writing ARM assembler code specifically for the kind of ARM CPU you have is arguably better. Modern compilers are very adept at optimizing the code they compile. It is unlikely you would do a better job if you wrote the assembly language code yourself. The C language is a good choice for ease of coding versus performance, memory footprint, and access to ARTIK internals.

The companion Apress *ARTIK Reference Guide* describes techniques to exploit the capabilities of the C-language compiler to make your code easier to maintain and port to different variants of the ARTIK modules.

CHAPTER 16

■ ■ ■

Programming with Node.js

Developing with Node.js

The ARTIK modules are equipped with a Node.js interpreter as part of the standard OS configuration. Use the Node.js tool to run applications written in JavaScript directly inside your ARTIK module. Because it is an open-source project, there are installable runtime environments for all current development platforms. Figure 16-1 shows the Node.js logo.

Figure 16-1. *Node.js logo*

Using Node.js may be an attractive solution for creating experimental applications very quickly, as the learning curve is easy and there are a lot of people out there who know how to code JavaScript. JavaScript has had a lot of work done on it to improve its performance and capabilities. It is useful for prototyping your designs to test out your ideas. If the performance is good enough then it could be shipped in that form, subject to a risk analysis to test it for security. Otherwise, rewrite the critical performance and security parts in a more suitable compiled language and run them as a native application. Find out more about Node.js here:

```
https://nodejs.org/en/about/
https://en.wikipedia.org/wiki/Node.js
https://nodejs.org/api/
```

The JavaScript interpreter inside Node.js is based on the Google V8 engine (See Figure 16-2).

Figure 16-2. *Google V8 logo*

It is important to know the provenance of the JavaScript interpreter you are using, because there are many different implementations. This fragmentation results in different functionality being available on each interpreter. Find out what features are supported by your JavaScript interpreter so as to avoid depending on unsupported functions or objects. Read about the Google V8 JavaScript interpreter here:

```
https://en.wikipedia.org/wiki/V8_(JavaScript_engine)
http://code.google.com/p/v8
```

JavaScript is based on ECMAScript at its core, and there are several versions published by the European Computer Manufacturers Association (ECMA). JavaScript interpreter developers then layer additional functionality on top of that, some of which is proprietary. Some JavaScript language support is based on W3C specifications that describe bindings between the language and the Document Object Model (DOM), and interpreters may support experimental features that are currently being worked on by the standards organizations. Proprieteray V8 features are defined by Google. Often, you will see interpreter owners declare that their product is standards compliant, but this is an opaque description unless the specific standards are enumerated. This statement is technically true if the interpreter is only compliant with ECMAScript or W3C but is not necessarily completely supportive of any others.

The Node.js runtime environment compiles the JavaScript down to executable machine code that runs directly in the CPU. This is very efficient, and your code will run extremely fast compared with the traditional way of interpreting JavaScript line by line at runtime.

The Architectural Design

The Node.js architecture is event driven, and its I/O calls are all designed to be non-blocking. Scripts will not halt while they wait for incoming data. Instead of waiting, scripts register an event to be called when the incoming data is ready to be accessed. This is essentially like AJAX programming in a web page. Learn about the different coding strategies so as to understand this paradigm. This behavior is different than that of a linear coding strategy where everything is a nested function call on a stack. In this scenario, your event-handling code can be called at any time and in any order, none of which is under your control.

Your event handler will only be called after you have made a request that it listens for. The timing and order of calls back to your event handlers cannot be predicted, because they are dependent on the duration of a request-return loop on a remote resource. This architectural design allows a Node.js application to run as if it were a real-time web app.

Compiled Binary Code

Unlike the GCC-complied C-language approach, your JavaScript code needs to be executed in Node.js every time you want to run it. Internally, the Google V8 engine will compile the JavaScript into machine code, but you cannot save this as a compiled application because it happens at runtime inside the interpreter and is discarded after use.

There is a command-line tool called nexe that is in an early stage of development. It will compile your Node.js code into an executable binary, but there is still a lot of work to be done before it is finished. Find out more here:

```
https://github.com/jaredallard/nexe
```

Checking the Version of Your Node.js Installation

Before starting to build applications either directly in Node.js by itself or combined with Temboo, your Node.js interpreter should be installed and working properly on your ARTIK. Version 0.8.0 or later is needed in order for Temboo to work correctly. You should have Node.js installed already as part of the ARTIK base operating system, but it might need updating. According to the Node.js release summary and downloads page, there are much later versions of Node.js available. Before installing a later version, you should make a note of the currently installed version so you can reinstate it later if necessary. The authoritative list of releases is available here:

```
https://nodejs.org/en/download/releases/
```

Follow these instructions to check what version of Node.js you have:

1. Type the following command to see what version of Node.js you have:

   ```
   node -v
   ```

2. You should see this output or something similar:

   ```
   v0.10.36
   ```

3. If your version is lower than 0.8 or if you know there is a later version of Node.js than the one you already have, you can download new versions at the following URL. Navigate into the release folder on the web server for known good and stable builds. The npm tool is included in the installer by default:

   ```
   http://nodejs.org/download/
   ```

4. If you are installing Node.js on your Windows development workstation without intending to run your code as a command line script in Cygwin, then get an MSI installer for the Node.js runtime instead.

5. Mac OS X users can use a packaged installer as an alternative to running a command-line install script. That installer package is also available at the download site. Get more help installing Node.js here:

```
http://nodejs.org/
http://www.thegeekstuff.com/2015/10/install-nodejs-npm-linux/
https://nodejs.org/en/download/package-manager/
```

Extending Node.js

The Node.js interpreter has useful utility libraries included by default. Extend it by adding other packages. The Node Package Manager (NPM) gathers those packages from the repositories where they are hosted, downloads them, and installs them so they are ready for you to include in your projects.

Installing NPM

Your ARTIK should come with the Node Package Manager already installed, but if it is not there or if you want to upgrade it, follow these steps to download a script using the `curl` command. That script is executed right away to install NPM for you. It carries out various checks along the way and reports any show-stopping errors for you to fix before running it again:

1. Log in to your ARTIK from the terminal.

2. Check the version of NPM you have with this command:

```
npm version
```

3. To install NPM, type the following command exactly. This should also work on a Linux or Mac OS X workstation if you want to build a test environment. You should also be able to run it within Cygwin on Windows:

```
curl -L https://www.npmjs.com/install.sh | sh
```

4. The script figures out what kind of environment you have for executing scripts.

5. It checks the NPM configuration settings in case they have already been set up. If they have, the existing values are preserved for reinstatement after the install is done.

6. The installer script then checks to see whether you already have Node.js installed. It must be present before running this NPM installer script again. Some Node.js installers will install NPM for you anyway. Pausing at this point and reinstalling Node.js might accomplish the same thing you are trying to do and update your Node.js interpreter at the same time.

7. Because this script is designed to work in all operating systems, it then checks to see if the tar utility for unpacking archives is available.

8. The script will build directly from source files. It checks for the availability of the make tools before trying to use them.

9. Having earlier established that Node.js is installed, the script checks to see if your version is high enough and warns you accordingly if it does not meet the required specification.

10. The script figures out which NPM installer version to download based on a compatibility table it requests from the repository.

11. The appropriate archived installer package is downloaded and unpacked before building and installing the contents.

■ **Note**   On the Beta version of the ARTIK modules, this installation process fails because the installer script tries to use the UNIX which command to locate the node interpreter. Because that command is not present in this ARTIK version, the test fails and the installer thinks that Node.js is not installed, even though it is. You may need to explore other ways to install NPM if you need it on your ARTIK module. More details are available here: https://nodejs.org/en/download/package-manager/

Node Packages and Modules

Once you have NPM installed and working, you can use it to manage your Node.js toolkit. Check to see what modules you have installed with this command:

```
npm ls
```

Install a node package if you need it with this command:

```
npm install {package_name}
```

Find out more about NPM and the packages available for download with it here:

```
https://www.npmjs.com/
https://docs.npmjs.com/
https://github.com/npm/npm/wiki/Troubleshooting
```

Installing the WebSocket Module

The WebSocket module is required to develop applications with Node.js and transmit data to SAMI. Install the WebSocket module with this command:

```
npm install ws
```

Let's Write Some Node.js Code

Now that the Node.js and NPM tools are all up to scratch, your ARTIK is ready to run JavaScript-based code. Follow these steps to build and run a Hello World application in Node.js:

1. Open a terminal window on your ARTIK module.

2. Use the vi editor to create a file called hello_world.js.

3. Put this code into the file:

   ```
   console.log("Hello World!");
   ```

4. Save the file and quit out of the vi editor.

5. Run your code in Node.js with this command:

   ```
   node hello_world.js
   ```

6. You should see the text "Hello World!" echoed on your console screen.

Get more learning resources online. There are lots of books available to teach you the fine points of Node.js programming. If you already have experience developing JavaScript in web pages, then you have a head start. This is a different context, however, and some techniques from web-page building are not appropriate while others will be unfamiliar.

Reading a Pin Voltage with Node.js

To read a pin voltage, locate the address of the analog-to-digital convertor (ADC) for the pin you want to read. Include the pin number within the virtual file-system path you compose:

```
/sys/devices/12d10000.adc/iio:device0/in_voltage{pin_number}_raw
```

The complete path to the input for pin 7 is this:

```
/sys/devices/12d10000.adc/iio:device0/in_voltage7_raw
```

The sysfs virtual file-system base address for analog pins is different for the ARTIK 5 and 10 modules. Note the different hex-coded hardware addresses. Table 16-1 shows the alternative file-system locations.

Table 16-1. Analog Pin Addresses

Module	Virtual File System Address
ARTIK 5	/sys/devices/12d10000.adc/iio:device0/in_voltageX_raw
ARTIK 10	/sys/devices/126c0000.adc/iio:device0/in_voltageX_raw

Because this value is accessible as a virtual file, it can be exploited very easily with the Node.fs extension module in your ARTIK. The result is logged to the console output on your ARTIK. Listing 16-1 shows some example Node.js code for an ARTIK 5. Modify the file path to accommodate the different base path for an ARTIK 10.

Listing 16-1. Node.js Example

```
// Load the file-system support module
var fs = require('fs');

// Define the path to the analog pin
var myVirtualFile = "/sys/devices/12d10000.adc/iio:device0/in_voltage7_raw";

// Callback function to process output
function logTheOutput(err,data)
{
    console.log(data);
}

// Asynchronously read the pin voltage with this function
function readPinVoltage()
{
    fs.readFile(myVirtualFile,'utf8', logTheOutput);
}

// Run the interval timer every second
setInterval(readPinVoltage,1000);
```

Save this script as read_pin_7.js and then run it with this Node.js command:

```
node read_pin_7.js
```

Sending Data to SAMI with Node.js

This can get complicated when you combine multiple connections. Fortunately, there is a very good blog article by Martin Kronberg that shows you how to do just that and provides sample code. The main blog article describes how to read the analog input pins and links to another page that describes how to create a manifest. The sample code is hosted on Git. This approach builds JavaScript Object Notation (JSON) formatted messages for dispatch to the remove service. Here are the URLs where you can download the code:

```
https://www.hackster.io/martinkronberg/artik10-sami-eab8f7
https://www.hackster.io/monica/getting-started-with-sami-grove-weather-
station-e0b4e3
https://github.com/martinkronberg/node-code/blob/master/read_and_send_to_
sami.js
```

Here is a step-by-step guide to registering a new device with SAMI:

1. Sign on to the SAMI developer portal with your Samsung account:

    ```
    https://devportal.samsungsami.io/
    ```

2. Add a new SAMI device type where the manifest can live.

3. Input the human-readable name to describe it.

4. Give it a unique name that you know does not exist anywhere else.

5. Add a data field to describe the data you intend to transmit. Use temperature value, as shown in the example.

6. Define the data type.

7. Click the Next button.

8. Save the new manifest.

9. Open another browser window.

10. Sign on to the SAMI user portal with your Samsung account:

    ```
    https://portal.samsungsami.io/
    ```

11. Connect to a new device.

12. Enter the details of the manifest you just created.

13. Generate a SAMI device token.

14. Make a note of the device ID that is displayed. You will need this shortly.

15. Make a note of the device token that is displayed. You will need this shortly.

16. Install and use the WebSocket module with NPM if necessary:

```
npm install ws
```

17. Define the path to the WebSocket API in a global variable:

```
var webSocketUrl = "wss://api.samsungsami.io/v1.1/
websocket?ack=true";
```

18. Define your device ID in a global variable to use it wherever you need it:

```
var device_id = "{your_device_ID}";
```

19. Define your device token in a global variable:

```
var device_token = "{your_device_token}";
```

20. Your script can now load up the WebSocket module and create a new object with it:

```
var WebSocket = require('ws');
```

21. Make a new connection and add logging callbacks for when the socket is opened and closed, and for when a message arrives:

```
ws = new WebSocket(webSocketUrl);

ws.on('open', function()
{
    console.log("WebSocket connection is open ....");
    register();
});

ws.on('message', function(data, flags)
{
    console.log("Received message: " + data + '\n');
});

ws.on('close', function()
{
    console.log("WebSocket connection is closed ....");
});
```

22. Build a message to register the device with SAMI:

```
var registerMessage = '{"type":"register",
"sdid":"'+device_id+'", ↩
"Authorization":"bearer '+device_token+'",
"cid":"'+getTimeMillis()+'"}';
```

23. Send the registration request:

```
ws.send(registerMessage, {mask: true});
```

24. Make a timestamp to use with the data message:

```
ts = ', "ts": '+getTimeMillis();
```

25. Build the payload data body as a simple JSON message:

```
payload_data = {"button": button, "light": light};
```

26. Wrap the payload data body in a SAMI message envelope:

```
var payload = '{"sdid":"'+device_id+'"'+ts+', "data":'+ ↩
JSON.stringify(payload_data)+', "cid":"'+getTimeMillis()+'"}';
```

27. Send the data message:

```
ws.send(payload, {mask: true});
```

The fundamentals of sending messages to SAMI are not hugely complex. Download and inspect the Node.js example source code from the blog article to see these calls in context.

Summary

The Node.js approach is a neat way to get started with developing prototype applications to run in your ARTIK. This is most appropriate when you come from a web development background and do not yet know how to code in C language. You may already know how to code in JavaScript. There are special considerations and new functionality to grasp, however. You will also have to extend your repertoire of JavaScript coding skills as you are no longer writing code that runs within a web page; it runs in an application container. More importantly, you may not have a display on which to present things. Function calls you are familiar with for debugging, such as alert(), are problematic because there is no display surface for you to see them on. Access to files for input and output becomes much more important.

CHAPTER 17

■ ■ ■

Programming with Python

Developing with Python

The Python interpreter is installed as a standard part of the ARTIK operating system. You can run your Python-based applications directly inside the ARTIK module without needing to install additional software. Upgrade the Python interpreter as new versions become available. Figure 17-1 shows the Python logo.

Figure 17-1. *Python logo*

Python is one of the most popular programming languages. Each language has strengths and weaknesses and is useful for particular kinds of logic design. Choosing the right language depends on the kind of problem you are trying to solve. If you choose the wrong one or you only ever use one language for everything, you might be making a lot more work for yourself.

■ **Note**   If the only tool in your toolbox is a hammer, everything looks like a nail. To put it another way, hammering wood screws into pine boarding as if you were using nails to hold it together will create a very nasty looking piece of furniture.

Python is designed to be useful for general-purpose development. It sets out to require fewer lines of code to create your application than the equivalent C++ language or Java source code would require. Python encapsulates things like file access as objects. Use object-oriented design or the more traditional procedural approach with Python depending on your architectural needs.

If there are any caveats to using Python, they are much the same arguments as for using Node.js. Because this is an interpreted language, the performance will be limited when compared to a compiled language such as C. The raw source of your code is visible to intruders. That will at the very least give them clues about the deeper parts of your product, even if they cannot gain sufficient permissions to alter your code. A fundamental rule of thumb is to prototype in interpreted code but ship compiled applications to make things inherently more secure and performant.

Python is probably best suited to building script frameworks with which to call up compiled components. Use it in place of conventional shell scripts if they are not capable of implementing the kind of logic you need. Prototyping your application logic in Python before incorporating it into compiled code can save you some development time, because you can compose your experimental code and run it directly without needing a build process.

Checking Your Python Interpreter

The Python interpreter is installed by default on your ARTIK module. Follow these instructions to see what version of Python you have installed:

1. Request the version:

    ```
    python --version
    ```

2. You should see something like this:

    ```
    Python 2.7.10
    ```

The version you have in a production ARTIK may be later than this version, which was installed in a Beta prototype ARTIK 5 module.

Installing the Python Package Manager

Enhance Python by adding extension libraries. This is much easier to do if you have the pip package manager installed. Follow these instructions to install pip:

1. Open a terminal window and log in to your ARTIK command line.

2. Type this command exactly:

    ```
    wget https://bootstrap.pypa.io/get-pip.py
    ```

3. The wget command downloads the get-pip.py script. This script contains a self-loading archive of the latest version of the pip installer.

4. Now run the self-loading installer:

    ```
    python get-pip.py
    ```

5.   The installer locates the blob of encoded binary code and extracts it to a temporary file.

6.   The installer unpacks the archive and installs the pip tools.

7.   At the end of the process, the self-loading installer cleans up the temporary files automatically. If necessary, remove the get-pip.py script yourself with this command:

```
rm get-pip.py
```

Installing Python Packages

Once you have pip installed, use it to install new packages:

```
pip install {some_package_name}
```

The pip utility can also remove packages you no longer need, like this:

```
pip uninstall {some_package_name}
```

Conditionally install different packages based on the version of Python you have installed. Get more information about PIP here:

```
https://en.wikipedia.org/wiki/Pip_(package_manager)
```

Use pip to access the Python Package Index. This has extension packages uploaded by Python developers all over the world. Before starting to write an extension yourself, check the index to see if it has already been done:

```
https://en.wikipedia.org/wiki/Pip_(package_manager)
https://pypi.python.org/pypi
https://python-packaging-user-guide.readthedocs.org/en/latest/
```

Run a Simple Python Test

It is time to write a small test application to exercise Python. Just enough to prove that it works. In fact, the Python interpreter was already tested thoroughly by using it to install the pip package manager. Follow these steps to build and run a Hello World application in Python:

1.   Open a terminal window on your ARTIK module.

2.   Use the vi editor to create a file called hello_world.py.

3.   Put this code into the file:

```
print "Python says Hello World!"
```

4. Save the file and quit out of the vi editor.

5. Run your code in Python with this command:

```
python hello_world.py
```

6. You should see the text "Python says Hello World!" echoed on your terminal screen.

Get more learning resources online. There are lots of books available to teach you Python programming.

Reading a Pin Voltage with Python

To read a pin voltage, locate the address of the analog-to-digital convertor (ADC) for the pin you want to read. Include the pin number within the virtual file-system path you compose:

```
/sys/devices/12d10000.adc/iio:device0/in_voltage{pin_number}_raw
```

So the complete path to the input for pin 7 is this:

```
/sys/devices/12d10000.adc/iio:device0/in_voltage7_raw
```

The sysfs virtual file-system base address for analog pins is different for the ARTIK 5 and 10 modules. Note the different hex-coded hardware address. Table 17-1 shows the alternative file-system locations:

Table 17-1. Analog Pin Addresses

Module	Virtual File System Address
ARTIK 5	/sys/devices/12d10000.adc/iio:device0/in_voltageX_raw
ARTIK 10	/sys/devices/126c0000.adc/iio:device0/in_voltageX_raw

Because this value is accessible as a virtual file, it can be exploited very easily with Python, which has a similar file I/O sub-system to ANSI-standard C language. Listing 17-1 shows a snippet of Python code for an ARTIK 5. Modify the file path to accommodate the different base path for an ARTIK 10, and then use the write() method on the file object to set pin values. Refer to chapter 15 for detailed guidance on GPIO pin functions and addresses and convert those into Python code for yourself.

Listing 17-1. Python Code Snippet

```
// Define the path to the analog pin
myVirtualFile = "/sys/devices/12d10000.adc/iio:device0/in_voltage7_raw";

// Create a file object
target = open(myVirtualFile, 'r');

// Read the pin voltage (only eight characters required)
target.read(8);

// Dispose of the file
target.close();
```

Summary

Python is the last of the classic programming languages we will look at for now. Add Perl or other languages from open-source projects that you can cross-compile to run in the ARTIK. Interpreted languages will be easier to get working. Adding other compiled languages to the ARTIK or to your Eclipse IDE just requires that they can cross-compile into ARM executable code and that the right CPU model is supported.

The next goal is to deploy ARTIK applications in a production context and build an Internet of Things connected network. The first of these illustrations will use SAMI, because it is provided by Samsung and can be integrated with any language that can make an HTTPS: request. The other one is Temboo, which is a complete programming and deployment environment that exists online. Let's look at SAMI first.

■ ■ ■

## CHAPTER 18

Integrating with SAMI

About SAMI

The ARTIK operating system comes with a suite of tools that implement the Samsung SAMI interface. You can share data from each ARTIK with other networked devices through the SAMI data exchange. Figure 18-1 shows the SAMI logo.

Figure 18-1. *Samsung SAMI logo*

SAMI reconciles the behavior of all your IoT devices in order to exchange compatible data regardless of who developed the devices. This interoperability and security are based on data-driven development. The data format and transformations are described in a manifest, which decouples the framework from hard wiring the support for different devices. SAMI is also extensible enough to support new and as yet unknown devices.

© Cliff Wootton 2016
C. Wootton, *Beginning Samsung ARTIK*, DOI 10.1007/978-1-4842-1952-2_18

When designing a new product idea, think beyond single, self-contained devices. Data belonging to different users and devices can be shared to a much greater extent when you aggregate the data with hub like SAMI. Rule-based configurations can then trigger actions. The SAMI data exchange then becomes much more than a simple data-conversion nexus. Samsung describes this as data fusion, and it is a key enabler of what you can do with your ARTIK.

Designing the SAMI capabilities into your applications is possible no matter what language you use to develop them. The REST API interface that SAMI supports is easy to access with a simple web request that is already available in all languages, or can be added very easily.

Read these Samsung blog articles for more examples of how to integrate SAMI with your projects:

```
https://blog.samsungsami.io/topics/data/
```

What Is SAMI?

Because SAMI is a data-driven development platform with simple open API endpoints and SDK libraries, it can send and receive diverse data, regardless of the source. The SAMI tools integrate applications and hardware to exchange data in order to enrich the user experience. Your smartphone can share data with wearable devices built with an ARTIK module, and both can transmit data that is then imported into another device at your workplace or home. Figure 18-2 shows the various data flows that transfer information between devices, users, and the SAMI data exchange.

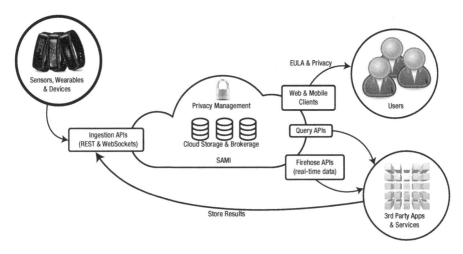

Figure 18-2. *SAMI data flows*

SAMI is a data-exchange platform that enables any online device, ARTIK module, or attached sensor to push data to the cloud for aggregation with data from other devices.

SAMI is open and agnostic. To save data or send a message to the cloud, do it in the format most convenient to you. SAMI will do the work of interpreting it, and it can interoperate with other manufacturers' devices.

This foundation is powerful enough that the Samsung SmartThings Open Cloud ecosystem has been built on top of it.

Interacting with SAMI

There is a variety of ways to interact with SAMI. As a developer, adding SAMI support to your devices and software applications is easy. You introduce those products to SAMI via the Developer Portal, which is a web-based user interface to the SAMI registry. End users can register their SAMI-compatible devices and applications with their personal account via the User Portal. This is a web-based dashboard where the aggregated data flowing between your SAMI-compatible devices and applications is managed. Only the devices and applications that you register with your account will contribute to this aggregated data set. Both portals require a Samsung account to log in. You should create one as soon as you can. Instructions are provided in Chapter 4 ("Understanding Security"). The signup process is simple. Find out more about the User and Developer ortals here:

```
https://developer.samsungsami.io/sami/sami-documentation/
developer-user-portals.html
```

How SAMI Works

SAMI defines a new paradigm for developers to create services and applications. It offers a new dimension that thinks beyond a single device and also enables developers to connect and analyze all sorts of data. This is called data-driven development (D3).

- Client applications can access and aggregate historical data from different sources, thus opening a new perspective on big data.

- Client applications that subscribe to a WebSocket can receive data in real-time, enabling different modules and applications to talk to each other.

- SAMI gives users complete control over their data. By granting access to modules and applications, users promote an ecosystem of services around data.

- Through the definition of a manifest, developers can support diverse modules and data.

Use SAMI to track any kind of device, from health and fitness trackers to home appliances and fixtures. Control your data by toggling access with simple on/off switches. Grant permissions based on your devices or on the applications you use. Watch your data as it is collected with the live views. The SAMI dashboard provides elegant, attractive, and easy-to-use data-visualization tools that make it simple to track your data.

The core services in SAMI are flexible in working out what kind of data you are transmitting and process whatever data or message format you use. The transactions are all sent and received in real-time (subject to the limitations of your network).

SAMI Developer Documentation

Sign up for a Samsung account and log in to the Developer Portal. Your account will give you access to the supporting SAMI documentation here:

```
https://developer.samsungsami.io/sami/sami-documentation/
```

The documentation is organized into sections so as to navigate it more easily:

- Overview of all the component parts of the SAMI system

- The API specification

- Descriptions of native SDK libraries to help you build applications in a variety of languages

- Tools and tutorial exercises as examples

- Sample projects

- FAQs

Security

When you use SAMI for data aggregation, the device setup takes advantage of the security features that SAMI provides. SAMI supports secure device registration to ensure secure communication to and from devices:

- The device is checked against the registration to ensure it is genuine.

- The device owner can be challenged to verify that they have the device in their hand.

- Every message exchanged between the device and SAMI is verified.

- The security certificate cannot be forged or copied because it is managed by the ARTIK Embedded Secure Element (ESE) technology.

If you are a device manufacturer, follow these steps to create your own secure device-type manifests:

- Obtain a client certificate for your device type.

- Obtain an access key for your device type.

- Use the Developer Portal to update and manage your device type to support secure device registration.

- Implement software logic in your device for secure registration with SAMI.

- Implement software logic in your device for secure message exchange with SAMI.

Read the following guidance in the developer documentation for more detailed instructions on how to secure your devices:

```
https://developer.samsungsami.io/sami/sami-documentation/
secure-your-devices.html
```

Authentication

Authentication within the SAMI ecosystem is very simple. It describes just two privileges: read data from SAMI entities or write new data to them. Removing both permissions effectively puts your device or application offline. Grant both permissions if necessary. Without these permissions you are prohibited from using the SAMI API calls.

User accounts can access data that they own without any additional permissions. An administrative user account can be granted limited permission to manipulate data owned by other user accounts on their behalf.

Users can grant permissions to applications to share information with the application about the user profile and registered devices list.

Messages

Messages transport the data that is incoming from devices. SAMI treats applications as if they were devices from the data-messaging perspective. Functionally, it makes no difference how the message originated since it ends up in the same place and is described in the same way. Messages may also describe outgoing data that SAMI dispatches to a remote device. Messages are tagged with the following identifying metadata, which is carried as a payload:

- Device ID

- User ID

- Application ID

The metadata assists in the browsing and filtering of messages when aggregating them to produce timeline tables and charts.

You may want to impose rate-limiting constraints on your messaging traffic, which helps improve performance overall. You do not want to flood your SAMI account with unnecessary traffic, which would deny the service to new traffic if it is too busy handling incoming data to aggregate it for feedback before the next arrival. Apply limits to the throughput based on these criteria:

- Per user

- Per device

- Per application

Read more about message traffic, send/receive logic, and rate limiting here:

```
https://developer.samsungsami.io/sami/sami-documentation/rate-limiting.html
https://developer.samsungsami.io/sami/sami-documentation/
sending-and-receiving-data.html
https://developer.samsungsami.io/sami/sami-documentation/
data-collection-with-trials.html
```

User

A SAMI user is represented by a Samsung account. Create these users yourself whenever you need them. If you are developing and testing, you may want to create one account for development and another for testing as if you were an end user. Or perhaps you want to segregate user accounts so they are only used for testing a sub-set of your ARTIK- and SAMI-based products. Carefully document your account setups to avoid confusion later on about why you created them. Documenting everything should become a habit.

■ **Note**   Making plenty of notes will pay dividends later on when you need to come back to something and work on it again. It also helps to clear the mind of distractions. Documenting some work after it is completed also walks through the process again in your mind and may reveal something you forgot to do.

User ID

This is the identifying value that must be unique on the SAMI system in order to connect with a specific Samsung user account. Incoming messages will be associated with this account via their metadata. Only those messages that are tagged with this user ID are considered to be a part of the aggregated data set for this user.

Applications can quote this user ID to acquire the public parts of the user profile and device list. With that information, they can then create and manage an application profile for that user.

Devices

Developers create devices and describe them using the device-type manifests. Your end users purchase or obtain these devices in many different ways, but each must make sure that their own personal, unique device is paired with their own SAMI account. They must not be able to see someone else's devices, nor should anyone else be able to see their devices. This pairing creates a unique one-to-one relationship that maps a device to a single SAMI account. SAMI devices can act as data sources. These devices will be one of the following types (or even a combination of them):

- Sensor
- Appliance
- Application
- Service
- Hub

An ARTIK module might be a single stand-alone device with sensors that create feeds for SAMI to manage. Alternatively, that ARTIK module might be the front end for a collection of legacy devices, none of which could talk to SAMI on their own. In that scenario, the ARTIK module acts as an intermediary, and data appears to stream from the ARTIK but is actually forwarded on behalf of another (possibly much less smart) device. The legacy devices might be implemented as individual sensors belonging to an ARTIK module.

The following referenced blog articles go into much more detail about how to set up an ARTIK module as an aggregation hub and how to integrate that with SAMI:

https://blog.samsungsami.io/topics/security/

Device Type

A device type groups devices into categories. These identify a unique product type. Liken this to the model number for a production run of devices you have designed and manufactured. The device type only identifies a generic type of device, not a specific instance of it. This identifier allows properties and behaviors to be defined for all devices of the same type.

Develop private device types on SAMI, with security supported as the standard. Any data or message can be sent and received in real-time subject to the latency and speed of the network route between the remote entity and the SAMI server.

Samsung has created SDK libraries for many devices that already have manifests ready to access and use right away. This is useful at the outset and may provide all that you need. As your designs become more sophisticated, you may outgrow these prototypes. Add more of your own as you develop new and unique devices and applications. Create your own device types via your Developer Portal dashboard.

Device ID

A device ID describes a unique instance of a device type. Where the device type describes generic behaviors, the device ID identifies one of many devices in that family. Two ARTIK-based wearable devices would each have a different device ID even if they were both of the same device type. This identifier is fundamental to creating a Secure Device Registration (SDR).

Add new devices to your User Portal dashboard. As you create them, each one will be granted a specific and unique ID. As the user, you are responsible for keeping the name and description of that device up to date.

Applications

Applications can run inside an ARTIK-based product or in other contexts, such as workstations or devices made by other manufacturers. They all communicate with SAMI using API calls, just like any other SAMI-compatible device.

Build applications that can read historical and real-time data from any connected device. SAMI is a platform rich in API endpoints for managing user and device connectivity while you focus on your application design and feature set.

Application ID

Each application is assigned a unique identifier by SAMI when you create it in your User Portal dashboard. This ID value is used to acquire an OAuth2 access token. Without that token you cannot send a message to the SAMI system. You also need the user to have been granted access to your application first.

Each developer can request as many application identifiers as needed. Document them carefully as you acquire them to avoid mixing them up and embedding them into the wrong device.

OAuth2 Access Tokens

It is not necessary to deeply understand how OAuth2 works. It is a robust and proven security technology. It is used industry wide and is well maintained. It is embedded inside SAMI and creates access tokens that your application or device can use to authenticate the messages being transmitted inward to SAMI. Request a token and embed that in the messages you transmit. Tokens have a limited lifetime, and after a short while they will expire and cannot be reused. It makes sense to always request a new one at the start of any transaction-handling process.

Manifest

The internal mechanisms within SAMI must function in a predictable way. The SAMI engineers cannot know in advance what you want to build or what kind of data you will transmit to SAMI. They would have had to incorporate data types and variable names that cover every potential developer's needs. That is an impossible task.

Instead, SAMI provides the means to map your data formats and descriptors to internal representations and gives you the tools and responsibility for managing that descriptive configuration. SAMI calls this a *manifest*.

Build a manifest to describe each of your own device types. In fact it is your responsibility to do this, because SAMI cannot do it for you. Register the manifest via your Developer Portal. After that, your users can select that device type when adding devices to their profile. Applications can request the manifest to discover the kind of data values your device type expects. A manifest describes a type of device. If you have multiple identical devices, they will all share one manifest and use their device ID to distinguish one from another. Different types of devices require different manifests because the device type maps to an appropriate manifest.

You cannot send data to SAMI unless there is a manifest to describe it. SAMI uses the manifests internally to steer the data-parsing activity. Without a manifest, SAMI has no way to understand what format your data has been presented in. This mechanism decouples SAMI from your data, because it is no longer hard wired. Because it is data driven, the data parsing is infinitely configurable.

You create a manifest by adding a new device type to your Developer Portal. In that definition, you describe the kinds of data being delivered. There are predefined standard fields to use, or you can synthesize your own new ones. The form-based manifest editor makes this process very easy.

A simple manifest only has data fields. Add user-defined actions to create a more advanced manifest. After your manifest is complete, publish it to make it available to the general public or they will not be able to see and select it in their own profiles. Once your manifest is complete, the manifest editor will simulate a call and display to you a sample JSON response. This is going to be invaluable when you want to build receivers into an application, as you can define a manifest and capture the output for testing.

Once a manifest has been created, it cannot be deleted. Upload a new one to supersede the behavior. The older ones must be maintained to ensure data integrity, because they may have been used for data that has already arrived and been processed into the SAMI data-storage repository. Deleting a manifest associated with that data would render the data orphaned and unusable. It is imperative that you think through your manifest design before creating any. Otherwise, you risk filling your account with garbage data and unusable legacy manifests. If you expect your manifests to change and therefore be replaced, develop a consistent naming scheme that incorporates a version-numbering index so you can keep things neat and tidy.

These online resources provide additional material that describes the manifest and how to use it:

```
https://developer.samsungsami.io/sami/sami-documentation/the-manifest.html
https://blog.samsungsami.io/development/data/2015/04/21/
send-actions-to-devices.html
https://blog.samsungsami.io/development/portals/2015/08/06/
see-all-the-standard-fields-and-actions-in-sami.html
https://blog.samsungsami.io/portals/development/data/2015/03/26/
the-simple-manifest-device-types-in-1-minute.html
https://developer.samsungsami.io/sami/demos-tools/manifest-sdk.html
https://developer.samsungsami.io/sami/demos-tools/
manifest-advanced-example.html
https://developer.samsungsami.io/sami/demos-tools/your-first-iot-device.html
```

Raw Data

Your incoming messages are formatted according your own needs. These may use product-specific names for the value containers, and the format will be one of several that are compatible with the SAMI incoming data–parsing processes.

Normalized Data

SAMI uses the descriptions in the manifest to parse your incoming data and transform it into a standard format. This normalization process converts your variable container names to internally compatible names. Your application might describe a variable as temp, but SAMI translates that into temperature. The data is also stored in a normalized format based on JSON. Values are also converted where necessary. This makes the data storage consistent regardless of its provenance.

A developer can request either the normalized data or the raw data because SAMI stores both in the database.

The SAMI API

Applications, services, and modules can exchange data with SAMI through simple API endpoints. Access the details of that API specification and other helpful information about the API at the following URLs:

```
https://developer.samsungsami.io/sami/api-spec.html
https://developer.samsungsami.io/sami/sami-documentation/
administrative-apis.html
https://developer.samsungsami.io/sami/sami-documentation/
sending-and-receiving-data.html
https://developer.samsungsami.io/sami/demos-tools/api-console.html
```

Using the administrative calls in the SAMI API, you have the ability to retrieve a user's profile, update applications for a user, and retrieve a list of a user's device types and devices, as well as the data they have sent to SAMI. This is useful for creating threads of related messaging events or browsing the contents of the message traffic on a remote device.

Access historical data according to a specific timestamp or range and apply analytic tools to observe trends. Perhaps you are monitoring a remote system where you are trying to diagnose an intermittent fault. Logging the observations and analyzing them for patterns is a useful diagnostic approach.

You also can send actions to SAMI that will be routed to the destination device to trigger something to happen. In a home-automation context, that might turn on a light or activate a streaming video camera.

Developer SDK Libraries

There are Software Development Kit libraries (SDK) available for the main platforms with which you are likely to build applications. Language support for others is in development. Table 18-1 summarizes the supporting kits or alternatives to them for each language.

Table 18-1. *SAMI Language-Supporting API Kits*

Kit	Availability
Java/Android	Available now for development of applications to run in Android-based devices
Objective-C/iOS	Available now for developing iOS applications to run in Apple mobile devices
PHP	Available now for building server-side support in web-based solutions
Ruby	Available but currently in Beta testing
Python 2	Available but currently in Beta testing
Python 3	Available but currently in Beta testing
C language	Use libCurl and manufacture the API calls as described in the documentation. This would work inside an ARTIK or any other application that has libCurl and network access available.
Node.js	Construct the payload and SAMI envelope manually and dispatch it via a WebSocket connection.
UNIX command line	Use the wget and curl commands to dispatch messages to SAMI from a shell script, or write small C-language utilities and call them from scripts or command lines directly.
Mac OS X	Use the C-language approach with libCurl. You may be able to use some of the capabilities of the iOS library.
Objective C	Encapsulate your sessions in objects and write their methods in C language, and use libCurl.
Swift language	Manufacture the payloads and wrap them in a SAMI envelope in a similar way to the raw C language or Node.js approach, then deliver them via a WebSocket connection.

The SAMI developer documentation at the following URLs has details of the SAMI SDK libraries and how to obtain them for use in your own projects. The API specifications will provide enough insight for you to construct payloads and SAMI envelopes. Study the worked example by Martin Kronberg on the Hackster·IO blog to see how to do this with Node.js:

```
https://developer.samsungsami.io/sami/native-SDKs/
https://www.hackster.io/martinkronberg/artik10-sami-eab8f7
```

SAMI Tools

Samsung has provided developer tools that assist you in getting your devices and manifests working more quickly. The Developer Portal dashboard itself is one of those tools, and you may have already used it to create experimental resources. The User Portal is a dashboard for managing the devices that provide data to be aggregated under your SAMI user ID. The API Console helps you to exercise API calls and see their results, and the Device Simulator gives you a way to send test data to SAMI as if it had come from your device before you even create it.

The Developer Portal

This is where you construct prototypes that describe your own devices. Introduce handlers for the data that your device will want to send to SAMI through the creation of a manifest. Manage these additional resources from your developer account:

- Applications that you develop and vend on the application store for other users to access

- Device types that you create and share with other developers

A Samsung account is required in order to access SAMI as a developer. You must be signed in to see the developer support pages. SAMI developers can do more powerful things with their ARTIK-based product development. User Portal access is all about configuring the data exchanges with your own personal devices. Developer Portal access is concerned with creating new applications and device types for your customers to use.

Here are the steps for device development when you integrate new devices with SAMI:

1. Define the device type via the Developer Portal to associate the device with a user account in the User Portal.

2. Obtain an access token via the User Portal.

3. Make API calls to send data to SAMI.

Developing an application that connects to SAMI follows slightly different steps:

1. Discover the device-type data by accessing the manifest to find out the required field names.

2. Create the application in the Developer Portal.

3. Request permissions.

4. Obtain an access token using the OAuth2 messaging protocols.

5. Make the API calls to SAMI.

6. Collect the response data that SAMI sends back to the calling application.

Find out more about the Developer Portal at the following:

```
https://developer.samsungsami.io/sami/sami-documentation/
developer-user-portals.html
https://blog.samsungsami.io/portals/development/2015/02/12/
how-to-use-the-developer-portal.html
```

The User Portal

This is where you securely pair a personal device you own with your secure SAMI account. Within your SAMI account, you have collections of resources to configure and edit. SAMI maintains these collections for you as a casual user of the system:

- Devices that are allowed to exchange data with your SAMI account

- Rules governing actions that can be triggered when incoming messages arrive

- Charts showing trends based on incoming data

- Data logs containing lists of raw messages and actions performed by them

- Exports where you have aggregated data into a tabular form for external processing

Add new items to these collections or alter the configuration of them whenever you want to. Access SAMI via the User Portal to do this. If you want to register new SAMI devices or monitor the data being received, go to the User Portal and sign in with your Samsung account:

```
https://portal.samsungsami.io/
```

Click on the Get Started or Sign In buttons to access your data via the portal. Find out more about the User Portal here:

```
https://developer.samsungsami.io/sami/sami-documentation/
developer-user-portals.html
https://blog.samsungsami.io/portals/datavisualization/2015/01/09/
opening-the-user-portal.html
```

API Console

The API Console is a web-based tool for testing SAMI API calls to verify that you are using them correctly in your own code. Quickly retrieve important information such as device IDs and normalized messages in the format that your device would see them in if it made a call to the API. It also works as a hands-on reference for required and optional parameters discussed in the API specification. Go to the online API Console and try it out here:

```
https://api-console.samsungsami.io/sami
```

Device Simulator

The SAMI Device Simulator is a command-line tool developed in Java. It is meant to help you send messages to SAMI on behalf of any device in the system. You can run this from the command line in a terminal window on your developer workstation. If you have a viable connection from your prototype ARTIK module to the SAMI infrastructure, this would work in your ARTIK too. Read more about it here:

```
https://developer.samsungsami.io/sami/demos-tools/device-simulator.html
```

Manifest Validator

Validating your manifest is a vital step before you upload it to SAMI. There is a Java command-line tool to download and run with your manifest as the input. The tool will check that your manifest is correctly constructed and tell you if it thinks there is anything wrong with it. Think of this as being a bit like a source-code compiler. See this SAMI developer documentation for more details and how to download the tool for use in your development workstation:

```
https://developer.samsungsami.io/sami/demos-tools/manifest-sdk.html
```

User Portal: Managing Devices

Register your device to get an ID and token value to use when you transmit data to SAMI. Keep a copy of your device ID and device token so you can use them again later.

Read the "Connect to SAMI" section in the SAMI tutorial that describes how to make an IoT weather station. This shows you how to create a temperature sensor entry in SAMI and transmit data to it from your device:

```
https://blog.samsungsami.io/architecture/tutorial/beginner/2015/04/30/
make-an-iot-weather-station-with-sami.html#connect-to-sami-its-free-really
```

Once you are logged in to the User Portal, SAMI invites you to add your IoT devices. This permits them to access your SAMI account and exchange data with it. Return to this starting page by clicking on the Devices button in the menu bar at the top of the page. Figure 18-3 illustrates the initial connection dialog.

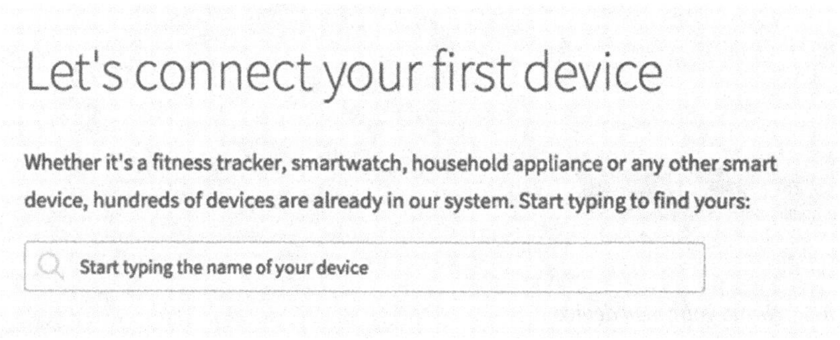

Let's connect your first device

Whether it's a fitness tracker, smartwatch, household appliance or any other smart device, hundreds of devices are already in our system. Start typing to find yours:

> Start typing the name of your device

Figure 18-3. Let's connect your first device

If you have no devices attached to your account, SAMI invites you to connect your first one. Since this book is about programming your ARTIK module, add that as the first device in your SAMI account. Use that device to transmit data to SAMI directly from your applications.

Click in the search box and choose the kind of device you want to associate with your account from the menu. Filter the list by typing the first few letters of the device type. Click on the one you want. Choose Artik from the available list (shown in Figure 18-4).

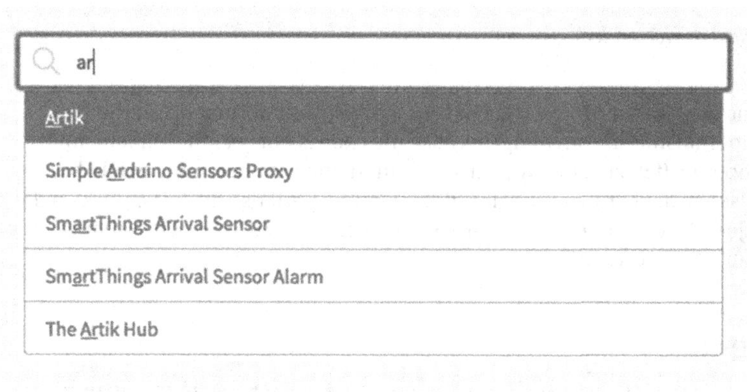

> ar
>
> Artik
> Simple Arduino Sensors Proxy
> SmartThings Arrival Sensor
> SmartThings Arrival Sensor Alarm
> The Artik Hub

Figure 18-4. Choose a device type

SAMI then automatically creates a device name cell and pre-fills the name based on the chosen device type. Replace this with your preferred unique device name up to 32 characters long. Figure 18-5 illustrates how SAMI shows you how many characters you have left as you type the name.

Figure 18-5. *Name your new device*

Click on the CONNECT DEVICE button when you are ready. You should see your new device added to the Connected Devices panel (see Figure 18-6).

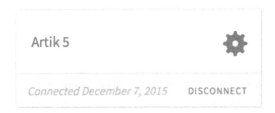

Figure 18-6. *New device added*

Click on the device name to view the data as it transmits information. At the moment, it is not transmitting anything, because the code is not yet fully implemented in the ARTIK module. If it had already been configured, the data streaming would be evident here. Use the data browser to select different time periods and dates. Click on the gear icon to adjust the device settings or click on the DISCONNECT button to remove this device from your SAMI account.

Device Details

Clicking on the gear for a device presents the Properties panel, shown in Figure 18-7. This panel contains vital information that your application will need in order to transmit data into a specific SAMI account. Your data messages will be tagged with your SAMI account name, password, and the device type ID. SAMI uses the device type ID to invoke an appropriate data parser. You will also tag your messages with a unique device ID that identifies each instance of a device type ID. This tags the data for more than one instance of the same type of device.

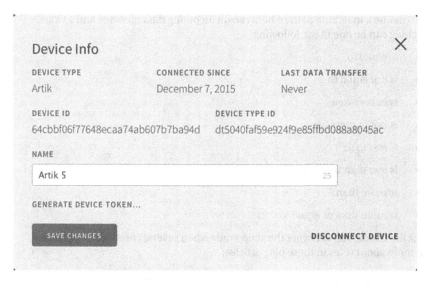

Figure 18-7. *Device properties panel*

Click on the GENERATE DEVICE TOKEN button to create a secure token that your device will use to tag the data it transmits to SAMI.

Note your device ID and token and device type ID values so you can use them in the application running on the ARTIK module. Use this panel to rename or disconnect your devices as well as to revoke the device tokens.

Click on the SAVE CHANGES button when you are done.

User Portal: Managing Rules

Once you have set up a device, describe the rules that manage the incoming data. When a SAMI rule matches True, an action can be triggered as a consequence. Figure 18-8 illustrates the relationship between the various participating sensors (SAMI calls these *buttons*) and output controls (SAMI calls these *lights*).

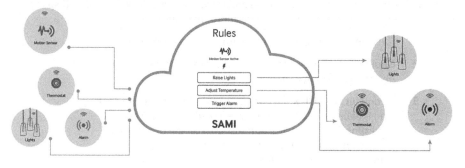

Figure 18-8. *SAMI rules mechanism*

Rules define a matching pattern between an incoming data message and a value. The matching can be one of the following:

- is equal to

- is not equal to

- is in message

- is not in message

- is less than

- is less than or equal to

- is more than

- is more than or equal to

Stack the conditions to trigger the action only when several conditions hold true. Find out more about rules in these blog articles:

```
https://blog.samsungsami.io/data/rules/iot/2015/09/23/
sami-rules-make-your-devices-work-together.html
https://blog.samsungsami.io/rules/iot/2015/10/13/
sami-rules-your-devices-can-speak-up.html
```

Rule-based Actions

An action can send a message back to an ARTIK module as a response or onward to another device. Messages can only be routed to devices you have previously registered. Perhaps your action can send an e-mail that can go anywhere. Simply pressing a button connected to your ARTIK module could transmit a message to SAMI that delivers an e-mail somewhere on your behalf.

Actions can also be stacked so a trigger can do a variety of things each time it is invoked. This makes SAMI extremely powerful.

Adding New Rules

Click on the RULES button in the heading menu bar. Your current rules will be displayed if you have any. Follow these steps to create additional rules:

1. Click on the Create New Rule button to access the rule editor.

2. Choose one of your devices from the menu. Your new rule will be associated with that device.

3. By default, an ARTIK has two properties that collate the data. One is called button and the other is called light. These correspond to inputs and outputs. Choose the one that you are creating a rule for. You now have a value defined to test with a conditional operator.

4. Specify a conditional operator from the listed options.

5. Add a value that the condition will be tested against.

6. When the condition tests the incoming data message against the rule, you want it to perform an action. Enter the details of the action you want to trigger.

7. Add a title for your rule so you can find it again in among all your other rules. It makes sense to plan this and use sensible naming conventions, but SAMI will not impose any of these on you itself. Create a registry of your own to manage a collection of naming conventions for your products.

8. Use a more lengthy description to document your design. SAMI pre-populates this based on the conditions and actions you have already defined, but you can replace that with your own text.

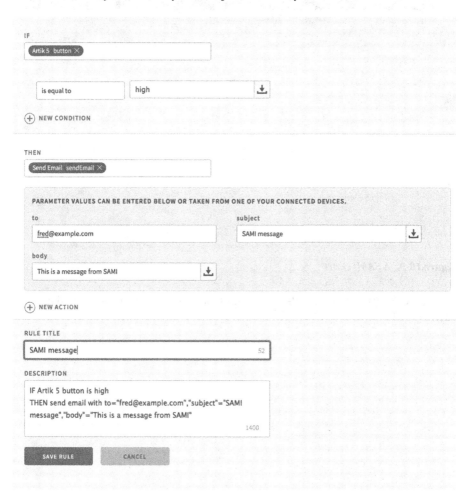

9. Click on the SAVE RULE button when you are done.

10. Your rules browser then shows you the new rule in an abbreviated listing together with all your other rules.

User Portal: Displaying Charts

Your incoming data streams are visible in the SAMI Charts panel. Choose this from the menu bar. Figure 18-9 shows an example chart from the weather station project.

Figure 18-9. A SAMI chart

Figure 18-10 is a more complex chart. This time, the chart is recreated from data logged and stored in the SAMI database.

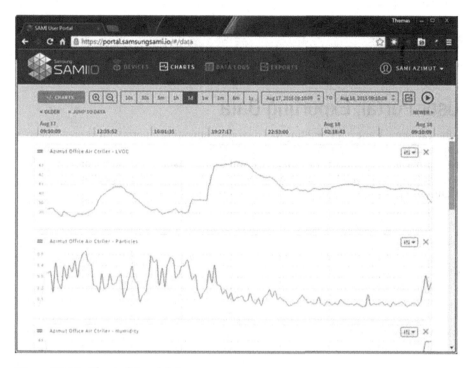

Figure 18-10. Chart of stored data

User Portal: Viewing Data Logs

Data logs are an alternative to viewing a graphical chart. They list the raw data that SAMI is managing. This can be useful when you are debugging SAMI transactions. Each individual message transaction is separately recorded in the log. Figure 18-11 illustrates part of a data log with the events filtered; a calendar defines a date range.

Figure 18-11. Table view of a SAMI data log

Find out more about the data-logging capabilities of SAMI here:

```
https://blog.samsungsami.io/portals/datavisualization/2015/04/07/
check-out-table-view.html
```

User Portal: Exporting Data

After gathering some data, auditing that data and generating reports with a spreadsheet application is easier if you can extract it from SAMI in a useful format first. The Export tools provide a way to choose a time range and data format and extract the data in a spreadsheet-compatible form. Requesting an export presents the page shown in Figure 18-12.

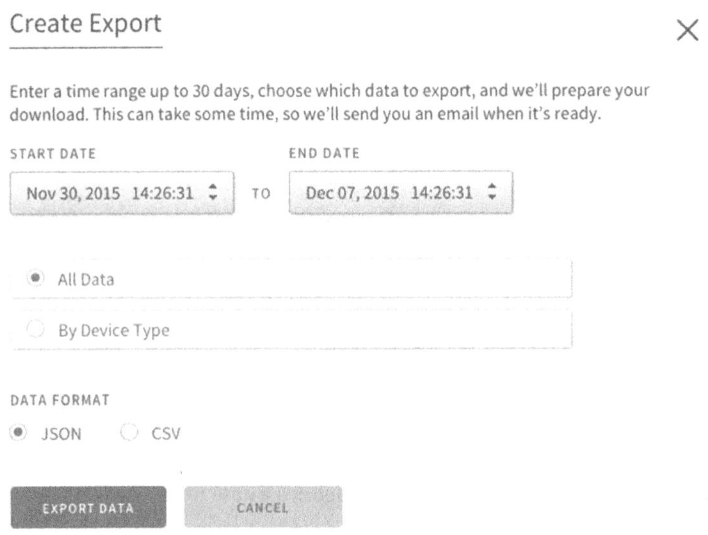

Figure 18-12. *Export SAMI data*

When you click on the EXPORT DATA button, SAMI works in the background, sending you an e-mail message when it is done. When you receive the e-mail, return to your SAMI account and download the exported data.

Developer Portal: Managing Device Types

SAMI is open and device agnostic. It integrates data sources and destinations on devices made by other manufacturers. Potentially any mobile or permanently sited device can join the franchise. Participating devices can upload data to SAMI in any format that works for them and SAMI will then parse that data to integrate it. This makes SAMI an important nexus in the data-exchange process. Develop your own private device types with security already supported. Collaborate and share device-type capabilities with other developers to enrich the SAMI community.

Click on the + NEW DEVICE TYPE button to tell SAMI what your device type is called, then start building a new manifest to describe it further.

Developer Portal: Managing Applications

Create applications that unite devices around a common shared exchange of data. Your SAMI applications are limited only by your own imagination. From the Developer Portal, name your first application, add a device type, and get ready to do new things with real-time and historical data. Registering the application with SAMI grants a set of credentials to embed in your application so as to transmit messages that are uniquely associated with it. Analyze and apply rules to those data feeds in order to add the centralized SAMI mechanisms to your application portfolio, such as the following:

- Use SAMI to control a device by sending actions from your application.

- Subscribe to activity on a device via SAMI notifications.

- Use simple communications over WebSocket and REST API endpoints.

Click on the APPLICATIONS button in the menu bar to get help with developing new SAMI-based apps. Be aware that by introducing your application to SAMI, it is available for other users on the application store:

```
https://developer.samsungsami.io/sami/sami-documentation/sami-basics.html
https://developer.samsungsami.io/sami/demos-tools/
https://developer.samsungsami.io/sami/api-spec.html
```

Connecting to SAMI from Your Applications

Connect to SAMI from any application that can generate an HTTP: request and access the REST API that SAMI supports. These development environments are introduced in this book, but there are other alternatives:

- Online access via Temboo (see Chapter 19)

- Native development with C language (see Chapter 15)

- Native development with Python (see Chapter 17)

- Native development with Node.js (see Chapter 16)

Acquiring an Access Token for Your Application

Access tokens in SAMI are generated with OAuth2. First, make an authentication call to initiate the process. Then, respond to a callback when OAuth2 is ready to deliver the token back to you. Provide the account ID for the User Portal account that is paired with the calling application. You make the authentication request like this:

```
https://accounts.samsungsami.io/authorize?client_id={your_account_id}↵
                    &response_type=token&redirect_uri=artik_app://redirect
```

The SAMI responder will extract the callback URI from the redirect_uri parameter and use that to construct a call back to your device. It knows you want an access token because that was what you requested for the response_type value. Therefore, your device needs to be ready and listening on an HTTPS: port and must map a response to this URL:

```
artik_app://redirect
```

SAMI will call that response handler with URL parameters that tell you the expiry time and the access token. You will not get a token back if the application is unrecognized by the user account. SAMI will call back with a URL that looks like this:

```
artik_app://redirect#expires_in={milliseconds}&token_type=bearer ↵
&access_token={access_token_val}
```

The token is typically only valid for a few minutes at most. You should request a new one if you make a fresh inquiry.

Getting Data from SAMI for Your Application

Your application can request data from SAMI with a simple HTTPS: request that sends back a JSON-style response. You need the access token you just obtained and a known good device ID to validate the request. The request construction is shown in Listing 18-1.

Listing 18-1. SAMI Request Format

```
https://api.samsungsami.io/v1.1/messages/last?count=1&sdids={valid_device_id}

headers:
{
    "Authorization":"bearer {access_token}"
},
```

If the request is successful, you should also receive a response body with a JSON data block. Listing 18-2 shows an example layout. Your results will have real values inserted instead of the placeholder tags.

Listing 18-2. SAMI Response Body

```
"data":
{
   "value1":{some_value},
   "value2":{another_value}
},
```

Sending Data to SAMI from Your Device

Construct a JSON-formatted message containing your data and wrap it in an HTTP: envelope, then transmit it to the SAMI REST API. To create the message body, you will need a valid device ID value, which you should have created earlier via your account on the Developer Portal. Your sensor values are passed within the data array. The timestamp is used inside SAMI to organize the messages according to their chronological sequence. An example message body structure is shown in Listing 18-3.

Listing 18-3. SAMI Example Message Body

```
{
   "sdid":"{a_valid_device_id}",
   "data":
   {
      "value1":{some_value},
      "value2":{another_value}
   },
   "ts":{time_stamp}
}
```

The HTTP: envelope needs the device token in order for SAMI to associate the incoming message with the correct user account. The same message body is shown in Listing 18-4. This is wrapped in an HTTP: envelope ready for dispatch using the curl command.

Listing 18-4. SAMI Message Body Delivered via curl

```
POST: https://api.samsungsami.io/v1.1/messages

headers:
{
   "Authorization":"bearer {device_token}"
},
```

```
body:
{
    "sdid":"{a_valid_device_id}",
    "data":
    {
        "value1":{some_value},
        "value2":{another_value}
    },
    "ts":{time_stamp}
}
```

Try Out More Examples

The SAMI developer documentation has a section with more tutorial code samples for you to experiment with. The SAMI GitHub has useful repositories of source code for you to download. These are applications that demonstrate advanced ways of using SAMI in practice. Each application is separately available on GitHub, and the collection is designed to be modular. This is an ideal starting point, and you can take the applications apart and reuse them in your own project designs:

```
https://developer.samsungsami.io/sami/samples/
https://developer.samsungsami.io/sami/demos-tools/
https://developer.samsungsami.io/sami/demos-tools/
        your-first-application.html
https://developer.samsungsami.io/sami/sami-documentation/hello-world.html
https://github.com/samsungsamiio/
```

Want to Know More?

Find out all about SAMI from a dedicated website and the articles posted on the SAMI blog:

```
https://developer.samsungsami.io/
https://blog.samsungsami.io/
```

The developer documentation you should read to create your own SAMI-based data interactions is found here:

```
https://developer.samsungsami.io/sami/sami-documentation/
```

The discussion forum is located at the following URL in case you want to ask questions or see the answers to questions that other SAMI developers have posted:

```
https://developer.samsungsami.io/community/
```

Take a look at the Samsung SmartThings Open Cloud ecosystem. This is a useful foundation on which to build wired home systems, although in the fullness of time it is likely to be used for other kinds of integration across a range of mobile and static IoT devices. Find out more about that here:

```
http://www.smartthings.com/opencloud/
```

Summary

The Samsung SAMI system is an example of the kind of connecting hub that will become commonplace as the Internet of Things industry gathers pace. Already there are other similar services.

Partitioning different kinds of activity into different hubs prevents everything from failing when the one and only aggregation system in the world goes offline. These hubs can be interconnected themselves. Perhaps a factory can host a hub of its own with a gateway to other systems with which it needs to share an aggregated data feed.

If your design works with SAMI, it can very likely use other alternative aggregation systems. Create your own aggregation hub if you want to scale your product or service up to a large enterprise. Samsung has ensured that the crypto support in the ARTIK and the SAMI service architecture are compatible.

Samsung has integrated a lot of intelligent home solutions with the SmartThings devices and connected hub. Find out more in order to integrate your ARTIK-based solutions with it:

```
https://www.smartthings.com/uk
```

Check out the ARTIK partner company, Medium One. They support data streaming and real-time analytics. This would be useful in a manufacturing context:

```
https://mediumone.com/
```

The SIGFOX partner company provides cellular connectivity for reaching online services from mobile devices. As an ARTIK partner, their technologies will integrate with an ARTIK module more easily:

```
http://www.sigfox.com/
```

The next chapter will examine Temboo. This is an alternative to using SAMI, although it is oriented more toward the software development of the applications that run inside your ARTIK module. Build simple application components using the online Temboo GUI tools and then generate the code to compile and run in the ARTIK. That code could have SAMI calls integrated with it too.

CHAPTER 19

■ ■ ■

Integrating with Temboo

Hello Temboo

Temboo is an exciting new technology for developers to create reusable code with that can run across a range of devices and architectures. There is a lot to explore, and new features are being added all the time. You can see the logo in Figure 19-1.

Figure 19-1. *Temboo logo*

Temboo is accessed via the web-based dashboard on the Temboo website. There you connect together various components without needing to write code. Temboo generates the source code for you to copy to your ARTIK module and compile into an executable application that runs natively inside the ARTIK. Find out more about Temboo here:

http://www.temboo.com/

The whole Temboo user experience is very well conceived and rather beautifully engineered. Once you have chosen a target platform, everything reconfigures itself around that choice. This reconfiguration includes the code-generation tools and access to the library of additional plugin functionality (choreographies).

© Cliff Wootton 2016
C. Wootton, *Beginning Samsung ARTIK*, DOI 10.1007/978-1-4842-1952-2_19

Developing with Temboo

With Temboo, it becomes very easy to reach more than 100 web-based services and resources, such as Facebook, Dropbox, or census data published by various open government initiatives. Temboo acts as a central location that gathers these data resources or makes connections to them on your behalf. Use the tools on your ARTIK module to connect to your Temboo account and ask it to act as an intermediary for you.

The coding process is very visual and takes place online in a web-based dashboard. The outcome can be shared very easily. You can build sophisticated solutions without ever writing a line of code. There is also a Software Developer Kit (SDK) for programmers who like to write code themselves. The visual approach will not prevent traditional coding from taking place. It just gets you started more quickly. Use Temboo without the SDK just by calling API endpoints via a REST interface. Use the curl command for this, but wget and even a custom, handmade HTTP GET call via raw Berkeley Software Distribution (BSD) sockets would work. Watch these tutorial videos for insight into how powerful Temboo is:

https://www.temboo.com/videos

Temboo is a technology stack for connected devices and the Internet of Things. Generate production-ready code for robust IoT applications in minutes by going to the Temboo website and choosing components that Temboo uses to construct your application's source code.

The Temboo IoT technology stack makes the computing power of the cloud easily accessible from ARTIK hardware. A lightweight Temboo library is installed on every ARTIK module, enabling developers building ARTIK applications to quickly and easily connect their hardware to any web-based resource.

Temboo packages complex processes as choreos. This is an abbreviation for choreographies. Assembling these choreos is somewhat like building with pre-formed bricks. They already have built-in smartness. Connect them to create an application.

Explore choreo processes on the Temboo website, and then generate production-ready code to execute those processes in your ARTIK IoT applications. Most of the code behind each choreo executes in the cloud and not directly in your ARTIK. Your devices only do what is necessary to communicate with Temboo. This approach conserves memory and builds more efficient and dynamic applications. By integrating Temboo into the ARTIK, you have a complete IoT programming solution ready to use from inside the Samsung ARTIK hardware ecosystem.

Registering Your Temboo Account

To use Temboo, you need to register an account at the Temboo website. Before registering, you should read about the privacy policy describing the information that Temboo collects about you. Their terms of service are also covered here:

https://temboo.com/privacy
https://temboo.com/terms

The registration process is simple, and the signup form is presented on the Temboo home page. Choose a unique name, add your e-mail address, and define a robust password. After you enter your account details and accept the terms and conditions, click on the Sign Up button. Note your password in a safe place or use one that is easy to remember.

By default, you will be signed up for a free account to start with. This gives you full access to the Temboo infrastructure but limits the number of calls you can make. Each time you run a choreo, it counts against your total. The free developer accounts start with 250 choreo runs per month. You will probably use these up rather quickly when developing your code. Purchase more if you are running your choreos often to test them. Different plans are available to purchase depending on the capacity you need. Go to your account page to upgrade from a free to a paid account. There is a special low-cost plan for developers to experiment with:

```
https://www.temboo.com/account
```

The Library page also gives you statistics describing your usage of choreos and how many calls you have made:

```
https://www.temboo.com/library/
```

Once you are logged in, access your account dashboard and see how much Temboo capacity you are using. This is available from the Activity page:

```
https://www.temboo.com/activity
```

Your Temboo Account Dashboard

The Account dashboard is where you manage your relationship with Temboo. Access it here:

```
https://www.temboo.com/account
```

You will be prompted for a password if you are not signed in already. Change your billing plan in here from the default free account and upgrade it to cope with more traffic. Running a choreo deducts a token from a total that you must keep in credit. When you run out of tokens, your choreos will stop running. When you deploy a product based on Temboo and ARTIK, it needs to be associated with an account that will be kept topped up with credits or your customers will find their devices will stop working. That account is probably not your own personal one. Figure 19-2 shows a typical account dashboard, although Temboo will update the design of this from time to time.

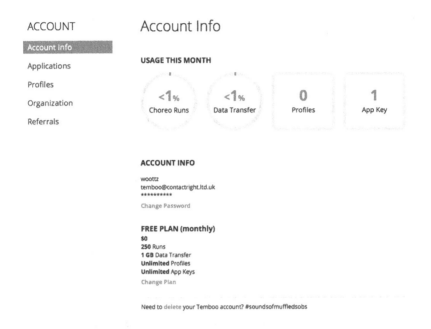

Figure 19-2. *Temboo account dashboard*

Click on the "Change Password" link to change your password or the "Change Plan" link to purchase additional capacity.

Click on the Applications item in the left navigation menu to configure your Temboo-compliant application credentials. Create multiple applications and give each of them a unique and secure identification key. These values must be compiled into your application via the TembooAccount.h header file that you include in your application's source code.

The Profiles menu item takes you to a page for creating profile containers where your application can offload data for storage.

Upgrade your whole Temboo experience to operate across an entire organization or enterprise. The default account is for only you to access and use. To embed Temboo into a product, you will probably need one of these power-user upgrades to create new users and share profile data between them and the rest of your organization.

Monitoring Your Activity

As you develop and run your Temboo choreo-based applications, you will gradually consume your credit balance. You may want to see a more detailed record of your traffic. Go to this page to see your activity metrics:

```
https://www.temboo.com/activity
```

The summary in Figure 19-3 shows how many different choreos have been executed and displays historical graphs of data usage measured in bytes.

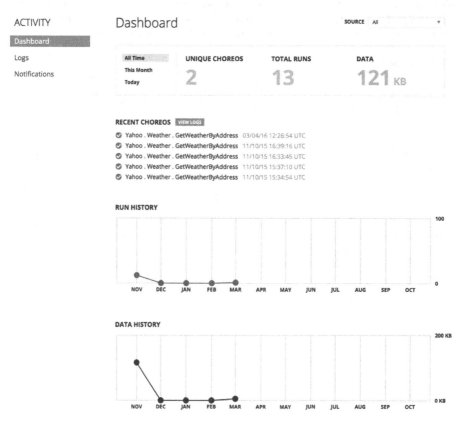

Figure 19-3. *Temboo activity dashboard*

Filter this report by individual applications or view the grand total. Sub-set the data to show it one month or one day at a time. The Logs view shows you individual calls to your choreos from your Temboo applications. These logs can be downloaded as a CSV file for you to import into a spreadsheet or management reporting system.

The Notifications panel helps you set up automated notifications by e-mail for when your choreos fail to execute correctly. Notify your own Temboo-registered e-mail address and up to ten others. Some of these can be automated email-handling robots in your monitoring system. Adjust the frequency of these notifications to arrive at hourly or daily intervals. You only receive messages if there are new errors to report.

Your Choreo Library Dashboard

If you go to the Library page on the Temboo website without being signed in first, Temboo cannot report any statistics about your usage of the choreos because it does not know who you are. You just get a page for exploring the library in a passive way:

```
https://www.temboo.com/library/
```

Logging in to your account and going to the Library page presents much more information. Your Library dashboard will look similar to the one in Figure 19-4.

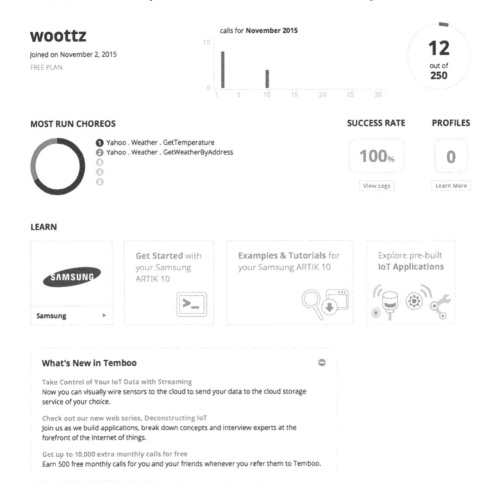

Figure 19-4. Library dashboard

The Library dashboard presents summary details of your Temboo account traffic. This is great for tracking how fast you are using your capacity and deciding whether to upgrade your account. Check at a glance whether your choreos are functioning correctly; any problems are accessible by clicking on the shortcut that displays the logs.

The lower part of the screen is for training you in how to get the best out of Temboo. The first box chooses a platform to work with and the rest of the boxes then reconfigure themselves around that choice to provide the most appropriate learning resources.

Supported Platforms

Temboo supports a variety of different hardware platforms. Choose your platform first, and then the Temboo website will take you through the process of building your application before generating the code to compile and embed. These target hardware platforms are supported:

- Samsung ARTIK modules

- Arduino

- Texas Instruments

- Android mobile devices

- IOS mobile devices

Temboo also generates raw code to incorporate into other projects written in these languages:

- C#

- Java

- JavaScript

- Node.js

- PHP

- Processing

- Python

- Ruby

- REST API

Each of these would require the inclusion of a Temboo SDK file to provide the necessary supporting calls. The code that calls the Temboo SDK is straightforward. Choose any of these from the tutorial interface at the Temboo website to see the code they create.

Some SDK libraries are already installed. Additional Temboo toolkits for embedding raw code can be downloaded from this page:

```
https://www.temboo.com/download
```

■ **Note** As of Spring 2016, Temboo only supports the ARTIK 10 modules and is developing the support for ARTIK 5 modules. The ARTIK 5 support will be released in due course when it is ready.

Supported Connectivity

As you build your application, you may want to incorporate wireless connectivity to remote services and systems. The following modes of connection are supported, and others may become available as the technology is developed:

- Bluetooth
- Ethernet
- GSM
- Wi-Fi

Online Data Storage

Shared data storage helps you avoid the need to be located in a single place where your bulk data is stored. Temboo already supports the following storage architectures. Others will surely become available as Temboo evolves:

- Microsoft Power BI
- Google BigQuery

You may also be able to exploit similar tools via the SAMI infrastructure.

Choreographies

Interacting with databases and other connected services happens via pre-built blocks of code that Temboo provides. These are like library functions or objects in an object-oriented programming (OOP) development environment, but they do much more because they are inherently connected. Temboo calls these blocks of reusable code *choreographies* and abbreviates that to the term *choreos*. There is a large library of choreos already in existence at the Temboo website. Each choreo manages a different online service or toolkit. Explore the library here:

```
https://www.temboo.com/library/
```

Table 19-1 is a list of the library contents that can be presented in various sub-sets by selecting a topic from the category menu item.

Table 19-1. *Temboo Choreo Library Index*

23andMe	EnviroFacts	LastFm	SunlightLabs
Amazon	Facebook	LinkedIn	Tumblr
AuthorizeNet	Factual	LittleSis	Twilio
Basecamp	FedEx	MailChimp	Twitter
Bitly	FedSpending	Microsoft	Uber
Box	FilesAnywhere	Mixpanel	UnlockPlaces
Bugzilla	Fitbit	Nexmo	USPS
Clicky	Flickr	NOAA	Withings
CloudMine	Foursquare	NPR	WolframAlpha
ConstantContact	Genability	NYTimes	Wordnik
CorpWatch	GitHub	OneLogin	Xively
DailyMed	Google	PagerDuty	Yahoo
DataGov	GovTrack	Parse	Yelp
Delicious	Highrise	PayPal	YouTube
Disqus	InfluenceExplorer	RunKeeper	Zendesk
DonorsChoose	Instagram	Salesforce	Zillow
Dropbox	Instapaper	SchoolFinder	Zoho
DuckDuckGo	KhanAcademy	SendGrid	
Dwolla	Kiva	Socrata	
eBay	Klout	Stripe	

The OAuth support is particularly useful. Interacting with an authentication system can be very tricky sometimes. If all of the details are managed for you via a choreo, it becomes easier to develop secure applications–and that has to be good for all of us!

Temboo also provides libraries of utility code to embed and call as part of your application:

- HTTP Forms submits for GET, POST, PUT, and DELETE
- Encode for URLS or base 64
- Authenticate via OAuth 1.0 and 2.0
- Hashing functions
- Text-processing tools
- JSON-parsing tools
- Random number generators

- Email send or receive

- Data-format conversion and transforms

- Validation

- Search and find with regular expression functions

- Date-handling tools

- XML parsing

- Data cleaning and formatting

Condition Handling

The Temboo conditions handling logic interacts with the ARTIK hardware to read sensor values and performs actions if the conditions are met. A choreo can then be triggered from a switch connected to your ARTIK or when a sensor has a particular value.

As you build your code, apply hardware conditions to the outcome of a Temboo choreo. This is all presented in a wizard-like user interface for constructing your application code. Figure 19-5 shows a pin selector built to look like an ARTIK 10. You can pick the pins visually and associate them with a condition; in this case, triggering an SMS message transmittal:

Figure 19-5. *Selecting an ARTIK pin to trigger an SMS message*

Remote Storage in Profiles

Temboo profiles are used to keep your API credentials for other services organized in a central place. Your Temboo account profile can also be used to store persistent data for your applications. You save memory in your device by uploading bulky data sets to your profile for storage and to share them with other devices.

Your profile access is managed via code you write that interacts with the Temboo libraries in the ARTIK. Be aware that since Temboo works across multiple platforms and architectures, storing something in your profile from one device can affect how a different type of device from a different manufacturer will respond.

This feature can also help you to economize on RAM usage in memory-constrained devices. It is also helpful when memory is volatile, and it reduces the chance of losing important data when devices cease to function or are mislaid.

Reprogram your device remotely by sending messages to your profile on the Temboo system, which then forwards them to your device based on rules you set up yourself.

Output Filters

The output from a choreo can be filtered to isolate just the data you want and discard the rest. That data can be cleaned and formatted for downstream processes to make use of without having to work around lots of formatting inadequacies.

This takes place in the Temboo server. The filtering reduces the bulkiness of message transfers to your device and avoids consuming valuable mobile data bandwidth. Your mobile data tariff–controlled capacity is eked out more sparingly and will go further.

Data Streaming

Temboo has collaborative arrangements with Microsoft and Google for streaming data to their cloud services directly from your application regardless of the hardware or platform it is running on. The Microsoft Power BI database integration is illustrated with a working example here:

```
https://temboo.com/hardware/microsoft-power-bi-getting-started
```

This shows how to authenticate your connection with a Microsoft Power BI database using OAuth protocols. Set up a Microsoft BI client account first, then connect to it from your application. Temboo provides a link to a tutorial for setting up your Microsoft Azure and Power BI credentials.

The process is simplified because Temboo has created a choreo to manage the authentication once you have set that up with the client ID you got from Microsoft. Although the next step in the online example describes how to do this with an Arduino, you can choose the ARTIK platform instead to generate the right kind of code for your device. The setup process then shows you how to map a specific sensor pin on your hardware to a column name in your Microsoft Power BI database.

Now all you have to do is generate the code, load it into your ARTIK, and run it. You should then see your Microsoft Power BI database fill up with data as your ARTIK reads the sensor pins and dispatches the data via the stream.

The process is very similar for integrating with the Google BigQuery database, as shown in this online example:

```
https://temboo.com/hardware/google-big-query-getting-started
```

The authentication takes place with the OAuth choreo again. This assumes you have a Google BigQuery account already set up. Temboo provides another tutorial guide for that.

The code description that you integrate with Google BigQuery is formatted as SQL code. Extrapolate this technique and apply it to other database scenarios. Learning SQL is a valuable skill you can apply to many other database-driven projects whether they are Temboo based or not.

This level of detail in the Temboo tutorials is very useful. When you are just beginning to learn about a new and unfamiliar system, having step-by-step guides and lots of example screenshots is very helpful. Temboo has done a great job here.

Machine-to-Machine (M2M) with Temboo

Temboo now supports messaging between peers in order to have one of your mobile devices control another. Either or both can still share their data with the cloud-based services as before. The main benefit is that the devices can communicate with one another without the need for an Internet connection. This is useful where you have multiple devices that share data with each other. An industrial process control situation is a typical example. Sending messages up to the cloud and back down again is somewhat wasteful of network capacity. Machine-to-machine (M2M) communication accomplishes effectively the same transfer of data between two nodes for half the network traffic, since there is no up and down link needed, just a peer-to-peer link. Aggregate hundreds of devices distributed around a factory and then delegate the cloud connectivity to just a few of them to uplink data on behalf of the other devices. Read this blog article to see why this is such a great idea:

```
http://blog.temboo.com/post/134612682871/why-m2m-a-behind-the-scenes-
look-at-what-we-were
```

Temboo and ARTIK

The Temboo SDK is already installed in your ARTIK module. A few easy steps will turn it on:

```
https://www.temboo.com/hardware/samsung/getting-started
```

312

The Getting Started page shows you how to check that your ARTIK module is ready to use the Temboo resources. It also takes you through a simple example project to try it out. The example uses a combination of conditions, profiles, and output filters that are all provided by Temboo.

Temboo returns choreo result data to the Samsung ARTIK as a key-value pair. Read the incoming stream two lines at a time and strip off the ASCII control characters that are used for formatting and delimiting. The lines alternate between key-names and values, with the trailing control character telling you which is which to synchronize the parser (see Listing 19-1):

- The key names are followed by a newline (\n) and an ASCII unit-separator character (\x1F).

- The value items are followed by a newline (\n) and an ASCII record-separator character (\x1E).

Listing 19-1. Example Choreo Result Data Presented to the ARTIK

```
Name1\n\x1F
Value1\n\x1E
Name2\n\x1F
Value2\n\x1E
```

The Temboo library does a lot of work for you as it unpacks this data. See the companion Apress *ARTIK Reference Guide* for more in-depth coverage of this topic. Temboo has a helpful discussion that goes into a lot more detail here:

```
https://temboo.com/hardware/samsung/interpreting-outputs
```

Temboo and ARTIK 5

When Temboo was initially launched, it only worked with the ARTIK 10 models. It is feasible to reconfigure it to run on an ARTIK 5 if you manually modify the code that it generates for an ARTIK 10 module. Temboo is working on ARTIK 5 support. It will be released and fully supported as the ARTIK production revision devices come on-stream. See this web page for details on how to modify ARTIK 10 code to run on an ARTIK 5:

```
https://www.artik.io/developer/documentation/developer-guide/using-temboo-
with-artik-5.html
```

Getting Ready to Tango with Temboo

To compile an application natively inside your ARTIK 10 module and link it against the Temboo SDK library, locate the library and describe the path to it in every compiler invocation. Set up the Temboo library as one of the default libraries to make life easier. This library will be ignored when you build applications without using Temboo.

Type this command to see what libraries are already configured. Each one needs a configuration file:

```
ls /etc/ld.so.conf.d
```

If you see `temboo.conf` listed, it has already been set up. If not, follow these steps to create a new configuration file:

1. Go to the library configuration files directory:

    ```
    cd /etc/ld.so.conf.d
    ```

2. Open a new file with the vi editor:

    ```
    vi ./temboo.conf
    ```

3. Press the letter [I] key to go into insert mode.

4. Type this line into the file:

    ```
    /opt/iothub/artik/temboo/temboo_artik_library/lib
    ```

5. Type these keystrokes to exit from vi and save the changes to disk:

    ```
    [Escape] [:] [w] [q] [Return]
    ```

6. After saving `temboo.conf`, add the directory containing the Temboo library to the system library search path with this command:

    ```
    ldconfig
    ```

Now when you build applications, the compiler will check to see if it needs any of the Temboo code. It will incorporate it from the library container described in the configuration file only if it is needed. Replacing the library will automatically have ARTIK 10 use the new version. Reconfiguration is not necessary provided the library has the same name as before.

As you configured your ARTIK network connection you should have noted all the details of the IP address and configuration in order to use them in a Temboo application. The `ifconfig` command with no options will present a list of network interfaces and their properties for you to check them again. Type that instruction on an ARTIK command line and not on your development workstation. The `eth0:` device will communicate via the Ethernet cable. The `wlan0:` device communicates via Wi-Fi if you have configured it.

■ **Note**   The location of the Temboo library in this example is based on what was observed in a prototype ARTIK module. It might have moved to another location. Read the instructions on the Temboo website and follow those if they describe a different location.

An Example of Code Generated by Temboo

The pre-built examples are a good introduction to working with Temboo. A simple Temboo choreography shows you how to request the weather in New York via the Yahoo weather service. This involves a call across the Internet to acquire source data. The Temboo server acts as an intermediary for us. Your login credentials will be used to call the Temboo server and ask it to make the inquiry for you.

Embed a Temboo account name into the code to authenticate and access your account. Clearly this should not be your private Temboo account if you are building code for distribution in an ARTIK embedded inside a product, but it is OK when you are testing. In the tutorial examples on the Temboo website this substitution happens automatically. Follow these instructions to build a simple application and generate the code for loading it into your ARTIK:

1. Log in to Temboo using the account you created earlier.

2. Find the Yahoo ➤ Weather ➤ GetWeatherByAddress choreo in the Temboo library:

   ```
   https://www.temboo.com/library/Library/Yahoo/Weather/
   GetWeatherByAddress/
   ```

3. Enter any address in the Address input field. Anything that Yahoo understands as an address that it can translate to latitude and longitude coordinates will work. Yahoo calls this the PlaceFinder method. In New York, type something like this 104 Franklin St New York, NY 10013. In the United Kingdom a street address and postcode works well. An address formatted like this will work: 10 Downing St, London SW1A 2AA. Yahoo provides a helpful page that describes how this works here:

   ```
   https://developer.yahoo.com/weather/documentation.html
   ```

4. Test the choreo by clicking the Run button. You will get details of the values returned by the choreo. An extract of the complete response looks like this:

```
<?xml version="1.0" encoding="UTF-8" standalone="yes" ?>
<rss version="2.0" xmlns:yweather="http://xml.weather.yahoo.com/
ns/rss/1.0" xmlns:geo="http://www.w3.org/2003/01/geo/wgs84_pos#">
<channel>

<title>Yahoo! Weather - London, GB</title>
<link>http://us.rd.yahoo.com/dailynews/rss/weather/London__
GB/*http://weather.yahoo.com/forecast/UKXX0085_f.html</link>
<description>Yahoo! Weather for London, GB</description>
<language>en-us</language>
<lastBuildDate>Tue, 10 Nov 2015 3:20 pm GMT</lastBuildDate>
<ttl>60</ttl>
<yweather:location city="London" region="" country="United Kingdom"/>
<yweather:units temperature="F" distance="mi" pressure="in" speed="mph"/>
<yweather:wind chill="59"  direction="230"  speed="15" />
<yweather:atmosphere humidity="82" visibility="6.21"
pressure="30.15" rising="0" />
<yweather:astronomy sunrise="7:07 am"  sunset="4:17 pm"/>
<image>
<title>Yahoo! Weather</title>
<width>142</width>
<height>18</height>
<link>http://weather.yahoo.com</link>
<url>http://l.yimg.com/a/i/brand/purplelogo//uh/us/news-wea.gif</url>
```

5. Switch on the IoT mode with the control at the top of the page:

IoT Mode **ON**

6. Running a choreo also generates the code to install in your ARTIK to do the same thing. At the top of the Choreo page, choose your target hardware device type.

7. Choose what kind of communications interface to use. The ARTIK modules only support Ethernet or Wi-Fi for long distances, but these both generate the same code for managing a connection so there is only one option needed.

8. Now configure any sensor triggering based on what Temboo knows about your ARTIK. Turn on the sensor configuration tool by clicking on the small plus symbol just above the input configuration block.

9. Choose an input to sense on the pin board at the right. Pins 0, 1, 2, 5, 6, and 7 can be selected as inputs. This selector is modal. When it is blue, the setting is locked. Click on the selected pin number to unlock it and change the color to magenta and then choose that pin.

10. Decide whether to sense in analog or digital mode.

11. Set the sensing condition value. For analog the range is 0 to 1023. For digital the value can be low or high. Add appropriate pull-up or pull-down resistors to your hardware, which will stop the input from floating and generating random values. Now, when the value on that sensor pin changes to match the condition, the choreo will run.

12. If you want to define a hardware action that happens when the choreo has finished running and returns the results, add it by clicking on the small plus-sign symbol underneath the choreo condition configurator.

13. Choose which of the returned conditions to base your hardware actions on. This menu selector is different for each choreo because they each return different condition values. Choose a comparison operator and value. When the temperature is larger than the value, the hardware action will be triggered, for example. The ARTIK can set the value of an output digital pin to a high or low value to operate a relay or turn on an LED indicator.

14. Now run the choreo again to generate the code.

15. Here is an extract of the example code that Temboo has generated. The code is written in C language and must be compiled on your ARTIK, as it includes the Temboo code installed there by default:

```
... Headers and defines go here ...

// SocketConnection is a struct containing data needed
// for communicating with the network interface
SocketConnection theSocket;

// There should only be one TembooSession per device. It
represents
// the connection to Temboo
TembooSession theSession;
```

```
// Limit the number of times the choreo is to be run.
This avoids
// inadvertently using up your monthly choreo limit
int currentRun = 0;
const int MAX_RUNS = 10;

// Defines a time in seconds for how long the choreo
// has to complete before timing
const int CHOREO_TIMEOUT = 300;

int inputPin = 7;
int outputPin = 8;

... Callable functions go here ...

TembooError setup()
  {
  // Initialize the TembooSession struct exactly once.
  TembooError returnCode = TEMBOO_SUCCESS;

#ifndef USE_SSL
  returnCode = initTembooSession(
          &theSession,
          TEMBOO_ACCOUNT,
          TEMBOO_APP_KEY_NAME,
          TEMBOO_APP_KEY,
          &theSocket);
#else
  printf("Enabling TLS...\n");
  returnCode = initTembooSessionSSL(
          &theSession,
          TEMBOO_ACCOUNT,
          TEMBOO_APP_KEY_NAME,
          TEMBOO_APP_KEY,
          &theSocket,

"/opt/iothub/artik/temboo/temboo_artik_library/lib/
temboo.pem",
          NULL);
#endif
```

```
    if (!digitalPinMode(inputPin, INPUT))
    {
      return -1;
    }
    if (!digitalPinMode(outputPin, OUTPUT))
    {
      return -1;
    }

    return returnCode;
  }

  // Call a Temboo choreo
  ... More Temboo proprietary code here ...
```

16. ARTIK sets the pin modes and operates the pins like an
    Arduino. Examine the source file to see how Temboo sets
    things up. Soon you will become familiar enough with this
    to create your own applications from scratch. This code
    fragment checks for the value of the temperature in the results
    and conditionally fires the hardware action:

```
if (0 == strcmp(name, "Temperature"))
{
    if (choreoResultReadStringUntil(session->
    connectionData, value, sizeof(value), ↵
        '\x1E') == -1)
  {
    printf("Error: char array is not large enough to
    store the string\n");
  }
  else
  {
    if (atoi(value) > 15)
    {
        digitalWrite(outputPin, HIGH);
    }
  }
}
```

17. Now download the Temboo code package to your computer.
    Temboo will package this in a Zip file. Your Zip file should
    contain these two files:

    getweatherbyaddress.c
    TembooAccount.h

18. Copy the Zip archive file to your ARTIK to access it from there. Do this from the command line of your development workstation. Substitute the IP address you noted earlier:

```
scp getweatherbyaddress.zip root@{remote_IP_address_of_
your_ARTIK}:/home
```

19. Now log in to your ARTIK (or resume an earlier session).

20. Go to the directory where the scp command copied the Zip file:

```
cd /home
```

21. Check that the Zip file is present with an ls command if you want to.

22. Now unzip the archive package:

```
unzip getweatherbyaddress.zip
```

23. Go into the getweatherbyaddress directory to see the source-code files:

```
cd getweatherbyaddress
```

24. Compile the code with this command:

```
gcc -L/opt/iothub/artik/temboo/temboo_artik_library/
lib -ltemboo ↵
-I/opt/iothub/artik/temboo/temboo_artik_library/include ↵
getweatherbyaddress.c -o getweatherbyaddress
```

25. Now run your compiled application:

```
./getweatherbyaddress
```

Shared Login Credentials

When you join Temboo, your account is credited with enough cycles to run a few Choreos to exercise your development project. That starter pack is not enough to sustain heavy usage so as you start to need Temboo more, you would purchase a low cost developer pack which gives you a stash of credits for testing. Every project you build in Temboo will be imprinted with your account credentials. When you deploy a product to manufacturering, your own personal account credentials should be replaced with an account that you have set up to manage Temboo Choreo runs on a commercial basis.

By default, the TembooAccount.h header file contains the login credentials for the account you just used to create this code example. You should edit this file to use the production account if you are building a software image that you intend to redistribute in thousands of ARTIK modules embedded in your product.

You should design your production software to abstract login credentials out of the source code and store them safely somewhere else that can be shared by all the processes that need them. Defining them in one place and referring to it with a simple loading instruction makes your product easier to maintain.

Missing cdefs.h Message

If you get a warning message about a missing cdefs.h file, it suggests that the glibc-headers are not yet installed. They should be there by default. You can reinstate them with this command if they have been compromised:

```
yum reinstall glibc-headers
dnf reinstall glibc-headers
```

Try the GCC compile again and then run your finished application.

Using CURL via a REST API Instead of C

Listing 19-2 shows an example of a similar choreo setup based on calling a URL endpoint with a curl command, where the string xxxxx should be substituted with your Temboo account profile name. This example is separated into multiple lines for clarity but should be executed as a single line when you construct the command yourself.

Listing 19-2. Constructing a curl Command

```
curl --basic ↵
    -u "myFirstApp":"e3271099b5f248778ec3d3e5b7103961" ↵
    --header "x-temboo-domain: /xxxxx/master" ↵
    --header "Content-Type: application/json" ↵
    --header "Accept: application/json" -X POST ↵
    --data '{ "inputs": [{"name":"Address", "value":"New York, NY"}] }' ↵
    "https://xxxxx.temboolive.com/temboo-api/1.0/choreos/Library/Yahoo/
    Weather/GetTemperature"
```

Find out more about REST API endpoints here:

```
https://www.temboo.com/restapi/reference
```

Use this API to get a list of available choreos, or drill down and find out about a specific one. Set your choreos running with a call to action via the REST API. If the choreo is likely to take a while, find out the current status to see if it is making progress. Gather the results from completed choreos or shut one down if you no longer need the output it generates.

Using Temboo with Node.js

Temboo works very well with Node.js and gives you access to all of the same platforms and choreos that are available with other development tools.

Once you have verified that you have Node.js installed and working on your ARTIK, download the Temboo Node.js SDK and use the choreo-building tools on the Temboo website to create a sample script. Download that script and run it in your ARTIK. The process is similar to the way you generate C code. Temboo provides a helpful guide to exercising a choreo that encapsulates the Google GeoLocation code here:

```
https://www.temboo.com/nodejs/getting-started
```

Sample Code to Experiment With

A code generator like Temboo is a good way to create blocks of reusable code, but it cannot build a complete and finished product on its own. Eventually your needs will become more complex and you will have to use several choreos within a project. Temboo may evolve one day to become more sophisticated and help you, but for now, it is good for creating components that you need to integrate yourself. If you use the Temboo library of choreos as a playground on which to experiment, you can create lots of example code files to inspect and take apart to build your own apps. As you experiment with each choreo, you are creating the body for a potential new function within your own source code. It is only a small step to take the example code and wrap it in a function block to call it from your own main process thread.

■ **Note**   For private experimentation, the Temboo code is a good way to learn. Read the licensing terms carefully if you plan to integrate Temboo into a commercial product. It is polite to ask permission before incorporating their code into your product and establishing any limitations on usage. It is better to ask first than to find out later that you have infringed upon someone else's intellectual property rights.

When you step it up a gear and want to integrate different hardware, sensors, and controls, the Temboo website provides a rich source of example IoT applications with instructions, breadboard diagrams, and details of the components you will need. Some of these are truly awesome in the potential for wiring the world with IoT devices. Find out more about these example projects here:

```
https://temboo.com/iot-applications
```

Log in to your Temboo developer account to see these examples. Watch the video first and then look at the bill of materials to see what components to order. Gather a stock of useful components so as to be ready to start building a project as soon as you have an idea.

Now that Temboo is becoming more popular, more helpful example code is being made available by developers working at the leading edge. Paul Stoffregen describes how to send an e-mail via Gmail from an Arduino with the Temboo library. Porting this to work on an ARTIK should be straightforward, because the code is all based on using Temboo choreographies:

```
https://github.com/PaulStoffregen/Bridge/blob/master/examples/Temboo/
SendAnEmail
```

Another example shows how to update a Facebook status from inside your Arduino. This example could be modified to run in an ARTIK instead:

```
https://github.com/PaulStoffregen/Bridge/blob/master/examples/Temboo/
UpdateFacebookStatus
```

This example shows you how to send an SMS message:

```
https://github.com/PaulStoffregen/Bridge/blob/master/examples/Temboo/
SendAnSMS
```

Here are tutorial videos to help you understand Temboo better:

```
https://www.temboo.com/videos
```

The Deconstructing IoT blog is also a good place to go for tutorial help:

```
https://www.temboo.com/deconstructingiot
```

Send an e-mail directly to the Temboo support team for more advice if you have questions about how Temboo works:

```
support@temboo.com
```

This blog article describes how to integrate an ARTIK 10 with Temboo and SAMI to create a weather station that feeds data directly into SAMI:

```
https://blog.samsungsami.io/iot/development/tutorial/architecture/2015/09/08/↵
    building-a-weather-station-with-sami-artik-10-and-temboo.html
```

Summary

I hope you will see the merits of using Temboo for your projects. It is an elegant and well-engineered tool that is also remarkably easy to use for creating quite complex sub-systems. If you build individual application components using their online GUI tools and generate the code to compile and run in the ARTIK, you'll have had a valuable learning experience. Temboo generates raw source code that can be integrated into your application piece by piece. Create a library of reusable components by wrapping the example Temboo code in function calls. Study the Temboo terms and conditions to understand the limits of what you are allowed to do with their code in a commercial context.

This chapter has illustrated accessing Temboo from C language and Node.js. Because Temboo uses a REST API, it can be used from any language that supports an HTTPS: web request/response call. Most languages have this capability already, or it can be added easily with plugin modules and code libraries.

## CHAPTER 20

Debugging Your Application

Debugging Your App

Setting up the debugging tools and processes for your application development is an important part of your workflow. If you have a reliable set of debugging tools available, getting your application running correctly is much easier.

The time-honored printing to console or logging to a debug file from an application running inside your ARTIK module are good approaches, but they will not help you inspect the state of the application internals and modify them on the fly. A graphical debugger is much more helpful. This needs to run via a remote connection to an application in another machine.

Embedded operating systems and applications are harder to debug because they are usually running in a context where you have no view of their output unless you add indicators to the application somehow. You could turn some attached LED indicators on and off, for example. Run your application in an emulator to shake out faults in your fundamental logic and design.

Attach a hardware debugger to the JTAG connector on your development system. The debugger will monitor the embedded CPU with an application that runs on your development workstation. You must buy the hardware, but if you work out how much time it saves you, the expense is worth it.

Software Debugging with GDB

This is generally easier if you are using an integrated development environment (IDE) such as Eclipse, because the debugger output is presented in a window within the IDE. It is much easier to work with.

The GCC toolkit includes a useful set of debugging tools. Use them to set break points and step through your code one line at a time. The GNU Debugger (GDB) is part of the software development tools and can be deployed by adding command-line options to the build process. This is done under the control of the Eclipse IDE or by adding a -g flag if you are using a command-line approach. Make sure you remove all these debugging hooks when you deploy your product to manufacturing.

© Cliff Wootton 2016
C. Wootton, *Beginning Samsung ARTIK*, DOI 10.1007/978-1-4842-1952-2_20

Use the following commands to compile the standard hello_world.c and hello_world.cpp source files with GDB support included. Note the additional -g option:

```
arm-linux-gnueabihf-gcc -g -o hello hello_world.c
arm-linux-gnueabihf-g++ -g -o hello_cpp hello_world.cpp
```

Deploy the application to your ARTIK and debug from the development workstation or from a logged-in session on your target ARTIK module.

There are many tutorials and books available on this topic. To become a power user, you must devote effort to learning how your tools work, and there is no substitute for practice. Here are some online resources to help you get started with GDB:

```
http://www.gnu.org/software/gdb/documentation/
http://sourceware.org/gdb/current/onlinedocs/gdb/
https://sourceware.org/gdb/wiki/Internals
http://www.thegeekstuff.com/2010/03/debug-c-program-using-gdb/
http://www.tutorialspoint.com/gnu_debugger/
```

Onboard Native Debugging with GDB

If you log in to your ARTIK and run the application from the command line there, invoke the debugger inside the ARTIK and trace the execution of your application as it runs. Follow these steps to invoke the debugger:

1. Go to the directory where you installed your application.

2. Use this command to run your application as normal (just to check it runs OK):

    ```
    ./myapplication
    ```

3. To run the same application in debug mode, use this command instead:

    ```
    gdb ./myapplication
    ```

4. You should now see the GDB message screen presented before any message your application displays:

    ```
    GNU gdb (GDB) Fedora 7.7.1-21.fc20
    Copyright (C) 2014 Free Software Foundation,Inc.
    License GPLv3+: GNU GPL version 3 or later <http://gnu.org/
    licenses/gpl.html>
    This is free software: you are free to change and redistribute it.
    There is NO WARRANTY, to the extent permitted by law. Type "show
    copying"
    and "show warranty" for details.
    This GDB was configured as "armv7hl-redhat-linux-gnueabi".
    ```

```
Type "show configuration" for configuration details.
For bug reporting instructions, please see:
<http://www.gnu.org/software/gdb/bugs/>.
Find the GDB manual and other documentation resources online at:
<http://www.gnu.org/software/gdb/documentation/>.
For help, type "help".
Type "apropos word" to search for commands related to "word"...
Reading symbols from my_bin ...done.
```

5. Use the GDB commands to set break points and run your
    application under control of the debugger. Your application
    may not run as fast as normal because of the additional
    debugging code overhead.

Remote Debugging with GDB

If you want to debug the application running inside your ARTIK from a remote
workstation (such as your hosting development system), first start a GDB server running
inside the ARTIK module. This would be a good approach if your application is running
in a device that operates in a stand-alone scenario without generating any output
messages and has no screen to display them on anyways. Follow these steps to turn on
remote debugging tools:

1. Go to the directory where you installed your application.

2. Use this command to run your application as normal
    (just to check it runs OK):

    ```
    ./myapplication
    ```

3. Start GDB Server on your ARTIK with this command,
    which will make it available on port 1234 and load up your
    application for debugging:

    ```
    gdbserver localhost:1234 ./myapplication
    ```

4. You should see a message from GDB server telling you it is up
    and running:

    ```
    Process target_process created; pid = 262
    Listening on port 1234
    ```

5. Now go to your development machine's command line
    and type this command to run GDB on the development
    workstation (host system):

    ```
    gdb
    ```

6. In the GDB command line, connect to the GDB server running on your ARTIK module with the `target remote` command. The format of the command is like this:

```
target remote {target_IP_address}:{remote_port_number}
```

7. Assuming the IP address of your ARTIK is 192.168.1.38, you would type this:

```
target remote 192.168.1.38:1234
```

8. You should see something like this on your screen:

```
Remote debugging using 192.168.1.38:1234
0xb029a9a2 in ?? ()
```

9. At this point the application will pause and wait for you to give it some debugging instructions.

10. Set the application in motion with this command:

```
continue
```

IDE Support for Debugging

Modern IDE tools like Eclipse use the semi-hosting stubs to insert debugging hooks into the code and handle the callbacks. This is why you must strip out the debugging when you create a releasable application for your shipped commercial products. These are the recommended debugging tools to add to your Eclipse IDE, for example:

- QEMU
- SEGGER J-Link
- OpenOCD

Read the guidance on the Eclipse debugging page, which describes a variety of debugging strategies:

```
http://gnuarmeclipse.github.io/debug/
```

Emulating Your Hardware with QEMU

Running your application code in an emulator makes it much easier to debug things that would be embedded in a remote device. The emulator lets you run the code in the hosting development environment but keeps a leash on it in order to probe it with software debugging tools. Read the documentation that describes how QEMU works and how to install it here:

```
http://gnuarmeclipse.github.io/debug/qemu/
```

QEMU runs in a secondary terminal window and echoes the calls that are made to it onto that console. This is the end-point for the debugging stubs that were added to the application source code to satisfy the missing calls that the linker detected. There is an interesting technical paper from the Real Time Linux Workshop 2011 that describes how QEMU works:

```
https://static.lwn.net/images/conf/rtlws11/papers/proc/p09.pdf
```

This next web page provides installation details for QEMU and describes what to do for Windows, Mac OS X, and Linux:

```
http://gnuarmeclipse.github.io/qemu/install/
```

After installing QEMU, you will need to install debugging plugins for the GNU/ARM cross-compiler.

Using the JTAG Connectors

The developer reference boards are all equipped with JTAG hardware debugging connectors. The Type 1 developer reference board has a 14-pin connector for debugging the MIPS architecture. The Type 5 and Type 10 developer reference boards have 20-pin JTAG connectors that are compatible with the more powerful ARM CPU architectures. Acquire a set of adapter cables for plugging your hardware debugging tools into all the different configurations. The companion Apress *ARTIK Reference* book describes these connectors in more detail. Find out more about JTAG here:

```
https://en.wikipedia.org/wiki/Joint_Test_Action_Group
https://en.wikipedia.org/wiki/Open_JTAG
```

Hardware Debugging with SEGGER J-Link

The SEGGER J-Link shown in Figure 20-1 is a hardware probe designed to work with the JTAG connector on the developer reference boards. There are several models. One is designed for educational (non-profit) use. This is an inexpensive way to learn how this debugging technique works. There are other more powerful (and more expensive) probes for commercial application development.

Figure 20-1. *J-Link adapter for JTAG connections*

The J-Link debugging probes implement the ARM Serial Wire Debug (SWD) protocol and support tracing via the Serial Wire Output (SWO) pin. This is advanced debugging, and if you want to know more, study the SEGGER website. These hardware-debugging interfaces are not hugely expensive when you consider how much time they can save you. If you buy the educational version, the price is about fifty dollars. The commercial-use versions are more expensive, and there are several models starting at a few hundred dollars and increasing in price as they implement more features. This debugging hardware helps you design a product that you expect to make a lot of money from. It is a false economy to avoid buying the best tools available. This may be the only way to properly debug your product if it is designed to run completely stand-alone. Here are some links that can tell you all about it:

```
https://www.segger.com/jlink-general-info.html
https://www.segger.com/index.html
https://www.segger.com/j-link-edu.html
https://www.segger.com/jlink_base.html
```

Install the Eclipse support for J-Link in order to attach the hardware to your application when it is running in debug mode. Here are some Eclipse guidelines for you:

```
http://gnuarmeclipse.github.io/debug/jlink/
```

Find out more about the JTAG connectors here:

```
https://en.wikipedia.org/wiki/Joint_Test_Action_Group
```

Hardware Debugging with OpenOCD

This is another hardware debugging solution. It uses the same JTAG connection as the SEGGER J-Link probe.

Read more about OpenOCD and install this instead of the J-Link debugging tools if you find that there are problems that you cannot trace with J-Link. Sometimes, viewing the problem from another angle helps to see what is going wrong. These will be helpful:

```
http://gnuarmeclipse.github.io/debug/openocd/
http://gnuarmeclipse.github.io/openocd/install/
```

Cleaning Up after Debugging

Make sure you remove any debugging software from your application when you ship your product. If you can attach a debugging tool to it, the nefarious hacker community out there in the "Wild Wide Web" can also do that. You should also run your product through a complete regression test to see if any bugs come back after you have removed the debugging code. It may be that the debugging code was what allowed your application to run in the first place due to it having fixed something as a by-product of turning it on. These bugs are very hard to find.

If you have used object-oriented techniques to build your application, check specifically for memory leaks. These are extremely easy to add to your code without realizing it. Make sure that you properly de-allocate any memory when you tear things down at the end of a run of code. Your application will expect to run for an extended time, and an unfixed memory leak is going to kill it prematurely when the memory runs out.

Summary

You should always look for opportunities to develop and enhance your debugging skills. The more you improve your debugging skills, the quicker you can resolve potential problems. Ensuring that your application works before you ever ship products to customers is a huge cost saving. Sending updates to many hundreds or thousands of your customers can become painfully expensive. Making sure the code was bug free before committing it to production saves you a lot of money. You should also bear in mind the damage to your brand and product reputation that bad software can cause. Because debugging happens late in the product lifecycle, it is one of the tasks that is often skipped or truncated because project deadlines are looming. Quality assurance and technical documentation are two other project tasks that can easily become neglected in the rush to get a product out the door. Do the sensible thing and hone your debugging and QA skills to make great products that your customers will love. Let them be ambassadors who tell all their friends to buy your products.

CHAPTER 21

■ ■ ■

Deploying Your Application

Getting Ready

Eventually you will reach the end of your debugging process. You are now ready to deploy your product to the manufacturing facility. A quality and security audit is appropriate at this point just to make sure your design is protected against unauthorized access.

After you build the final version of the application and run the audits, deploy the binary to the target ARTIK module and test it there. For mass production, the image you want installed needs to be loaded as the modules are manufactured, unless you want to set up a production line process of your own. There are several easy ways to deploy, and several other possibilities with varying levels of security risks attached:

- Use the scp command to network copy.
- Mount an SD card and copy locally in the ARTIK.
- Mount a flash drive via the USB connection.

You could deploy applications to the ARTIK directly from the Eclipse IDE so the entire process is automated, but this is only realistic while you are developing the application software.

Deploy Files to ARTIK with scp

The secure copy scp command is useful for deploying your application to a development ARTIK module provided it is reachable across your local area network. You should be able to do this whether it is a wired connection via Ethernet or a wireless connection via Wi-Fi. The format of the scp command is as follows:

```
scp {source_file_to_copy} {account_name}@{remote_IP_address}:
/{destination_directory}
```

© Cliff Wootton 2016

C. Wootton, *Beginning Samsung ARTIK*, DOI 10.1007/978-1-4842-1952-2_21

Deploy Files across the Network

There are other ways to deploy your content to the ARTIK. A file-sharing service in the ARTIK, with the ARTIK storage mounted on your development workstation, would be very convenient. There is a risk that you would forget to deactivate this before shipping. It is not the optimum solution for use on a production line.

Alternatively, write a scheduled script to run in the ARTIK and pull something from a network-reachable location. This is safer but is an unnecessary process when the remote location is no longer reachable. It is also not particularly secure, because a hacker could subvert it. At least build in authentication to make it safer.

The file transfer protocol (FTP) is an alternative to the scp command. Turn on an FTP service in the ARTIK module first and then use an FTP client application on your development workstation. Make sure your shipping product does not have an open FTP service running.

If you want to automatically update your ARTIK from the development workstation, use rsync running on a scheduled or event-triggered basis in your development workstation. This is a good solution because it will ensure the ARTIK module is updated whenever your content changes if you monitor the file system and use that as a trigger. Install a responder in the ARTIK to receive the files and store them, but remember that this is another item to remove when you go into production.

Deploy Files to Your ARTIK with a Micro SD Card

Deploying with a Micro SD card is a more secure solution. The ARTIK 5 and 10 modules have support for mounting and reading Micro SD memory cards. There is a Micro SD socket on the developer reference board. The downside is that every ARTIK will need to be plugged into a developer reference board or your system will need to implement a Micro SD card socket, which adds expense to your design. Micro SD cards compatible with these specifications can be used:

- No larger than 32GB in capacity

- File system initialized as W95 FAT32

▪ **Note** Historically, the technical documentation indicates that both 16GB and 32GB are the maximum depending on the vintage of the specification you read. If you have problems with a 32GB Micro SD card, try using a 16GB Micro SD card instead. You may only need a 1GB or 4GB card, which should be fine.

You will need a card reader so your development system can load Micro SD cards with the files to transfer to your ARTIK. The examples shown in Figure 21-1 are compact designs that are compatible with only one kind of card. Other readers support multiple types of memory cards.

Figure 21-1. *Example Micro SD card readers*

Your Micro SD card must be set up with a Master Boot Record partition system and then formatted with an MSDOS FAT file-system partition. Keeping things simple and only having one partition on your Micro SD card is a good idea. Follow these steps to prepare and load your Micro SD card and transfer the files to your target ARTIK module:

1. Plug the Micro SD card reader into your development system.

2. Plug the Micro SD card into the reader.

3. Configure a blank Micro SD card with a Master Boot Record partition scheme.

4. Create a single MSDOS FAT file-system partition with a sensibly short name.

5. Copy the files you want to transfer onto the Micro SD card.

6. Dismount/eject the Micro SD card to properly flush the file system before unplugging it.

7. Install the Micro SD card into the ARTIK development system.

8. Type this command to list the visible file systems on your ARTIK:

    ```
    fdisk -l
    ```

9. The Micro SD card should present itself like this:

    ```
    Device          Boot  Start     End       Blocks    Id   System
    /dev/mmcblk1p1  8192  65535999  32763904  b         W95  FAT32
    ```

10. Use this command to view more detail about the Micro SD card:

    ```
    blkid
    ```

11. You should see a more extensive output like this:

```
/dev/mmcblk0p1: SEC_TYPE="msdos" LABEL="boot" UUID="AC7E-B03B"
TYPE="vfat" PARTLABEL="boot" PARTUUID="d117f98e-6f2c-d04b-a5b2-
331a19f91cb2"
 /dev/mmcblk0p2: LABEL="rootfs" UUID="ddd680fb-4343-4c74-b816-
e8c81f1ccc5c" TYPE="ext4" PARTLABEL="rootfs" PARTUUID="25718777-
d0ad-7443-9e60-02cb591c9737"
 /dev/mmcblk1p1: LABEL="UNTITLED" UUID="3974-16F0" TYPE="vfat"
 /dev/mmcblk0: PTUUID="00042021-0408-4601-9dcc-a8c51255994f"
PTTYPE="gpt"
 /dev/mmcblk1: PTTYPE="dos"
```

12. Create a mount point in the ARTIK file system where the Micro SD card will be mounted with this command. Name the mount point as something other than SD if you prefer a different name:

```
mkdir /mnt/SD
```

13. Type this command to mount the Micro SD card at the specified mount point. Note your command will be slightly different if the Micro SD card has a different device name identifier or if you chose to name the mount point other than SD:

```
mount /dev/mmcblk1p1 /mnt/SD
```

14. The contents of the MSDOS FAT file system should now be available at the mount point.

15. Check that with this command:

```
ls -la /mnt/SD
```

16. Copy files on and off of the Micro SD card with the cp command.

17. When you are done, safely unmount the Micro SD card with this command:

```
umount /mnt/SD -l
```

18. Now remove the Micro SD card from the ARTIK development system.

Deploy Files to Your ARTIK with a USB Flash Drive

Loading your data with a USB flash drive is similar to mounting a Micro SD card, but a few details are different. You can only do this with an ARTIK 10 module. Your USB flash drive should be compatible with these specifications:

- Partition map should be set up as MSDOS compatible
- Just one single partition (multiple partitions are confusing)
- File system initialized as W95 FAT32 or MSDOS FAT

Follow these steps to prepare and deploy your files:

1. Plug your USB flash drive into your development system.

2. Configure the USB flash drive with a Master Boot Record partition scheme.

3. Create a single MSDOS FAT file-system partition with a sensibly short name.

4. Copy the files you want to transfer onto the USB flash drive.

5. Dismount/eject the USB flash drive to properly flush the file system before unplugging it.

6. Plug the USB flash drive into the ARTIK development system's USB connector.

7. Type this command to list the visible file systems on your ARTIK:

   ```
   fdisk -l
   ```

8. The USB flash drive should be visible in the /dev directory. The name will start with sda or sdb followed by a number that is incremented every time a new drive is attached:

   ```
   Device      Boot  Start     End       Blocks Id  System
   /dev/sda1   2     60751871  30375935  b      W95 FAT32
   ```

9. Use this command to view more detail about the USB flash drive:

   ```
   blkid
   ```

10. You should see a more extensive output like this:

    ```
    /dev/loop0: UUID="2fd71144-7dfa-4caa-90c6-08c822a7b9ca" TYPE="ext4"
    /dev/mmcblk0: PTTYPE="dos"
    /dev/mmcblk0p1: UUID="847cfc70-1bda-4096-9a57-cff780001e5a" TYPE="ext4"
    /dev/sda1: LABEL="UNTITLED" UUID="8417-1618" TYPE="vfat"
    ```

11. Create a mount point in the ARTIK file system where the USB flash drive will be mounted with this command:

    `mkdir /mnt/mydrive`

12. Type this command to load the USB flash drive at the specified mount point:

    `mount /dev/sda1 /mnt/mydrive`

13. The contents of the USB flash drive should now be available at the mount point.

14. Check that with this command:

    `ls -la /mnt/mydrive`

15. Copy files on and off of the USB flash drive with the cp command.

16. When you are done, safely unmount the USB flash drive with this command:

    `umount /mnt/mydrive -l`

17. Now remove the USB flash drive from the USB port on the ARTIK development system.

Prototypes vs. Production

The end product is an image of your design that can be replicated many thousands of times. Installing manually is great for building and testing prototypes. It is a less than ideal solution for production. Contact your Samsung sales representative to discuss whether it is possible to have your software imaged onto the devices as they are manufactured. The downside of this is that the further away it is from your control the harder it is to make last-minute changes or reworks to the software. However, it may just be expedient to load software as part of your production line.

Integrating the ARTIK into your Products

The developer reference boards are intended to help you build prototype code and learn about the ARTIK modules. They are not practical for building into shipping products. What you build into your finished shipping product will most likely be derived from experiments you do with an ARTIK module mounted on a developer reference board. The ARTIK would then be integrated directly into your product design. Look closely at your ARTIK development system and you will see some multi-pin connectors underneath the ARTIK module. The companion Apress *ARTIK Reference Guide* describes the pinouts of these Panasonic AXT connectors. Recreate those physical connections in your products to plug the ARTIK module directly into your product.

Summary

This chapter covers the deployment of your finished design. Now you can show off your design and exchange ideas with other developers before starting a new project or moving on to the next cycle of design changes on this one. In the next chapter we draw things to a close and make plans for the next stage of our ARTIK project development.

CHAPTER 22

Next Steps

What Do You Want to Make?

Now that you have your ARTIK development environment assembled and working, start developing your applications. This introductory book concentrates on getting your system up and running. It is now up you to work out what you want to build with it.

The companion Apress *ARTIK Reference Guide* supplements the coverage in this book. There was far more information than a single book could accommodate without it becoming too big. The sheer bulk of available material made it necessary to split the coverage. The *Reference Guide* delves much more deeply inside the ARTIK modules and describes more of their inner workings. Use what you learned from this book to go and explore your ARTIK module to see what you can do with it.

There are already many intriguing ideas out there. Can you come up with something new and original and carve out your own niche in the industry? Table 22-1 lists some examples of already existing projects to inspire you. Invent something new and original of your own that will amaze and amuse your audience.

Table 22-1. *Existing Project Ideas*

Idea	Find Out More Here
Smart shoes	https://boogio.com/
Wired home	https://www.smartthings.com/uk
Baby clothing	http://mimobaby.com/
Hearing aids	http://news.rice.edu/2015/04/08/vest-helps-deaf-feel-understand-speech/
Sensory	http://www.bbc.co.uk/news/technology-26487218
Industrial IoT	http://www.ge.com/digital/sites/default/files/industrial-internet-insights-report.pdf
Engineering	http://www.ge.com/digital/

(continued)

© Cliff Wootton 2016

C. Wootton, *Beginning Samsung ARTIK*, DOI 10.1007/978-1-4842-1952-2_22

Table 22-1. (*continued*)

Idea	Find Out More Here
Future-casting	`https://www.artik.io/blog/2015/samsung-iot-2020-and-beyond`
Skateboards	`http://www.inboardskate.com/`
Model railways	`https://en.wikipedia.org/wiki/Digital_model_railway_control_systems`
IoT drones	`http://www.broadcom.com/`
Digital health	`http://www.bbc.co.uk/news/uk-wales-35061369`
Thermal image	`http://www.bbc.co.uk/news/business-35049606`
Farming	`http://www.weenat.com/`

Table 22-2 maps some potential scenarios for applying each kind of ARTIK module to tasks that are most suitable for each module.

Table 22-2. *Potential Product Ideas*

ARTIK	Application
1	Bluetooth tags
1	Low-end mobile devices
1	Industrial systems
1	Wi-Fi location beacons
1	Activity bands
1	Fitness trackers
1	Smart home endpoints (sensors and controllers)
1	Pet monitoring
1	Smart toys
1	Medical sensors
5	Smart home hubs
5	High-end smart watches
5	Drones and model aircraft
5	IP cameras
5	Interactive games
5	Digital signage
5	Medical devices connected to a hub

(*continued*)

Table 22-2. (*continued*)

ARTIK	Application
5	Telecare hubs
10	Home servers
10	Smartphone systems
10	Media hubs
10	Shared gaming systems
10	Virtual reality
10	Augmented reality
10	Personal medical-system hubs
10	Broadcast video ingest tools

Finding Out about More Project Ideas

Look for ARTIK tutorials online and try to reproduce the example projects in your own lab. Take what you learn from them and extrapolate the knowledge to synthesize your own designs. Soon you will be able to call yourself a Master ARTIK Developer.

The Temboo website is gradually releasing more worked tutorial examples. This approach is interesting, because it is well organized and built within a framework. Evaluate the same project concept in a variety of different architectures to choose the best one. To understand how the Temboo project builder works in more detail, make an ARTIK version and a PHP or Arduino or raw C language variant to compare the differences.

Another rich source of project ideas is the Hackster·IO website. There are only a few ARTIK projects there so far, but that is only because the ARTIK module is a new product. As developers get to know it better, more project examples will be posted. Use these search queries to list the ARTIK-related projects:

```
https://www.hackster.io/search?q=artik
https://www.hackster.io/search?q=sami
```

Search for SAMI-related projects on Hackster·IO as your project may span a diverse set of remote devices. Some of them may be applications running on a mobile phone or tablet. Hackster·IO covers many different platforms.

There are great example projects on the Instructables blog website as well. That collection will grow as more developers create projects and post them on the site. Subscribe and pay a small fee to get access to the more advanced materials. You can access a great deal of the site for free and then upgrade your membership when you are ready. This is all in the same kind of spirit as paying shareware fees to use open-source software; it is good to put a little something back into the pockets of people who work very hard to bring these resources to you. Find out more here:

```
http://www.instructables.com/member/SamsungIoT/
```

There are a lot more tutorials that illustrate how to use SAMI on the Hackster·IO, Temboo, Instructables, and Samsung developer websites.

Becoming a Partner Organization

If you have projects, products, or services that you think may be of benefit to the ARTIK developer community, then perhaps it is worth joining Samsung as an ARTIK partner organization. Check out the existing partners for an idea of the kind of products that are appropriate.

Becoming a partner gives you early access to ARTIK technology, as Samsung releases it to partners first. Contact the product team from the partner page to request the partnership registration:

```
https://www.artik.io/partners
```

Scroll to the bottom and click on the Registration button to send a partnership request to Samsung.

Going Deeper into ARTIK Development

The goal of this book was to introduce you to the ARTIK development tools and boards that Samsung has engineered to help you exercise your ARTIK and connect your existing systems to it.

To develop a product based on the ARTIK modules, your hardware design will have a mounting connector where the ARTIK module can be plugged in. You will need the mechanical dimensions and pinout details of the Panasonic AXT connectors on the underside of the ARTIK module. Each kind of ARTIK module is different, and you cannot interchange them without re-engineering this connector configuration. Deciding the best technology to use at an early stage of your project is important.

The companion Apress *ARTIK Reference Guide* book (designed as a follow up to this introductory book) covers these and other more advanced topics.

The current state of the ARTIK is that we are working with a Commercial Beta. This implies that things are certainly going to change. Indeed, during the writing of this book, a lot of things have been updated, even at the very last stage. We can expect more things to be revised as Samsung complete the engineering work and evolve the Commercial Beta product to a version 1.0 release. If you use the tutorials in the book and they do not work correctly, bear in mind that your ARTIK may have later software installed. Provided Samsung keep the developer documentation updated, you should be able to rely on that as the definitive source of knowledge.

My Challenge to You

Writing this book has been a hugely enjoyable process. Executing a project like this leads to significant learning outcomes. Even as you complete your first ARTIK-based project, you should have significantly expanded what you know.

Your journey will be different than mine, and you will discover things that I missed. Your challenge is to find topics that interest you within the context of ARTIK development and become an expert in them. When you discover new things about the ARTIK, get in touch with Apress and talk to them about writing a book about your new-found area of expertise.

There is so much still to be covered in the ARTIK world, and the developer community is only just beginning to discover what it can do. The Internet of Things is going to bring a disruptive change to everyone's lifestyles. The ARTIK community is at the spearhead of this, and it is going to be an exciting ride.

Index

A

Access tokens, 280, 296
ADC. *See* Analog-to-Digital
    Convertor (ADC)
Advanced Linux Sound
    Architecture (ALSA), 34
Analog Pin Addresses, 263, 270
Analog-to-digital convertor (ADC), 270
Apache Subversion (SVN), 171
API Console, 286
Apple Lisa computer, 65
Arduino IDE
    analog output pin values,
        setting, 212–213
    analogRead() function, 213
    Arduino pins
        Type 1 developer reference
            board, 204–205
        Type 5 and Type 10 developer
            reference boards, 206–207
    Arduino sketch compiler, 215
    ARTIK module configuration, 201
    board version, 208
    configuring and installing, 199–200
    cross-compiling, 204
    delay() function, 214
    digital output pin values,
        setting, 211–212
    digitalRead() function, 211
    IDE preferences, 197–199
    installation steps, 196
    interrupts, detecting, 214
    JRE, 195
    JVM, 195
    libArduino SDK, 204
    native sketch compilation, 203
    network upload method, 202

pin modes, 210–211
powersaving mode, 215
serial object, 209–210
serial upload method, 203
SPI, 214
switches and LED indicators, 216
systemCommand() function, 208
troubleshooting
    CPU utilization, 217
    digitalRead() function, 217
    logic levels, 218
    pin numbering, 217
    porting projects,
        architectures, 218
ARM software, 62
ARM Toolchain, Mac OS, 182–185
ARTIK
    Alpha and Beta prototype modules, 3
    Arduino compatible pins, 2
    Arduino suppliers, 59
    ARM software, 62
    booting up, 104–105
    breadboard/PCB, 60
    command-line user interface, 2
    cross-compiler tools, 62
    development system, 66–67
    developer reference board, 63–64
    development systems, 5
    digital multimeter, 61–62
    forensic techniques, 2
    hardware and software solution, 2
    JTAG probes, 2
    kernel driver code, 63
    kernel startup, 101–103
    LAN, 66
    Linux and Mac OS, 5
    Linux kernel, 241
    open-source technologies, 2

ARTIK (*cont.*)
  oscilloscope, 62
  reference guide, 6–7
  SAMI/Temboo ecosystems, 1
  Samsung account, 5
  self-directed study approach, 6
  software installing, 157–158
  starting up, 99
  static discharge and blowing, 59
  UNIX command-line shell, 62
  UNIX systems administration, 4
  USB interfaces (*see* USB serial
      interfaces)
  USB Vendor Identifiers, 78–79
  virtual file-system mapping, 241
  Windows, 4
  wire Color Conventions, 60
ARTIK 1 module
  block diagram, 22
  bluetooth location-based beacons, 21
  design, 22
  embedded operating system, 22
  functional organization, 22
  memory storage, 23
  spatial sensors, 23
  wireless communications, 22
  WVGA video output driver, 23
ARTIK 5 module
  block diagram, 25
  computing capacity, 26
  Fedora Linux, 25
  functional organization, 25
  GPU, 26
  hardware video codec support, 27
  memory storage, 27
  networking protocol support, 26
  radio frequency (RF) shielding, 24
  Samsung secure element protocols, 24
  wireless communications, 25–26
ARTIK 10 module
  audio codec support, 32
  block diagram, 30
  computing capacity, 31
  design, 29
  file-based edit/storage systems, 28
  GPU, 31–32
  hardware video codec support, 33
  HD video output, 28
  home intranet server, 28
  internal sub-systems, 29–30
  29mm x 39mm form factor, 28

networking protocol support, 31
OpenGL implementation, 32
OpenHAB and OpenStack
    networking, 31
operating system, 30
PMIC support, 34
Samsung secure element protocols, 28
video playback formats, 28
wireless communications, 30
ARTIK development
  online tutorials, 343
  product ideas, 342–343
  project ideas, 341–342
ARTIK ecosystem, 15
ARTIK firmware release versions
    history, 155
ARTIK module
  Arduino modules, 20
  artificial intelligence, 16
  ARTIK 1 (*see* ARTIK 1 module)
  ARTIK 5 (*see* ARTIK 5 module)
  ARTIK 10 (*see* ARTIK 10 module)
  audio coding support, 34
  centralized SAMI connecting hub, 15
  communications challenges, 19–20
  community websites, 18
  connected cloud service, 19
  consumers benefits, 21
  core-enabling technology, 21
  ecosystem, 15
  embedded UNIX operating systems, 16
  ESE, 15
  input/output sensors, 16
  IoT, 15–16
  Panasonic AXT multi-pin connectors, 35
  Samsung, 16
  security and privacy, 18
  security management, 34
  sensory capabilities, 19
  software support, 17–18
  Temboo ecosystem, 15
  types, 16
  video coding support, 34
ARTIK module CPU architectures, 170
ARTIK networking, 109
ARTIK operating systems
  Fedora Linux, 37
  Nucleus real-time, 35–36
  Snappy Ubuntu, 38
  Tizen, 38
  Yocto project, 37–38

ARTIK processor hardware identifiers, 208
Authentication, 277

■ B

BLE. *See* Bluetooth low energy (BLE)
Bluetooth low energy (BLE), 111
Bluetooth wireless interface
      configuration, 139–141
Boot mode switches, setting, 103–104

■ C

C language programming
    coding strategies, 239
    simple application, creation, 240
    temperature sensor, coding, 254
Cloud-based Services, 43
CoAP. *See* Constrained application
      protocol (CoAP)
Code-editing tools, 160–161
Command line
    ARM Toolchains, 219
    curl commands, 225
    Mac OS X, 220
    top-level directory structure, 222–223
    Ubuntu linux, 219
    UNIX, ARTIK
        date setting, 228
        debugging messages, 227
        memory usage, checking, 228
        quitting and aborting
            processes, 226–227
    UNIX I/O streams and
        redirection, 221
    UNIX, windows, 221
Command-line ARM toolchains, 219
Command-line interface (CLI), 161
command-line shells, 167–168
Constrained application
      protocol (CoAP), 26, 31, 113
Cross-compiling, 169–170
curl tool, 224

■ D

Data-driven development, 275
Data Encryption, 44
Datagram Transport Layer
      Security (DTLS), 44
Debian linux, 220

Debugging
    cleaning up, 331
    embedded OS and applications, 325
    GNU Debugger (GDB), 325
    IDE, 325, 328
    JTAG connectors, 329
    OpenOCD, 331
    QEMU, 329
    SEGGER J-Link, 329–330
Debug *vs.* Release, 170
Deploy files
    ARTIK with scp, 333
    micro SD card, 334–336
    network, 334
    prototypes *vs.* production, 338
    USB flash drive, 337–338
Developer portal
    description, 275
    managing applications, 295
    managing device types, 294
Developer reference board, 63–65
    ARTIK 1 module
        Connections, 51
        Panasonic AXT connectors, 50
    ARTIK 5 and 10 modules
        Beta versions, 51, 53
        connectors, 53–54
        jumpers, 56
        LED indicators, 55–56
        switches, 55
    connectivity, external hardware, 56
    and module versions, 48
    static discharge damage, 47
Development workstation. *See* ARTIK
Digital multimeter, 61
DNS configurations
    GUI network-management tools, 126
    IP link report, 128–129
    network device names, 129–130
    static configuration, servers, 127–128
    system
        impact, 126
        UNIX operating system, 126

■ E

Eclipse IDE
    ARTIK development, 180
    cross-compiling, 175
    default Toolchain, setting up, 188
    eclipse smart home, 190

Eclipse IDE (*cont.*)
getting help, 175
GNU ARM eclipse plugin,
installing, 181–182
installing, 175–176
MIPS architecture, 190
new ARM project, 190–193
new tools adding, 179
on Mac OS X, 176–178
semi-hosting stubs, 189–190
setup instructions, 186–187
windows build tools, 181
workspace preferences, 178–179
Embedded Secure Element (ESE), 15, 45
Ethernet connection configuration, 117
Extending Node.js
node packages and modules, 261
NPM installing, 260–261
WebSocket module, 262

F

File system mapped properties
CPU configuration, 223
processor speed, 224
virtual file listing, 223
File transfer protocol (FTP), 334
Firmware security, 44
Firmware versions, 155
Folder separator characters, 161–162
Folders *vs.* Directories, 161
FT232R USB UART, 72–74
FTDI. *See* Future Technology Devices
International (FTDI)
FTDI Driver, 74–75
Future Technology Devices
International (FTDI)
Arduino boards, 72
vs. OS X Versions, 75
USB serial device properties, 72

G

GDB
Onboard native debugging, 326–327
remote debugging tools, 327–328
General Electric (GE), 12
Ghost disks, Mac OS X, 149
GNU ARM Eclipse IDE support, 181
GNU ARM Eclipse plugin,
Mac OS X, 181–182

GNU compiler collection (GCC)
application-building tool, 232
ARM compiler support, 234
ARTIK module, 232
compiler warnings, 236
language support, 233
logo, 232
simple program
(Hello World), 235–236
supporting libraries, 233–234
Temboo session, 236
up and running, command, 234
Xcode tools, Mac OS X, 232
GNU Debugger (GDB), 325
GPIO pins
analog pin addresses, 250
Arduino domain, 243
ARTIK 5 and analog read, 10, 250
connections, 244
digital value reading, 247
digital value setting, 247
direction setting, 246
Edge detecting, 248
mapping, 243–244
reading analog pins, 249
sys virtual file system, 243
writing, code, 245
GPU. *See* Graphics
processing unit (GPU)
Graphical debugger, 325
Graphics processing
unit (GPU), 26, 31–32

H

Hardware Debugging
OpenOCD, 331
SEGGER J-Link, 329–330

I

IDE. *See* Integrated development
environment (IDE)
IETF. *See* Internet engineering task
force (IETF)
IIoT. *See* Industrial Internet of
Things (IIoT)
Industrial Internet of
Things (IIoT), 13
Integrated development environment
(IDE), 160, 169, 325

Internet engineering task
  force (IETF), 117
Internet of Things (IoT)
  Cisco, 11
  climate change and energy
    supply issues, 12
  defining point, 11
  GE Predix and Apple HealthKit, 12
  industrial, 13
  lifestyles changes, 12
  map concept, 9–10
  medicine and care community,
    revolution, 12
  network architecture and
    design, 11
  revolution, 10
  Samsung ARTIK, 9, 11
  sensors, 11
  statistical cusp, 11
IoT. See Internet of Things (IoT)
IP address configuration
  DHCP, 122
  ethernet IP interface, 123
  IP network configuration
    report, 122–123
  IPv6 operation, 125
  static IP address, 124
IPv4 addressing notation, 118–119
IPv6 addressing notation, 120–121
IPv6 via Low-power Wireless Personal
  Networks (6LoWPAN), 31

■ J

Java
  Arduino IDE tools, 172
  ARTIK, 174
  installation guidelines, 173
  JRE, 172–173
  version
    on Linux, 173
    on Mac OS X, 172
    on Windows, 172
Java development kit (JDK), 172
Java runtime environment (JRE), 172
Java virtual machine (JVM), 195
JDK. See Java development kit (JDK)
JRE. See Java Runtime
  Environment (JRE)
JTAG Connectors, 329
JTAG hardware-debugging probe, 109

■ K

Kernel booting, 100–101

■ L

LAN. See Local Area
  Network (LAN)
Library function toolkit
  analogRead() Function, 253
  digitalRead() Function, 252–253
  digitalWrite() Function, 252
  GPIO configuration and value
    management, 250
  main application code, 251
  manifest constant
    definitions, 251
  setDigitalPinMode()
    Function, 251
Links vs. Aliases, 164
Linux
  terminal emulator application
    logging, 96
  minicom (see minicom
    application)
Local Area Network (LAN), 66
Login credentials, 105
6LoWPAN protocol, 114

■ M

Mac OS resource forks, 165
Mac OS X, 220
  Alpha prototype board, 69–70
  drivers vs. device names, 75
  FT232R USB UART, 72
  FTDI, 73, 75
  Prolific 2303 Driver URLs, 70
  security issues, 69
  terminal emulator application
    dialup connection tool, 86
    logging, 89
    output redirection, 91
    process ID (PID), 88
    Screen Command Logging, 90
    Script Command Logging, 92
    scroll-back buffer, 90
    Stream Duplexing, 91
Manifest validator, 286
mDNS. See Multicast domain name
  system (mDNS)

Message Queue Telemetry Transport (MQTT), 26, 31, 113
Micro SD card readers, 335
Micro USB OTG adapter cable, 78
Minicom application
  apt-get, 93
  ARM CPU architecture, 97
  configuration, 94–95
  Source Code Files, 93
  Windows, 82–85
  yum tool, 93
Mobile to mobile (M2M), 112
MQTT. *See* Message queue telemetry transport pprotocol (MQTT)
Multicast Domain Name System (mDNS), 26, 31, 111

N

Native sketch compilation, 203
Network configuration
  CoAP, 113
  dynamic name auto-discovery support, 111–112
  IPv4 addressing, 118–119
  IP v6 addressing, 120
  M2M, 112
  MQTT, 113–114
  port numbers, 121–122
  protocol support, 112
  Telnet via SSH, 138
  ZigBee and thread protocols, 114
Network connection strategy, 110
Networking protocol support, 109
New-Line characters, 166
Node.js
  architecture design, 258
  compiled binary code, 259
  developing, 257
  Google V8 logo, 258
  Hello World application, 262
  instructions, version checking, 259
  JavaScript interpreter, 257
  logo, 257
  new device registering, SAMI, 264–266
  pin voltage reading, 262–263
Node.js. Extending Node.js
Normalization process, 282

O

OAuth2 access tokens, 280
OMA Lightweight M2M protocol (LW M2M), 26, 31, 112
OpenHAB. *See* Open home automation bus (OpenHAB)
Open home automation bus (OpenHAB), 31, 115–116
OpenOCD, 331
OpenStack (Swift) framework, 31, 116
Operating systems
  case preservation and sensitivity, 163
  upper-and lowercase issues, 162–163
Oscilloscope, 62
OS kernel startup, 101–103

P

PIP. *See* Python package manager (PIP)
PMIC. *See* Power management integrated circuit (PMIC)
Port numbers, 121–122
Power management integrated circuit (PMIC), 33
Programming, ARTIK
  code developing, 169
  code-editing tools, 160–161
  code management, 171
  debug *vs.* release, 170
  file names and paths, 162
  file-system path, 161–162
  software development environment, setting up, 159–160
Prototypes *vs.* production, 338
Pulse-width modulated (PWM), 210, 213
PuTTY application
  ARTIK development, 84
  file-naming meta-characters, 85
  logging, 85
  Windows, 82–83
Python package manager (PIP), 268
Python programming
  ARTIK module, 267
  code snippet, 271
  developing, 267–268
  Hello World application, 269–270
  interpreter, 268
  logo, 267
  object-oriented design, 267

pin voltage, reading, 270–271
Python packages installation, 269

Q
QEMU, 329

R
Radio frequency interference (RFI), 24
Real-Time Operating System (RTOS), 22
Redhat package manager (RPM), 157
Remote systems, libCurl
    calling libCurl, 255–256
    curl commands, 254
    libCurl client-side library, 254
Remote web servers
    wget and curl tools, 224
REST API interface, 274
RFI. *See* Radio frequency
         interference (RFI)
RPM. *See* Redhat package
         manager (RPM)

S
SAMI
    access tokens, 296
    API, 282
    application, 280
    authentication, 277
    connecting to application, 295
    data-driven development, 275
    data flows, 274
    developer documentation, 276
    Developer portal (*see* Developer
        portal)
    device
        ID, 280
        pairing, 279
        type, 279
    manifest, 280–281
    messages transport, 277–278
    normalization process, 282
    OAuth2 access tokens, 280
    request format, 296
    response body, 297
    REST API interface, 274
    Samsung SAMI logo, 273
    SDK libraries, 283
    security features, 276

sending data, 297–298
tools
    API Console, 286
    developer portal, 284–285
    Manifest validator, 286
    SAMI Device Simulator, 286
    user portal, 285
tutorial code samples, 298
user ID, 278
User portal (*see* User portal)
SAMI API, 282
SAMI cloud-based protocols, 24, 28
SAMI cloud-based service, 19
SAMI data-aggregation system, 15
SAMI data exchange, 274
SAMI Device Simulator, 286
SAMI Request Format, 296
SAMI Response Body, 297
SAMI tools
    API Console, 286
    developer portal, 284
    Manifest validator, 286
    SAMI Device Simulator, 286
    user portal, 285
Samsung ARTIK modules, 16
Samsung ARTIK platform, 1
Secure copy, SCP
    file download, ARTIK module, 237
    file upload, ARTIK module, 237
Security
    cloud-based services, 43
    data encryption, 44
    data safe, 43
    device authentication, 44
    ecosystem, 42
    embedded secure element, 45
    firmware, 44
    hardware crypto engine, 45–46
    OAuth2 protocols, 42
    open technologies, sharing, 43
    operating system, 43
    risk factors and Dystopian
        futures, 41
    SAMI, 42
    Samsung account, SAMI
        services, 44–45
    segregated trust zone, 46
SEGGER J-Link, 329–330
Semi-hosting Stubs, 189
Serial object TTY addresses, 209–210
Serial peripheral interface (SPI), 23, 214

Shell command prompt-formatting
 meta-characters, 168
Shutdown commands, 106–107
Shutdown console logging messages, 108
Shutdown warnings, 107
Software Development Kit
 libraries (SDK), 283
SPI. *See* Serial peripheral interface (SPI)
Switch OpenStack cluster server, 116
Switchover, 122
System administrator console, 99
Systems on Modules (SOM), 16
sys virtual file system, 242

T

Target CPU, code, 170
Telnet, 138
Temboo
 account dashboard, 303–304
 account registration, 302–303
 activity dashboard, 305
 and ARTIK, 5, 312–313
 missing cdefs.h file, 321
 choreo-based applications, 304
 Choreo Library Index, 308–309
 code generation, 315–320
 condition handling, 310
 curl command, 321
 data streaming, 311–312
 deconstructing IoT blog, 323
 developing, 302
 IoT applications, 322
 libraries of utility code, 309
 library dashboard, 306
 logo, 301
 machine-to-machine (M2M), 312
 Node.js, 322
 notifications panel, 305
 online data storage, 308
 output filters, 311
 platforms support, 307
 profiles, remote storage, 311
 shared login credentials, 320–321
 supported connectivity, 308
 Tango, 313–314
 web-based dashboard, 301
Terminal emulator application
 installation, 82
 Linux, 92–97

old-fashioned tele-typewriter
 devices, 81
Toolchain
 ARM installing, Mac OS, 182–185
 definition, 180
 setting up, 188
Trusted execution environment
 (TEE), 15, 46
Typical developer kit, 49
Typographers quotes, 166

U

U-boot universal boot loader
 messages, 99–100
Ubuntu Linux, 75–77, 219
Updating, ARTIK 5/10
 boot switches, 152
 instructions, upgrade OS, 152–155
 SD card reader socket, 152
USB-Serial Controller D, 70–71
USB serial interfaces
 drivers *vs.* device Names, 76–77
 FT232R USB UART, 73–74
 Mac OS X, 69
 Prolific Technologies driver, 67
 Ubuntu Linux, 75–77
 Windows, 68
USB Vendor Identifiers, 78
User portal
 description, 275
 displaying charts, 292–293
 Export SAMI data, 294
 managing rules
  matching pattern, 290
  rule-based actions, 290
  rules creation, 290, 292
  rules mechanism, 289
 SAMI data logs, 293

V

vi editor
 command mode keystrokes, 230–232
 exit and save, 229
 GUI, 229
 insert mode, 229
 UNIX system, 228
 use, 229
 vim command, file open, 228–229

W, X

wget tool, 224
Wi-Fi, 66
Wi-Fi networking configurations
    advanced, 136
    Apple Airport wireless network, 135
    Broadcom driver, 135
    "Failed to Connect" message, 135–136
    Martin Kronenberg documents, nmcli
        command, 133–134
    reconfiguration, reboot, 136–137
    setting up Wi-Fi
        communications, 130–132
    troubleshooting, 135
Windows, 68
    Terminal emulator application
        PuTTY (*see* PuTTY application)
Wireless networking
    ARTIK modules, 110
    BLE, 111

IEEE 802.11 Wi-Fi, 111
mDNS, 111
power consumption *vs.* range, 110
protocols, module type, 111
ZigBee and thread
    protocols, 111
Writing downloaded images, SD card
    on Linux, 144–146
    on Mac OS X, 146–149
    partition maps, OS X, 149
    repartition, SD card, 149–151
    on windows, 143–144

 Y

Yocto long-term support
    initiative (LTSI), 38

■ **Z**

ZigBee and thread protocols, 66, 114

Get the eBook for only $5!

Why limit yourself?

Now you can take the weightless companion with you wherever you go and access your content on your PC, phone, tablet, or reader.

Since you've purchased this print book, we're happy to offer you the eBook in all 3 formats for just $5.

Convenient and fully searchable, the PDF version enables you to easily find and copy code—or perform examples by quickly toggling between instructions and applications. The MOBI format is ideal for your Kindle, while the ePUB can be utilized on a variety of mobile devices.

To learn more, go to www.apress.com/companion or contact support@apress.com.

Printed in the United States
By Bookmasters